Tales about Ron LeFlore, Ron Hunt
and other Expos yarns from 1969-2004

NEVER
Forgotten

Danny Gallagher

SP
Scoop Press
Toronto, 2021

Never Forgotten: Tales about Ron LeFlore, Ron Hunt and other Expos yarns from 1969-2004

Copyright ©2021, Danny Gallagher

Published by Scoop Press. For information, please call 365-881-2389.

Printed and bound in Canada.

Cover design and formatting by Dawna Dearing, First Wave Grafix.

Front cover photos: Ron Hunt on left taken by Denis Brodeur from an Expos magazine. Ron LeFlore pictures courtesy Canadian Baseball Hall of Fame. Back cover photo: Jim Cox and Barry Foote taken by Denis Brodeur from an Expos magazine.

ISBN: 978-1-777-4132-1-7

*To: Charles Bronfman, John McHale, Jim Fanning
and the 1981 Expos in this the 40th anniversary year
of the franchise winning the NL East title.*

Design by Jostens

Author Danny Gallagher has paid tribute to the 1981 Expos by having a 40th anniversary commemorative ring made up by Jostens, which has a contract with Major League Baseball. There are various ring possibilities so check out the options at:

jostenscanada.com/expos

Prices include shipping, warranty, your name and number on the side and a $10 charity donation to one of Gallagher's many causes. Charles Bronfman, the majority owner of the Expos for more than 20 years, has purchased a silver ring and was hoping to get it in time for his 90th birthday June 27, 2021. Bronfman's number will be 83, alluding to the Seagram 83 Canadian rye whiskey his company produced for years.

Table of Contents

Gary Carter's headstone in a beautiful cemetery in Tequesta, Florida

Foreword

That hyphen you see between 1969-2004 represents a lot of memories during the 36 seasons the Expos operated.

That's what I have done in this book is accumulate memories from the start of the franchise to the end of the franchise, just like I did with my last 2020 release Always Remembered.

I see the passion of Expos fans all the time on Twitter and Facebook. I draw on that passion for my books. I draw on my own passion for my books.

I see the passion in the memorabilia collections amassed by Maxwell Kates, Maurice Dumas, John Rotari, Guy Bourque, Joel Passino, Burton Peck, Perry Giannias, Daniel Plamandon, Russ Hansen, Don Rice and so many others too numerous to mention.

I can also tell you this: that I wouldn't be writing all of these books about the Expos if I hadn't been an Expos beat writer from 1988-94 and continued to write stories for Globe and Mail in Toronto, the Montreal Gazette and other media outlets, including the Canadian Baseball Network website.

We don't know what the future of Major League Baseball in Montreal looks but it won't stop me from continuing to write about the Expos.

We are happy that former Expo Warren Cromartie started beating the drums for the return of the Expos close to 10 years ago and we are happy that prospective owners Stephen Bronfman and Mitch Garber are ready to take over a new team.

Enjoy the book.

— Danny Gallagher, March, 2021

LET'S GO EXPOS!
(VICTORY SONG)

LET'S GO EXPOS!
(Victory Song)

Lyrics by Joe Jammer/Dwight Druick
Music by Joe Jammer

Let's Go Expos! Let's Go!

Play ball! Expos all the way
Batter up! We're gonna beat these guys today
Summertime, what a fine way to go
Catch the boys playing ball at the Big O
What a day! What a game! What a show!
It's a victory - Let's Go Expos!

Baseball is the name of the game
And the Expos play it to win
So Mom and Dad, Sister and Brother
Let's watch them do it again
They got offense, defense -
Power at the plate
Pitching's on the ball
And they're doing it great
A little muscle here
A lotta hustle there
They put it all together
To be Champs this year...

Everybody knows
We are the Expos!
You know we play for real
Just watch us on the field
You know the Expos play to win
It's a victory - Let's Go Expos!
An Expos victory - Let's Go Expos!

Lyrics by Joe Jammer/Dwight Druick
Music by Joe Jammer

Executive Producers For Sopro, Inc.:
Bud Monaco / Red Rose / Garry Flanagin

Graphic Design: "Boris" Boden

Webmaster: Steve Goodey

www.sopromusic.com

Copyright: SoproMusic 2002

Hilarious free-agent draft

On the 30th anniversary of the 1968 free-agent draft that allowed Montreal to take college and high school players from the U.S., Dan Ziniuk penned an eloquent, hilarious piece for his hometown Ottawa Citizen.

On the same page, Montreal newspaper legend Ted Blackman was commissioned to write a fun-filled tome that only Blackman could write, about what transpired that same day at the Americana Hotel on 7th Ave. in downtown New York June 7, 1968.

This event was actually overshadowed by some very sombre news that shocked America and the world: the assassination of Robert F. Kennedy. On the entertainment side, The Fifth Dimension was in New York to make their Manhattan debut of their smash hit Up, Up and Away.

What happened at the draft, as Ziniuk wrote it, was the "story of the first and only time an armchair general manager actually took part in the business of Major League Baseball." Ziniuk went on to say that "the delegation selecting on behalf of Montreal's brand-new National League franchise couldn't have been more conspicuous."

That armchair QB just happened to be Blackman because even though Montreal had been granted a National League franchise on May 27, just 11 days earlier, the team had no official owner in place until Charles Bronfman came to the rescue months later. John McHale and Jim Fanning had yet to be officially brought on board and the Expos name had yet to be chosen.

"Every table had 12 people at it. Every team had a manager, a general manager, a farm-system director, a director of scouting and at least five scouts sitting there," Blackman told Ziniuk about the pres-

Denis Brodeur photo/Lesley Taylor collection

It apparently was not Opening Day at home in 1969 but here's an interesting photo of people watching an Expos game at Jarry Park. Front row, left to right, are Montreal mayor Jean Drapeau, Charles Bronfman's mother Saidye, Norah Michener, former Canadian Governor-General Roland Michener, Bronfman's father Samuel and former Prime Minister Lester Pearson. Second row, left to right, man in camel hair coat unknown, Bronfman's father-in-law Herman Baerwald, Bronfman's wife Barbara, Charles Bronfman, Expos president John McHale and at the far right is a young Brian Mulroney, who became Prime Minister in 1984.

Expos' amateur draft picks from June 7, 1968

Player	Position	Round	Where drafted from
Michael Swain	RHP	Fourth	Ohio State University
Frank Ward	RHP	Fifth	Southern Poly Tech (Marietta, Georgia)
Roger Nelson	C	Sixth	Lincoln SE High (Nebraska)
Kevin Bryant	SS	Seventh	Winter Haven High (Florida)
William Kendall	3B	Eighth	University of Minnesota
Ross Hoffman	1B	Ninth	University of California
Carlton Exum	RHP	10th	Evans High, Orlando
Dave Hartman	LHP	11th	Iowa State University
John Palmer	LHP	12th	University of Minnesota
Louis Woltz	3B	13th	Georgia Perimeter College
Joseph Marecki	SS	14th	Miami-Dade College
Richard Turner	RHP	16th	Eau Gallie High, Florida
Bill Seagraves	RHP-3B	17th	Edgewater High, Orlando
Michael Fulford	3B	18th	Miami-Dade College

Source: Baseball-Reference.com. Richard Trembecki was selected but the pick was declared null and void because Canadians weren't eligible for the draft.

ence of established major-league teams. "We had Gerry, Johnny, a lawyer and a newspaper guy."

Gerry was Gerry Snyder, the Montreal city council member who had lobbied baseball's team owners for years that Montreal deserved a team. Johnny was Johnny Newman, a football fanatic. The lawyer was Jonathan Robinson, Bronfman's attorney. Pierre Jerome, who worked for Air Canada in public relations, was sent to the dais for the first round.

"Being perfectly bilingual, he (Jerome) got up and rambled on in French for about five or six sentences," Snyder told Blackman. "Nobody in the room knew what the hell he was talking about."

Then in English, Jerome let everyone know what he was really trying to say was that Montreal was passing on the first round.

When it was all over, the Montreal folks had drafted 15 players and signed six of them. The first pick was Michael Swain, who snubbed Fanning's offer of $500 to sign and never received another offer.

"I wasn't contacted for what seemed like months and I was anxious to sign and get playing," Swain told Ziniuk. "I remember how I finally heard from them, probably a month to six weeks after the draft."

Swain decided to re-enter the draft in 1969 and signed with the Mariners but never made it to the majors.

Blackman had flown to New York to cover the draft but ended up helping out an outmanned, undermanned contingent from Montreal. It was comical, although Fanning had helped the folks at the MLB Scouting Bureau by supplying the names of prospects that Montreal could choose from so that they wouldn't be totally inept at the table, Blackman told Ziniuk.

Canadian Baseball Hall of Fame

Jim Fanning and John McHale pose with the Expos logo, design and hat

"Obviously, the commissioner's office, having awarded Montreal a franchise, wasn't about to watch Montreal get humiliated," Blackman continued. "All around the table, everybody said, 'OK, let's look for a guy who's over 6 feet, weighs 200 pounds and is a pitcher, and let's see what happens from there.'"

Yes, Montreal's representatives sure needed help. The assembled representatives from the other teams chuckled when Blackman went up to the dais and announced that Montreal had selected Canadian Richard Trembecki who played centre field for the University of Denver. The only problem was that Canadians were ineligible for the draft and his choice was ruled null and void.

"Lacking a general manager, a field manager or anyone with baseball front-office experience, only George Plimpton seemed to be missing from Montreal's draft table," Ziniuk wrote in his feature story.

"Hell, I wouldn't even have let them be in the draft," snorted Whitey Herzog, a Mets minor-league director, to a reporter. "They were put together that fast. They didn't have an organization put together yet."

When Montreal was awarded the franchise in late May, Bronfman was confounded and puzzled.

"Holy shit, I own a franchise. Now, what do I do?" he told Blackman one time. Hilarious.

Snyder was the city's representative at the owners' meetings in May and one of the reporters on hand was Dick Kaegel, who wrote that he was somewhat skeptical of Montreal's chances. He told his readers that Dallas-Fort Worth, Buffalo, Montreal, Milwaukee and San Diego appeared to be the front-runners for the two new teams that the National League would pick.

"Analysts paid little attention to Montreal," Kaegel said in a dispatch. "After all, Triple-A ball died there in 1960 and why would the NL go into Canada anyway when there seemed to be qualified cities in

Expos' picks in Oct. 14, 1968 expansion draft

Player	Position	Team taken from
Manny Mota	OF	Dodgers
Mack Jones	OF	Reds
John Bateman	C	Astros
Gary Sutherland	IF	Phillies
Jack Billingham	RHP	Dodgers
Jesus Alou	OF	Giants
Mike Wegener	P	Phillies
Skip Guinn	P	Braves
Bill Stoneman	RHP	Cubs
Maury Wills	SS	Pirates
Larry Jackson	LHP	Phillies
Bob Reynolds	RHP	Giants
Dan McGinn	LHP	Reds
Jose Herrera	OF	Astros
Jimy Williams	IF	Reds
Remy Hermoso	IF	Braves
Mudcat Grant	RHP	Dodgers
Jerry Robertson	IF	Cardinals
Don Shaw	RHP	Mets
Ty Cline	OF	Giants
Carl Morton	RHP	Braves
Larry Jaster	LHP	Cardinals
Ernie McAnally	RHP	Mets
Jim Fairey	OF	Dodgers
Coco Laboy	3B	Cardinals
John Boccabella	C	Cubs
Ron Brand	C	Astros
John Glass	P	Mets

the U.S.? Gerry Snyder, pink-faced and dressed in deep blue, explained Montreal's low-keyed approach."

In defence and in support of Montreal, Snyder said: "To start with, we've got double the population of the other cities. It's a new territory. We're not infringing on anyone's rights. We're not running a popularity contest for Montreal. We haven't been trying for a lot of headlines. All we're trying to do is convince 10 men (voting owners)."

At 10:30 a.m., the meeting was slated to begin but Dodgers owner Walter O'Malley, who was in Montreal's favour because he operated the Montreal Royals, was late. Kaegel wrote that an "anxious photographer wanted to know if they would start the meeting without O'Malley." NL president Warren Giles said they would wait for O'Malley. As Kaegel could see, the owners' meeting was held at a table full of "ice water, plump apples, official NL note books, Doublemint, Spearmint and Juicy Fruit gum."

Wanna know how long the owners debated the pros and cons of each franchise? Almost 12 hours until 9 p.m. when Montreal and San Diego were selected.

John Bocc-a-bell-a

Claude Mouton walked onto the field at Jarry Park one day, sidled up to John Boccabella and asked him, "The way I announce your name, does it bother you?"

Boccabella answered the public-address announcer this way, "It doesn't bother me but I'm not Babe Ruth. I'm batting .105."

Of course what they were referring to was the way Mouton introduced Boccabella to fans at Jarry Park as he approached home plate for an at-bat: John Bocc-a-belllll-a.

Boccabella told me that someone in the Expos front office went to Mouton one time and admonished him about his pronunciation.

"You can't be doing that. It's bush league," the Expos official told Mouton, as Boccabella relayed the story.

Anyway, Boccabella did get a kick out of it.

"I wasn't playing a whole lot," the former reserve catcher was saying as he wondered in amazement about the popularity of his name. "It was great. It was pretty cool. The fans went crazy. It was kind of like a legend type thing in Montreal. I would get cool letters from people. Rusty Staub, Le Grand Orange and me.

"Claude sent me a letter and I framed it. It was after he left the Canadiens. He did PR for them. You heard people all over the ballpark pronouncing my name. Claude didn't realize what he had done for the citizens of the United States.

"After I retired, Equitable Life Insurance would do all-star games in each city each year. They would bring back players. It was a big deal. One of those years, we went to the famous Napa winery in California and had a dinner and we're on the bus. Tom Seaver was there and Tommy Davis comes on the bus and saw me and said, 'John Bocc-a-belll-a.' The players knew, not just the fans."

Denis Brodeur photo/Lesley Taylor collection

**Catchers John Boccabella, left, Ron Brand and John Bateman
were called the Killer Bs.**

Boccabella was an original Expos catcher getting some playing time with fellow Killer Bs John Bateman and Ron Brand. Even though he wasn't a regular, Boccabella considered him a solid defensive player, although he admitted he had his offensive shortcomings.

"I never hit worth a damn," he said. "I had the ability to hit better. Nobody taught me. It was raw ability. I could have hit .280 with 30 homers a year if somebody had showed me what to do."

In 1969, Boccabella collected only 86 at-bats but by 1973, he emerged with more playing time with 403 ABs.

"I was always a really good catcher," he told me. "I could throw guys out and I was real quick. Almost on average, I'd throw the ball on the base every time, right on the bag.

"I'd get rid of the ball so quickly the ball would be right at the ground and runners would slide into the glove. People would say, 'How did you do that?' I used to throw Lou Brock out by 10 feet. Pitchers liked to throw to me, especially Mike Marshall. He didn't like Bateman."

Boccabella was right. I looked up his fielding stats on Baseball Reference and his caught-stealing percentage was exemplary. His percentage in 1969 was 48%, much higher than the MLB average. The old adage is that if a catcher's CS percentage falls close to 35%, you're doing good. In 1973, he was at 48% again and in 1973, it was 40%.

Boccabella said he was ready to retire following the '72 season because he said he was "just hanging on." That winter, Boccabella had interviewed for a job outside baseball and was ready to pack in his baseball career.

"The Expos sent me a contract for the same money as the last year," Boccabella said, laughing about it. "I said, 'Screw it. I'm retiring.' They called me back and said, 'We want you to be the catcher.' I told them I would be back if they gave me more money. I was making $20,000. They offered $5,000 more. Back then, it was a lot of money. I had committed to this job in California.

"The Expos called me back a few days later. They said they had gone through all the available catchers. I was the only guy and they said, 'You're the guy.' We'll give you another $5,000. $10,000 was a lot of money in those days, probably a few million today. $30,000 (for 1973) seems like meal money nowadays. They talked me into it. I said, 'I'll do it.' I was making $7,000 when I started."

Boccabella helped the '73 Expos become a Cinderella squad that threatened to win the NL East pennant but the dream fell short. The Expos stirred up Canada in this their fifth season of operation. Boccabella hit a solid .279 with seven homers and 46 RBI as the No. 1 catcher, appearing in 118 games and getting 403 at-bats, sharing time with Terry Humphrey and Bob Stinson.

Bateman had been traded in June of 1972 to Philadelphia in exchange for Tim McCarver but McCarver didn't figure in Montreal's plans for 1973.

On July 6, 1973, Boccabella hit two home runs in the sixth inning, one of them a grand salami.

That game was the highlight of his career and No. 2 was the three-run, walk-off homer he delivered at Jarry Park as the Expos stunned the Pirates 10-7 on Sept. 2, 1970. Boccabella was a late-game replacement for Bateman and drilled one "20 rows into the left-field seats" on a 2-0 fastball.

"That year 1973 was the most fun I had in baseball," Boccabella said. "That was probably the biggest story, 1973. We had a chance to win the division. Nobody was that strong."

That's right: the Mets won the division with an 82-79 mark, the Cardinals were 81-81, the Pirates were 81-82 and the Expos came in at 79-83.

Who should Boccabella run into in Daytona Beach in 1973-74?

"Gary Carter had signed and we were at spring training. We became really good friends." Boccabella said. "I was rooming with Carter. He was so full of energy, strong as an ox. He had this enthusiasm. We'd talk about religion."

Boccabella was back in camp with the Expos in Daytona Beach in 1974 after his great season in 1973 but near the end of spring training on March 27, he was swapped to his hometown Giants in exchange for Don Carrithers. The son of immigrant parents didn't play much in 1974 and decided to retire after the season ended.

Submitted photo
John Boccabella
with Saskatoon

"I disliked travelling," Boccabella said. "I had some really bad plane rides."

Boccabella had a wife, Joyce, a sweetheart from school days in Marin County, Calif., and three kids to worry about so it was time to get out into the real world and work for a living. He worked for 19 years as a marketing rep for Pacific Gas and Electric, retiring in 1993. Boccabella said he has been receiving his MLB pension for more than 30 years.

We can't leave this story about Boccabella without telling you that he played amateur ball in the Canadian city of Saskatoon, Saskatchewan in 1962. The team was called the Commodores and he was recruited by the great promoter Spiro Leakos.

And what a season Boccabella had on the Prairies. He hit .340, tagged 13 homers and drove in 63 runs in 62 games as Saskatoon compiled a 46-16 regular-season record only to lose to Lethbridge, Alberta in the final series.

"We had a great team. It was a fun summer," Boccabella said of his time in Saskatoon. "It was a summer season. It was not professional. We had a lot of college kids. We had a lot of scouts watching."

Before heading east to Saskatoon, Boccabella also had played that year for the University of Santa Clara, a Jesuit school. The team went 49-8 during the regular season and headed to the College World Series in Omaha, Nebraska where they lost 5-4 to the Michigan Wolverines in the championship game that lasted 15 innings.

The Chicago Cubs really took notice of what Boccabella did in '62. Prior to the 1963 season, the Cubs signed Boccabella as a first baseman. Playing out of Pocatella (Idaho) in the Pioneer League, Boccabella was a standout with 30 homers, 92 RBI and a .365 BA. Whew. Holy shoot.

"That was some season, prompting some announcers to refer to him as Boccabella from Pocatella, although he hailed from San Francisco. He earned a September call-up and stretched out a decent MLB career until 1974.

Nowadays, Boccabella tries to get to Holy Mass daily and he plays golf five times a week. He's in excellent health, heading into his eighth decade of life.

A grand season for Morton

In the 36-season history of the Expos, Carl Morton's dream campaign in 1970 was akin to Ross Grimsley's 20-11 season in 1978, Steve Rogers' 19-8 campaign in 1982 and Pedro Martinez's Cy Young-winning 17-8 in 1997.

Morton was king of the hill the season following their expansion debut. He was wonderful. He was exquisite. He was tremendous. He almost won 20 games on a bad, second-year expansion team. He was a go-to man for Expos manager Gene Mauch.

Morton was never quite the same before or after that with the Expos. But in 1970, he served notice that maybe he had some future ahead of him.

Morton was 18-11. If you're trying to figure out what Expos pitcher enjoyed the best season in franchise history, then you start with Morton. We could say this one season of wonders was at the top of the list because the team he was pitching for was only in its second season of operation. He should not have been expected to win anywhere close to 18 games.

"My first impression of Carl was that he was in unbelievable shape. Physically, he was a specimen. He was really into conditioning," recalled his 1970 teammate Rich Nye.

Morton's extraordinary season resulted in him winning the National League rookie-of-the-year award over notable competition such as Reds players Bernie Carbo and Wayne Simpson, Larry Bowa of the Phillies and Cesar Cedeno of the Astros. Morton took 11 of the 24 votes cast by the Baseball Writers Association of America.

Morton also received votes for NL MVP and the Cy Young award.

The big redhead from Oklahoma was a workhorse, throwing 284.2 innings in an era when pitchers were never enamoured with pitch counts

Canadian Baseball Hall of Fame

Carl Morton

Denis Brodeur photo/Lesley Taylor collection
Carl Morton looks in for the sign

and coming out in the sixth inning. He was looking to pitch nine innings everytime he hit the mound. He threw 10 complete games that season, struck out 154 in 43 starts, 36 handled by catcher John Bateman. He was marvellous in July with a 6-1 record. His season ERA was 3.60.

Okay, so he gave up 27 long balls, 17 to right-handed batters, 18 at home. He tended to be a bit wild, issuing 125 bases on balls, although he only threw two wild pitches.

By July, it appeared he was on his way to a 20-win season but he got bogged down by a number of no decisions and losses and had to settle for 18 Ws.

"The thing that made him different in baseball," Nye said, "was that he actually studied the opposition. One of the first managers to have any kind of log on what opposing pitchers did against his team was Gene

21

Mauch. He was early into that phase of looking at statistics, keeping a computer print out of what every batter did – where the balls were hit. It was like you had 10 players on the field. Mauch would be in the dugout moving his players around.

"When you think about that, where does Montreal finish up that year? We knew everytime Carl was going to be on the top of his game. He didn't have bad starts. A lot of times, we didn't score runs. His goal was always to throw nine innings. He was going to complete the game. Today, they say, 'Give me five innings.'

"He was spectacular in his delivery. He had a fastball, curveball, slider, changeup. Nobody was like him when he was in his zone. When he was pitching, nobody bothered him. He really got into that mental part of the game. He would sit at his locker before each start and nobody would talk to him. He had his head focusing down at his notes. He'd call it meditating.

"When he wasn't pitching, he was a comedian, he was happy, he had all kinds of fun playing with the guys."

As Tom Hawthorn said in his profile of Morton for the Society for American Baseball Research book Time for Expansion, Morton constantly read Psycho-Cybernetics, especially before his starts. It was a book dealing with the science of motivation and self-confidence by Maxwell Maltz, a cosmetic surgeon.

"Carl was a grinder. He was always positive no matter the situation," his 1970-71 teammate Jim Gosger said in an interview. "A great teammate. He was the one pitcher Gene looked to when we were struggling in 1970."

Morton had started his pro career with the old Milwaukee Braves' organization as an outfielder but the Expos grabbed him as a pitcher in the expansion draft Oct. 14, 1968. Newly installed Expos executives John McHale and Jim Fanning had been with the Milwaukee/Atlanta Braves for several years and were aware of what Morton could do.

Morton started the 1969 season with the Expos but after he went 0-3, he was optioned to Triple-A with Canada's Vancouver Mounties.

After that glorious 1970 season, Morton would stumble to 10-18 in 1971 and then 7-13 in 1972. The Expos soured on him and swapped him back to the Braves on Feb. 28, 1973 in exchange for Pat Jarvis. Morton found his groove again with the Braves, posting solid seasons of 15-10, 16-12 and 17-16 before faltering to 4-9 in 1976. He never pitched again in the majors.

Morton gave it a whirl with the Rangers, who got him in a trade, and then he tried out with his homestate Triple-A team, the Oklahoma City Sooners, in the hope of getting called up by the parent Phillies but it never happened. He attended spring training with the Pirates in 1978 but was released before the regular season started.

Like he did with the Expos and all his life, he stayed in great shape.

It was ironic that keeping in shape doomed him. On the morning of April 12, 1983, he collapsed in the driveway of his house after jogging. He was pronounced dead of a heart attack at Tulsa Hospital. Anybody who jogs or runs gets an accelerated heart rate. It's believed Morton was the first former Expos player to die, according to a spreadsheet posted on Facebook by Francois Melancon of Montreal. At 39, Morton is certainly the youngest Expo to date to pass away. He was the only Expo to die in 1983, Melancon said.

His Expos legacy? That wonderful 1970 season.

Taylor was an Expo in spring training in 1972

Thoughts are with Ron Taylor, who is suffering from Alzheimer's at a long-care home in the Toronto area.

He's one of Canada's most famous baseball personalities: a Blue Jays physician for decades and a World Series winner with the 1964 Cardinals and the 1969 Mets as a relief pitcher. Amazing athlete and man.

Taylor actually had a stab with the Expos at spring training in 1972 but it ends up that he never played in a regular-season game.

Taylor's contract was purchased by the Expos from the Mets on Oct. 20, 1971 and he went to spring training in 1972 but was released on March 28. Less than a month later, he signed with the Padres.

Taylor pitched in four games for the Padres but he was released in Montreal on May 14, the day he gave up three runs against the Expos, including homers by Ron Fairly and Mike Jorgensen.

Upon his release by the Padres, he arranged for entry into medical school at the University of Toronto. He graduated a few years later and then in 1979, he began a long run as the Blue Jays team physician.

Taylor is a member of the Canadian Baseball Hall of Fame, the Ontario Sports Hall of Fame and Canada's Sports Hall of Fame.

Sandy Koufax clone

Many people were saying Balor Moore would be the next coming of a famous star from the 1960s, a fellow left-hander.

"I had so many strikeouts, such good velocity and good movement that I was constantly being compared to Sandy Koufax," Moore was telling me in 2020. "I didn't have much knowledge of Sandy Koufax but I knew he was something special. We had no way of following baseball. We had never seen the Sporting News."

Moore came from a miniscule town of Deer Lake, Texas located a short distance from Houston.

Moore inked a deal with the Expos for $20,000 in 1968 and the signing made the front page of the Sports section in the now defunct Houston Post newspaper. He posed with a pair of Reds: Murff and Gaskill. They were wearing beautiful Expos sweaters but Moore told me the story of how his sweater was spoiled when the red ink bled red over everything else when it went in the wash the first time. He doesn't have that sweater anymore.

"My dad knew nothing about baseball, he knew nothing about the draft or how it worked. We didn't really get coverage in the newspapers," Moore was saying. "My dad was from a blue-collar neighbourhood and he was wondering what it was going to cost him for me to sign. He had no idea they were going to make me an offer.

"We had no agent, no leverage. We didn't know if that offer was good, bad or if we should hold off a bit."

For five years or so, Moore was highly scouted. Scouts like Murff and Gaskill put in a lot of miles to see him pitch. Three years earlier, Murff and Gaskill were credited with signing phenom Nolan Ryan for the Mets.

And there was no denying Moore's pitch count leading into the draft was high. He was accustomed to going the distance in all or most starts. In 1969, he was downright excellent.

With the Gulf Coast Expos, he was 7-0 with a puny 0.27 ERA in 67

IP. That's right: 0.27. And then with the West Palm Beach Expos, he was 2-1 with a 0.86 ERA in 21 IP. In the fall of 1969 in the Florida Instructional league, he was 3-5 with a 2.33 ERA in 58 innings.

Moore made his MLB debut on May 21, 1970 with much fanfare at the age of 19 years, 116 days. By 1972, he was in the rotation more often. That season, one of the highlights that was "memorable" for Moore was his streak of 25 scoreless innings. Pretty darn impressive. That was prime-time Moore, the Koufax type of pitching the Expos were seeking.

Canadian Baseball Hall of Fame
Balor Moore

He was in his third consecutive game of scoreless pitching when Phillies rookie Mike Schmidt broke the streak with his first MLB homer, a three-run shot that gave Philly a 3-1 win. Moore finished 1972 with 161 strikeouts and a very respectable 3.47 ERA. He was an outstanding prospect indeed.

In 1973, he was a full-time member of the staff in a season when the Expos threatened to win the NL East. If Moore had gone 16-7 or even 13-10, instead of going 7-16, the Expos likely would have won the division. He fanned 151 in 176.1 innings that season and his ERA shot up to 4.49. Too many walks hurt him: 109, compared to 59 in 1972.

From spring training 1973 to spring training 1974, Moore figures he threw about 350 innings: that total included innings thrown in spring training both of those years, the 1973 regular season and 1973-74 winter ball in Puerto Rico.

That year-long stint saw him throw a nine-inning perfect game in winter ball. He remembers it so distinctly that it only took 81 pitches. Only nine pitches were curveballs, meaning he was throwing a lot of heat.

As for that perfect no-no, "I got food poisoning the night before. I was sick, weak and dehydrated but still I talked the manager into my scheduled start."

Moore admits the year-long stint that resulted in those 350 innings

25

Houston Metropolitan Research Centre, Houston Public Library

Balor Moore, centre, poses with his step-father Mark Rogers and mother Bobbie Rogers and scouts Red Gaskill, left back, and Red Murff.

Houston Metropolitan Research Centre, Houston Public Library

Balor Moore, right, holds up his Expos contract he signed June 15, 1968 with scouts Red Murff, left, and Red Gaskill.

took a toll on his throwing arm. He was never quite the same after that.

"No rest in between," Moore said of his work from 1973-74.

Then during the course of the 1974 season, Moore's stature and status with the Expos fell. That's when his arm began hurting because of overwork. He only threw 13.2 innings that season. There was no improvement in 1975 and the Expos made the decision to sell his contract to the Angels on June 15.

"Tired arm and poor mechanics led to my arm injury," Moore reasoned.

In the end, Moore never came close to emulating Koufax in the majors over the long haul. He doesn't blame manager Gene Mauch for what happened. Instead, he said his problems were mechanics-related.

"I was used to pitching nine innings," Moore said. "I don't think the Expos intentionally abused me. I think the issue I had was mechanically. I tried to force things and I hurt my arm. I may have been rushed to the big leagues. I didn't have time to mature as a ball player.

"I walked a lot of hitters, struck out a lot, went deep in the count to a lot of hitters. Sometimes 160 pitches a game. I was getting a little tired and my mechanics were falling apart.

"I was with a lot of veteran-type players who didn't want to be there in Montreal, players who were on the downside of their careers. They were malcontents. That was more harmful for me to be around them. Gene Mauch also added a lot of tension to the clubhouse. Mauch wanted to win. He went with veteran players."

In August of 1975 while in the Angels organization, Moore underwent Tommy John surgery under the knife with Dr. Frank Jobe in California, a procedure that didn't seem to produce good results, although he had hoped he would get back to where he was.

Moore was also told by Jobe that he had a rib that was broken in two places after he complained of back pain. Moore said there was no rehab program following the TJ operation but Jobe told him he "should be fine." He tried to come back and pitch but he "wasn't doing very good." He said he came back "much too soon after surgery."

Moore finished out his career with the other Canadian team, the Blue Jays. So all in all, he played in Canada for Montreal, Toronto, Vancouver and Winnipeg. He has no regrets about how things turned out. Looking back, he said he "needed to play relaxed" but admitted he "didn't have that security" because "one more bad game and I was going back to the minors." He said he gave it "everything I had" when he pitched.

"I was clean. I never cheated the game," Moore said. "I always pitched like it was going to be my last game. I have zero regrets."

In what was an interesting interview Moore did years ago with London, Ontario writer Kevin Glew, Moore said people would ask him who he played for in the majors and he would blurt out "Toronto Blue Jays".

So I asked Moore why he said Toronto and not Montreal first since the Expos were his first MLB employer.

"Toronto had a different atmosphere, the culture," Moore said, adding Mauch was more interested in winning. "Being from a small town in Texas, this (Toronto) was more close to being a mid-sized city."

For many years, Moore has owned the Britton Pipe Company in Texas. He talks about spending a lot of time in the pipe yard, not the ball yard.

"How is your arm today?" I asked Moore.

"I never had any re-hab. I can't straighten my arm or touch my shoulder but the arm feels fine," he said. "The shoulder is shot but that's to be expected considering I was a high pitch-count pitcher. Lots of walks, strikeouts and deep counts."

Any all time favourite Expos teammate? "Terry Humphrey, Tim McCarver, Kenny Singleton, Tom Walker, Mike Torrez, (coach) Cal McLish."

Rusty and his White Russians

The date was believed to be Sept. 2, 1970 at Jarry Park in Montreal.

The Expos had recorded the third out in a certain inning and right fielder Rusty Staub was sprinting, not trotting, off the field. Staub was headed straight to the clubhouse, causing a commotion.

"What's going on?" Staub's teammate Jim Gosger asked somebody close by.

"He shit his pants," his teammate said.

"What?"

"He shit his pants," came a second answer.

Gosger started laughing as he spoke to this writer.

"It's a funny story," Gosger said. "He was playing in the outfield. We got the third out and he started running. Everybody was laughing. It was just like it happened yesterday. Rusty liked White Russians. That was his favourite drink. It caught up with him. He took off for the clubhouse. He definitely had to change his pants."

If you don't know what a White Russian is, here goes the ingredients: vodka, coffee liqueur and cream. The liqueur could be either one of Kahlua, Tia Maria or Bailey's Irish Cream. The drink has no Russian connotations with the name stemming from vodka, the main ingredient.

That was one of many memories Gosger has of his two-season stint with the Expos in 1970-71.

How about the time the Expos and the Mets were playing in the seventh inning and Expos manager Gene Mauch told Gosger to "get a bat" with fireballer Nolan Ryan on the mound. This was on a day when truckloads and truckloads of snow had to be removed to get Jarry Park in playing shape.

"Who do you want me to give it to?" Gosger said to Mauch about the

Montreal Expos photo

Jim Gosger

bat he was asked to get.

"I want you to hit," Mauch replied.

Gosger started chuckling as he relayed the story to me.

"I had so much memorable stuff like that," Gosger said. "It's like these memories happened yesterday. I truly loved Montreal, I loved playing up there. The people were great, the park was fun to go to. I have some friends who passed away. It kind of scares me."

Gosger wasn't a fan of Mauch's. He felt the manager was just too darn hard on his charges. Gosger, admitting Mauch was a "helluva strategist", called Mauch a "strict manager" and "not a player's manager, who had the audacity to call out his players on the field or in the dugout if they did something he perceived to be wrong.

"Players have feelings, too," Gosger said about Mauch calling out people. "There was a pop up one game near the dugout and Ron Brand was sitting down in the dugout and Mauch got all upset with him because he thought Brand should have let the fielder know what was going on. Brand didn't know what to say.

"Things like that stick out. It got to me. We were walking around on our tip toes. He was always negative. One day, he was walking in the outfield and he looked at my socks. I had them all year. He said, 'Go into the clubhouse and get a new pair.' He wanted me to change them. When he got mad, he had veins in his neck.

"One game (May 16, 1971) we were in Cincinnati, Ron Fairly was batting for us and Tony Cloninger was pitching for Cincinnati. Mauch shouted, 'Fastball' and Cloninger heard it. Cloninger was screaming and hollering at Mauch for calling his pitches. So next pitch, he drilled Fairly on the right cheek."

That's right. In boldface on the retrosheet.org text account of the game underneath the boxscore, it read: Ron Fairly hit on face by pitch, taken off on stretcher. Fairly had to spend time on the DL.

Not only was Cloninger mad but so was Fairly. Gosger said Fairly didn't want Mauch or anyone to call out upcoming pitches coming to him.

"My memories of Mauch are not good," Gosger said. "He was not into the personal status of the ballplayers. In other words, he didn't want to congratulate you."

Gosger has memories to last a lifetime. He played with or against some of the legendary figures in MLB history.

"I hit a home run off Whitey Ford. The first time I ever faced him. One of my favourite memories," Gosger said.

And that in itself was an achievement because Gosger, as a member of the Red Sox, was a platoon player. And he was a left-handed batter facing a veteran southpaw, one of the best in the game, on Oct. 3, 1965.

"I was the last hitter to face Satchell Paige (59 years old). That was in 1965 (Sept. 25). I never knew it would be a trivia question," Gosger said proudly.

"He was pitching for Kansas City. Charlie Finley brought him in as a publicity stunt for three innings. He only gave up one hit. Yaz got a hit (double) off him. I grounded out to second (as Paige ended his three-inning stint) and I was running to the dugout. I looked at him and he looked at me and he said, 'Good luck, young man'.

"For a man of his stature to say something to me, a young kid, 22 years old, it's something you don't forget. I was very proud of that, proud of that situation in my memory.

"Ted Williams was my hitting instructor at spring training in 1962. It was so memorable when you get in the batting cage for a few minutes. He never said anything until I came out of the batting cage. He was a great mentor. I had a picture taken with him. I still have the picture. I wish I could have gotten it signed."

Gosger was a member of the Athletics squad that played its final season in Kansas City in 1967. He was privileged to have Joe DiMaggio as his hitting coach with the 1968 Oakland Athletics and his teammates that season including Reggie Jackson, Rick Monday and Campy Campaneris. He had Larry Doby as a hitting coach in 1971 with the Expos. He had Yogi Berra as a manager with the Mets and his Mets teammates included Willie Mays and Staub, his buddy with the Expos.

Gosger was known to help keep clubhouses in check wherever he played and could he swing with those powerful arms!

"Jim swung so hard he'd hit a golf ball longer than LP (Larry Parrish)," said Russ Hansen, one of Gosger's friends.

Denis Brodeur photo/Peggie Bougie collection
Don Drysdale, left, and Duke Snider were Expos coaches and broadcasters

"I still get a lot of requests for signatures, about 4-5 times a week," said Gosger, who lives in Port Huron, Mich. "What is nice is that they (people) remember you. I never refused anything. There are a lot of guys who charge for autographs. Not me."

Red Sox star Ted Williams, left, Red Sox scout Neil Mahoney, Rusty Staub and his father Ray pose in 1961

Photo supplied by Staub family

HBP led to concussions and Parkinson's

You've heard of that expression, "He took one for the team."

Ron Hunt took one for the team too often, meaning the Expos, Mets, Dodgers, Giants and Cardinals. He took pitches in the ribs, head, wherever, any way possible to get on base. Often, Hunt would just stand at the plate and let the ball hit him.

With no power so to speak and choking way up on the bat, Hunt figured he would try to get on base anyway possible. It would take bravery and courage to stand at the plate and wince when a fastball hit him. Hunt was never gun-shy. He crowded the plate, daring pitchers to hit him or give him a pitch to hit.

All these years later, the beanings and subsequent concussions have led to Hunt getting beaned broadside by Parkinson's or so him and his wife Jackie have been told. The neurodegenerative disease is incurable. Keep him in your thoughts. He's been suffering from this nasty disease for over four years.

"I have problems with my memory," Hunt was telling me in an interview in January, 2021. "I've got the shakes. I take medication. I take pills. I do rehab once a week."

Sadly, Parkinson's has been cruel to Hunt. His memory in many instances has been robbed just like it is for Alzheimer's patients. When I asked him what he remembered about Jim Fanning, the Expos GM during his tenure, he replied, "Who is Jim Fanning?" When I asked Hunt what he remembered about Expos president John McHale, he replied, "Who is John McHale?"

A few seconds later, Hunt would tell me, "I don't remember who the general manager was."

When I asked Hunt if he had a favourite Expos teammate, he had no

Denis Brodeur photo in Expos magazine
Ron Hunt was hit by a pitch 243 times

Denis Brodeur photo in Expos magazine
Ron Hunt hit the dirt a lot after getting hit by a pitch

answer. When I asked him if there was a teammate he didn't like, he had no reply. See how devastating Parkinson's can be.

Parkinson's doesn't stop Hunt from his duties as a cattleman at the family's Whispering Pines acreage located about 40 miles from St. Louis.

When New York Post baseball columnist Ken Davidoff visited Hunt in 2020, he shot video of Hunt feeding his animals and driving his tractor – along with an excellent print story. So Hunt can get around. He's not confined to his house.

Hunt told Davidoff that he would often practise in front of a mirror to get ready to get hit by a pitch on purpose. Some opposing pitchers would often complain that Hunt never made any attempt to get out of the way.

"He was diagnosed about four years when he had a heart valve put in," Mrs. Hunt said of the Parkinson's scenario. "We thought nothing up to that point because we saw no symptoms but apparently they saw something in the hospital when he was recovering from the heart valve operation.

"It has progressed over the years. That's what Parkinson's does. He doesn't shake. I give him CBD oil. It stops the shaking. He has problems with his balance. That is his problem."

Mrs. Hunt says those beanings, according to their doctors, are blamed in part for the memory losses. There were a lot of concussions in high school where he played football, getting hit on the noggin too many times by opposing players. Even shakes, rattles and rolls of the

Denis Brodeur photo in Expos magazine
Gene Mauch had a lot of detractors

head when hit in the main part of the body can help cause concussions. Hunt was so good at football that he was courted by Ohio State and Northwestern.

"I will tell you this. There were a lot of concussions in high school," Mrs. Hunt said. "But the concussions he received in the pros were more severe than in high school.

"I remember one when he was with the Giants. It was in Philadelphia and I was listening to the game in San Francisco. Willie Mays had hit a

37

double and Ron got flagged home. It was a close play. Cookie Rojas of the Phillies took the cut-off throw and threw the ball and hit Ron right on the side of the head. The throw was right on the number, right at the plate. They did not wear helmets then.

"They took him straight to the hospital. They kept him there for a couple of days. His head was so swollen. He couldn't get a hat on. It was a just a few days and he was back in the lineup."

Hunt told me he was "knocked out" by Rojas' throw.

When I brought up all those HBP, as it's indicated in the boxscore from his days with the Expos, Hunt replied, "That was in 1971, right? I took the pitches all my life. I got hit a lot. They thought I was a Montreal person and they would hurt me but I couldn't let them know it."

Yes, that season, Hunt was hit 50 times, a major-league record for many years. And as he said, he would rarely if ever challenge the pitcher or tell them to knock it off if he got hit. If he hit the dirt, he would simply get up and trot down to first.

"I remember the old park, Parc Jarry," Hunt said. "I enjoyed the fans, the money, the hunting and fishing and I'm still in contact with (broadcaster) Jacques Doucet.

"I got fined, too. This catcher Bob Barton (with the Padres) was getting in my face so I asked Gene Mauch what I should do. He said to take his mask off and hit him.

"So I took his mask off and hit him in the face. I was fined $250 and suspended for two games. I paid the fine out of my salary. I asked Mauch to pay the fine and he said, 'Fuck you.' So I said to him, 'Fuck you.'"

Hunt's wife met her future husband at age 15 when they were attending high school and it's been a grand love affair ever since. The Hunts are very grateful for their long union. The husband, despite his memory loss, remembers he was married on the "happiest day of my life": Sept. 15, 1960. He also knows that his 80th birthday was Feb. 15, 1936. His memory didn't cheat him on those two dates.

Funny, eh, how the hard-drive of one's brain can fetch him some memories but not other memories. Weird.

"It was a fun life. Not many people can say their husband played in the big leagues," Mrs. Hunt said. "I've got scrapbooks from every year he played. The game was different back then. Now, it kind of sucks. They don't do the sacrifice, the bunt, none of that stuff anymore. That's boring. There's no strategy."

Hunt got hit 243 times during his career, a mark he held for years until Don Baylor passed him and finished with 267. Baylor, in turn, was overtaken by Craig Biggio, who currently holds the career record with 285. Nolan Ryan, who once gave Hunt the greatest compliment by saying he was a "great competitor", hit Hunt four times in 1971.

Hunt was also tough to strike out. He fanned only 382 times in 6,158

Canadian Baseball Hall of Fame

This is a photo of the 1973 Expos, who almost won the NL East. Front row left to right: trainer Joe Liscio, Bob Stinson, Boots Day, Mike Jorgensen, Tim Foli, coach Jerry Zimmerman, manager Gene Mauch, coach Dave Bristol, coach Cal McLish, coach Larry Doby, Ron Fairly, Pat Jarvis and equipment manager Harvey Stone. Second row: Coco Laboy, Ron Hunt, Pepe Frias, Ron Woods, John Strohmayer, Jorge Roque, Joe Gilbert, Pepe Mangual, Tom Walker, Mike Marshall and scout Dick Rock. Third row: Hal Breeden, Ernie McAnally, John Boccabella, Mike Torrez, Steve Renko, Ken Singleton, Terry Humphrey, Balor Moore and Bob Bailey. Among the missing from the photo are Bill Stoneman and Clyde Mashore.

39

plate appearances. Amazing.

"Ron, you know, caused things to happen," his wife said. "It was a job. His job was to get on base. That's why he was a lead-off hitter. His on-base percentage was over .400 (.402 in 1971, .418 in 1973). He really gave 100% for every team he played for."

Hunt thought the best salary he earned from the Expos was $6,800 and his wife dutifully noted that his highest salary was $59,000 with the Cardinals.

Hunt is drawing from his major-league pension and told me he's being helped out financially by the Baseball Assistance Team arm of Major League Baseball.

Here's hats off to an Expos hero from the 1970s.

DeMola's million-dollar arm

Steve Rogers used to joke but he was serious: he had two words to describe Don DeMola's arm.

"Three Digits."

As in heat that would reach 100 m.p.h. That's the gas DeMola could fire. He could bring it.

DeMola was so good that Expos manager Gene Mauch ranked him in the top five percent in velocity in Major League Baseball in an interview with Sports Illustrated back in the day.

"I loved those days but that prick Gene ruined my career. He killed my arm," DeMola told me in a great interview that lasted close to one hour, 45 minutes.

Yes, Mauch and the Expos worked DeMola way too much and screwed up his right arm. DeMola was drafted by the Yankees and spent some time with them in the minors. One day, during spring training in Fort Lauderdale, DeMola remembers Yankees catcher Thurman Munson coming out of manager Ralph Houk's office with a grin from ear to ear.

Munson told people that day that his contract was doubled to $28,000 per season from $14,000 after his solid rookie season. DeMola remembers momentous things like that and of course, at the time, DeMola was saying to himself that he and Canadian Dave Pagan wanted to be with the Yankees some day, just like Munson.

DeMola spent some time in the minors with the Yankees before being released because he was "pretty much an asshole and did a couple of stupid things" to get on the wrong side of management.

DeMola took some time off after his release to work at Penn Glass but he approached his high school coach Bob Dell about getting back into

Montreal Expos photos

Don DeMola

jackscalia.anet

Jack Scalia

"I started out as a baseball player. I was a pitcher, for the Montreal Expos. They had a lot of hopes, and so did I. I was touted as a future twenty-game winner, but an injury prevented me from going any further after three years. It was devastating, all the time and effort I put in, all the love and friendships. So after that, I lived in Sacramento for a while, digging ditches, working in a Campbell's Soup factory. One day I stopped into a modeling agency there called Maniken Manor with some pictures I had from baseball. Whatever potential I had as a model, I guess they saw it. I just went in for kicks because I heard you could make thirty dollars an hour, and I was only making five, breaking my back." – Jack Scalia, in a post of his on his website jackscalia.anet. Scalia became a high-end model and actor after leaving the Expos.

baseball. He began working out with a highly regarded baseball team near his hometown of Commack, N.Y.

One day he ran into Expos scout Tommy (T-Bone) Giordano, who was director of athletics at Amityville high school. Giordano asked DeMola to throw baseballs against a wall at Commack South high school and then later during the early part of the winter in 1972-73 indoors.

"The guy catching me in the gym was scared shitless of me," DeMola said. Why? Because of his heat.

Giordano asked DeMola if he could return the next day to pitch. Of course, DeMola said yes. So the next day Giordano shows up with Larry Bearnarth, the Expos minor-league pitching coach, who later became the team's MLB pitching coach. It didn't take long for Giordano and Bearnarth to be impressed with DeMola's stuff. In the dead of winter on Jan. 11, 1973, DeMola signed a contract with the Expos.

"After I threw the second day in a row, Bear told me I threw harder than anybody they had," DeMola said, chuckling.

Later that winter, DeMola showed up for minor-league spring training in Daytona Beach, Florida. One of the guys he was working out with was Jack Scalia, the son of Brooklyn Dodgers minor-leaguer Rocky Tedesco. Scalia, like DeMola, was a hotshot pitching prospect until he encountered arm and rotator-cuff problems that forced him from the game into an eventual career of modelling and acting.

DeMola started the 1974 season in the A ranks in West Palm Beach, a roster that included Canadian Larry Landreth, Gary Roenicke and Marcel Lachemann. That same season, DeMola spent some time in Double-A in Québec City. It was in the latter metropolis that DeMola remembered getting an apartment on top of a fancy steakhouse and he started to get to know a fellow by the name of Gary Carter.

Shortly after the conclusion of the 1973 season, DeMola flew with Carter from St. Petersburg, Florida to play winter ball in San Juan, Puerto Rico. This was a team that included the likes of Barry Foote, Dale Murray, Chuck Taylor, Mike Schmidt, Willie Montanez, Jay Johnstone and Larry Christenson. As you can see, they were not all Expos' organization players.

In his first game in San Juan after Christenson hurt his right arm, DeMola pitched against a team that featured Rico Carty, Chris Chambliss, Mickey Rivers and Dave Kingman. He threw 5.2 scoreless innings. After the game, DeMola is walking off the mound and teammate Bobby Wine goes up to DeMola and congratulates him, whilst a fan in the stands yells out, "Who the fuck is that guy?"

By DeMola's accounts, he was 4-2 in Puerto Rico with nine saves, 60 Ks and a 1.90 ERA and he gave up only 12 bases on balls. Then later that winter after his team won the Puerto Rican winter ball title, it also captured the Caribbean World Series in Mexico.

So DeMola goes back home to suburban New York for several weeks to take a break but before you know it, he was back in spring training in Daytona Beach, looking to make more impressions on the Expos brass. That spring, he went 4-0, facing the likes of Harmon Killebrew, Tony Oliva, Rod Carew and Carl Yastzremski.

DeMola figured he would make the team and head north but he wasn't convinced until he was finally told. He went on a road trip to Orlando to play the Twins. He was told that day in Orlando that one pitcher had to be told he wouldn't be starting the season in Montreal.

So as DeMola was sitting on a bus, bullpen coach Jerry Zimmerman, all "serious and very professional", tells DeMola Mauch wants to see him.

"Shit, are you serious?" DeMola asked Zimmerman.

"So down by the foul line, Gene puts his arm around me and says, 'I'm taking you with me.' I said, 'Whoa.' So I get back on the bus," DeMola recalled. "Don Carrithers was the guy who didn't make the team. First thing I did was find a pay phone and call my parents collect. It was early April. This is beautiful."

The Expos started the season on the road in Pittsburgh and then Chicago. In one of Mauch's scrums with the media, someone asked him, "How come no lefties in the bullpen?" Mauch's reply: "Lefty-rightie, they still have to face DeMola's fastball.'

"That was a compliment to my velocity," DeMola told me.

In a doubleheader at Wrigley Field, DeMola's time for MLB duty had finally come. He entered Game 1 in place of John Montague in the sixth inning of a game the Expos won 7-4 on April 13. The guy he's facing is Rick Monday, who later would become a noted Expos nemesis for what he did on Oct. 19, 1981.

"I still see the fastball up and away. He was way late," DeMola said of his one pitch to Monday. "He popped it up between third and the dugout and the shortstop made the out. In the second game, I relieved Mike Torrez, who took me under his wing. I didn't know anyone. I pitched the last two innings of the second game. It's the first time I had pitched twice in one day. My arm wasn't hurt but it was sore as hell. It was just hanging."

DeMola sent me a newspaper clipping that showed Cubs manager Whitey Lockman singing DeMola's praises after the second game.

"That guy DeMola is super. He's something special," Lockman told reporters.

DeMola carved out a pretty decent season in 57.2 innings. His ERA was 3.12 in 25 games and he struck out 47 batters. After the season, Mauch and the Expos asked him to go to Puerto Rico again. He was not fussy about doing it but felt he couldn't turn the club down.

"You couldn't say, 'I wanna rest.' They could shit-can you," DeMola said. "Why do you think Gene had me go to winter ball three winters in a row when I had a million-dollar arm? My second year in Montreal, my

Photo supplied by Don DeMola

**Don DeMola poses with
close friend Bob Costas**

Beautiful friendship

Back in 1967, future Expos prospect Don DeMola and future broadcasting star Bob Costas were going through baseball tryouts at Green Meadows junior high school in Commack, N.Y. DeMola had just finished throwing batting practice. Back then, he said he "wasn't the dominating pitcher I became in my later years." DeMola was cooling off on the bench and Costas was standing in front of him, waiting to hit next. Costas had choked up on the bat about 12 inches. "It was the only bat he could swing," DeMola said. "The coach was a ninth-grade math teacher with a stone-cold face named Charles Aurandt and he took over throwing BP when I had finished. He looks over and sees Bob swinging the fungo in the batter's circle and says, "Costas, go home. I don't need you.' Just like that. I felt so bad for Bob. He never got a chance but he would've never been allowed to use the fungo. What a prick Aurandt was. In high school, the school paper had a weekly challenge called Stump Costas. There were no computers, nothing, he knew it all. I used to ask him questions in the hallway that I didn't know the answers to. Just made-up questions. He knew the answers. My senior year, he used to do play-by-play at our basketball games, using a pencil with a big eraser on it as his mic!!!." DeMola and Costas remain friends to this day.

arm killed me the whole year. I couldn't say anything. Things were different then. You say something to Gene, he'd bury you. My elbow blows up in spring training.

"They still sent me to Triple-A with a bad elbow. After my first appearance in Denver, I had surgery. They mistreated me so badly. I should have been there (in the majors) with Cy (Steve Rogers). Bob Reece (a catcher) came up to me one time and he knew my arm was killing me. He said, "You've got more balls than anybody I've met.'"

Just like with Balor Moore several years earlier, DeMola was overworked and overused. DeMola figures he had two total months off in three years and "when I said my arm hurt, I got optioned. I loved those days but Gene ruined my career."

DeMola recalls that during one juncture in 1974 he had thrown 13 scoreless innings with no walks and a dozen strikeouts out of the bullpen. Regular rotation pitcher Steve Renko cut a finger and Mauch told DeMola he would start the next day. He allowed his first run in the sixth inning at which time he "twinged a muscle in the back of the shoulder."

Mauch took DeMola out of the game. DeMola said his "arm wasn't serious, just me cautious." DeMola was scheduled to start five days later but he still felt discomfort so he "decided not to pitch." Two weeks later, he's healthy and Mauch options him to Memphis to make room for Larry Biitner. At one point, Craig Caskey, on a 5-0 run in Memphis, was promoted. In the meantime, DeMola went 5-0 in Memphis with three shutouts but when the Expos brought him back up, he got no starts.

During spring training in 1975, newly acquired Willie Davis ran into DeMola and asked the pitcher, "Gonna win 15 games this year?" DeMola replied, "How can I do that if I'm in the bullpen." A puzzled Davis said, "With your stuff, you're in the bullpen?" One time, Mauch in commenting about the good stuff DeMola possessed, he told someone, "No human being was going to hit that pitch."

As DeMola looked back on comments made by Davis and Mauch, he said, "You don't forget shit like that. Something you don't hear everyday."

Expos pitching coach Jim Brewer, after seeing DeMola pitch, said, "he's throwing 100 and the ball is moving everywhere." Bill Robinson of the Pirates was walked one time by DeMola and when he got to first, he asked first baseman Bob Bailey, "Who the fuck was the last guy on the mound? He's throwing 100 and the ball's moving all over the plate."

At one point, as DeMola's elbow problems escalated, Fanning agreed to have him checked out in 1975 by a specialist, the senior team physician for the Houston Astros.

"They fly me to Houston to see Dr. Joe King. Back then, he did elbows and Dr. (Frank) Jobe in California did shoulders," DeMola said. "King did Nolan Ryan's elbow two months before mine and mine was his last. I saw him in April and I was operated on in May. King retired after my surgery. Jobe took over the elbows.

"I sat in Dr. King's office and after he examined me, he got Fanning on the phone," DeMola recalled.

"Jim, are you ready for this?" the doctor asked Fanning. "This is the second worst elbow I have see in all my time working in the big leagues."

Said DeMola, "I remember we were in Los Angeles in 1974 (July 17) and I was in the bullpen when Tommy John was pitching for the Dodgers. It was the third inning and he ran right off the field. He didn't call time. He hit the runway into the clubhouse and we found out he hurt his elbow. It was an experimental procedure that took some time for consultation because Tommy was basically the guinea pig (for TJ surgery)."

The year following DeMola's surgery, DeMola was pitching in Triple-A and Angels scout Marv Grissom was behind home plate scouting. Following the game, Grissom was telling people that DeMola is "throwing better than 80% of the guys in the big leagues."

It was after that same game that DeMola got into a fight with a teammate and sustained a fracture of his throwing hand. DeMola said "the reason for the altercation really without getting into it, he violated an unwritten rule among teammates in MLB."

DeMola had a few other stories to tell. Here's one about Carter.

"Gary and I were flying home and we were in an airport. We were walking down the concourse and I turn around and no Gary. Nowhere to be found. All of a sudden, here he comes trotting down the concourse toward me," DeMola recalled.

"Where'd you go," DeMola asked Carter.

"Some guy offered me $100 for four pictures," Kid replied.

"You took the money?" DeMola said with a puzzled look on his face.

"I mean this shit was going on back then," DeMola was telling me. "He was smiling ear to ear. He was very frugal when it came to money. It was, 'How much?' We were like brothers, always together, till he met Sandy (his wife)."

DeMola said Mauch didn't allow any buffet spreads in the clubhouse, only soup. Boy, he was strict. And apparently no coffee was allowed so many guys would sneak stuff in by going to the concession stands and hope Mauch wouldn't notice. DeMola said trainer Harvey Stone enjoyed bread and honey.

He said teammate Hal Breeden, who was known to take greenies, was "scared shitless of Mauch". DeMola told the story about Breeden "hiding between two refrigerators in the concession stands one day with no lights on and eating a tuna fish sandwich."

DeMola said that when Warren Cromartie was promoted as a September callup in 1974, he was a "hotshot motormouth." DeMola said Ron Hunt "hated Mike Torrez". Breeden's catcher's mitt was a "steel clanker"

One day in Houston, Mauch and DeMola were having a chat and Mauch related the tale of how Astros pitcher Larry Dierker "used to add and subtract all day long" as a way of agreeing with or shaking off a catcher's signs. If Dierker put a finger on his chest, it meant adding, meaning the signal was fine. If he hit his left thigh or flipped his hat, he was subtracting, meaning he didn't like the pitch. So DeMola took note throughout the game and said Dierker did this back and forth scenario 225 times. No kidding.

DeMola told the story of how Nate Colbert was advised by Mauch that he had to shave off his "Fu Manchu moustache" when he was acquired from the Padres. Colbert was also the subject of another story. One game, he was sitting down at the end of the dugout when he went up to Bailey and said, 'Beatle, I'm 3-for-5 against Al Hrabosky.' "

"So, Bailey," DeMola said, "moseyed on down to see Gene and told him Nate hits this guy pretty good. Colbert gets a bat (pinch hitter). Colbert hit the first pitch straight back. On the next pitch, he hit the 420-foot sign in centre field. He smoked it (for a triple)."

DeMola recalled southpaw lefty Joe Gilbert, who had a "funny, south-ern, slow-talking drawl". Gilbert got into contract talks with Fanning and Fanning told Gilbert "nothing is more important as experience. It's much more valuable than getting big raises". So as an analogy, Gilbert goes into a restaurant and orders a juicy steak and the waiter comes with a big bill and Gilbert isn't exactly loaded with money, but says, "My expe-rience with Fanning is that you don't need the money."

DeMola's days with the Expos ended in 1978 when he decided to consider one last stab with a tryout with the Orioles. DeMola had gotten turned off in 1977 with Triple-A Denver when he said manager Doc Ed-wards wanted to "challenge people to fights". DeMola called Edwards a "real comedy act".

The irony of all of this is that the following season, DeMola decided to give it one last crack in baseball by switching organizations. He agreed to a deal with the Orioles but when he found out Edwards was going to be manager of their Triple-A club in Rochester, N.Y., "I quit on the spot. I wasn't dealing with him. I quit, I was done. They ripped it (enthusiasm) out of me. It took the love out of the game for me."

After baseball's lights went out and the cheering stopped and when there were no more games, no more flights or buses, no more meeting teammates in clubhouses and dugouts, DeMola got into the real world of work.

Around the time his father died, DeMola met Dr. Allan Levy, the team doctor for both the NFL's New York Giants and the NHL's New York Islanders.

One day, Dr. Levy was in Cadillac Furs, looking to buy a mink coat for his wife Gail. The store owner, Jeffrey Scharfman, was a sports nut because he had Sporting News papers scattered all over the place.

""I just delivered Don DeMola's baby," Dr. Levy told Scharfman

"I know who he is. Can you call him?" Scharfman replied.

So Dr. Levy called DeMola and eventually Scharfman got talking with DeMola. Scharfman picked DeMola up in Freeport, Long Island and they drove to Lu Chow's Chinese restaurant for a bite to eat. Of course, Scharfman was looking to convince DeMola to work for him in the fur business.

"He hands me $100," DeMola said. "Next day, we go to another place and gives me another $100. Another weekend, he gave me an-other $100, a total of $300. I started feeling guilty. I'm looking at these coats. They came to me like a duck to water. I really learned how to cut the furs and sew them. I learned how to make a coat by myself.

"I later worked with wholesalers. I was very good in the mink business all over the U.S. for many years, dealing with furs, foxes, coyotes."

DeMola's story is one of perseverance and resilience that ended up in a baseball career shut down because Mauch and the Expos pushed him and pushed him to the point where his arm was being punished. He was overworked and overused.

When he should have been told to rest some winters, they asked/told him to report to winter ball. During games, they would have him warming up in the bullpen, pitching the equivalent of a few innings and never getting used in the actual game. Nowadays, that stuff never happens.

But as he noted, DeMola said he's one of less than 20,000 people who have played in the major leagues. He's grateful that he's part of that number.

"Nobody knows how hard it is to get there, how hard it is to stay. I was happy for the opportunities," DeMola said.

DeMola family photo
Don DeMola as a kid

Leaving on a jet plane

"Cause I'm leaving on a jet plane.
Don't know when I'll be back again.
Oh babe, I hate to go.
All my bags are packed, I'm ready to go."
— some of the lyrics from the song by John Denver
Leaving on a jet plane

The date was July 16, 1973. Infielder Jim Cox and pitchers Craig Caskey and Steve Rogers boarded a plane in Norfolk, Virginia bound for Houston.

It was an exciting time for the three Expos prospects because they had been given the good news on July 15 that they were being called up to the big leagues for the first time. Heady stuff. The dream of a lifetime was coming through for the trio.

One by one, Expos Triple-A Peninsula Whips manager Bill Adair had called the three into his office July 15 to tell them they were going to The Show. Some people like Caskey referred to the team's name as the Newport News Whips. True – that was actually the name of the town located on the outskirts of Virginia Beach. In a broad sense, the team owners decided to call the team Peninsula. It's a touristy part of Virginia and a hotbed for baseball with Tidewater next door as the long-time home of the Mets Triple-A team and the Braves had their team in Richmond. Norfolk has had minor-league ball there for years.

Cox had impressed the Expos brass in Montreal with 10 homers and 49 RBI through a good chunk of the 1973 season in Newport News. Caskey, a left-hander, was 11-7 and Rogers was 3-1. At that point, who would have known that Rogers would turn out to be the best player of the lot? Cox played small pockets of four seasons in the majors, all with the Expos. Caskey didn't play in the majors after 1973.

As Rogers recalled in early 2021, Caskey and Cox had been informed by Adair during the day about their promotion and it was even announced over the public-address system during the game on the 15th that they were being called up.

"There was a round of applause for Craig and Jim. Everybody was pumped up," Rogers remembered. "The game is over with, Bill Adair comes to me and says, 'I want you to go to the parking lot and get in the car. When the lights go out in the stadium, I want you to come back to the office.' I said, 'Okay.' So I wait out there with my wife at the time. I was saying, 'What is this all about?'

"The lights go on in the stadium. I go to the locker room, a cinder block locker room that you see in the minor leagues. I go in and the lights are on in Bill's office. I knock on the door. I said, 'Bill, what's the deal?' He said, 'You've been called up with Caskey and Cox but they haven't figured out who is going to be sent down.' I said, "Okay.' I'm excited but I can't get excited under the cloak of darkness. I had to keep it quiet. Bill said, 'Pack up.' So I pack up my stuff in a duffle bag for a week long road trip. That was baseball back then, cloak and dagger. It was a different time and a different era."

So then the next morning, Rogers goes to the airport, expecting to run into Caskey and Cox but Caskey and Cox aren't expecting to see Rogers. Hilarious. Little did Caskey and Cox know that Rogers would be joining them. They were surprised to see Rogers checking in his luggage.

"What are you doing at the airport?" Caskey and Cox asked Rogers.

"I got called up," Rogers replied.

"I told them the story. The night before had been weird," Rogers said about his meeting with Adair.

Rogers called the trip a blur but when the three of them walked through the lobby of their Houston hotel, the Marriott, things got even more odd. Rogers was laughing as he reminisced about running into Expos pitcher Balor Moore.

"When we got there, there were a lot of people in the lobby," Rogers recalled.

"I walked into Caskey and Cox and then I see you," Moore said to Rogers. "Damn. You know, I haven't been pitching good."

The bait was out. Moore, who was 7-16 in 1973 with the Expos, knew he was being demoted to Peninsula when he saw both Caskey and Rogers.

"The year before, Balor Moore had a tremendous spring training in 1972," Rogers told me. "They said, 'Wow.' We can use this kid. In Québec City in '72, he had this ERA of .6. He was off the charts. You couldn't even smell how good he was. They called him up the last four months (he was 9-9).

"1972 was a lockout year, a shortened season. They came to me and said they were going to send me to Québec City. They said, 'Don't worry, you don't have to be as good as Balor Moore was.' He had that .6 ERA. Oh crap, that's what put all kinds of pressure on myself, I was pressing, arguing with umpires. And then they come to me and say, 'Hey, we're going to send you to Triple-A (Peninsula).' I said to myself that's not a promotion. It's a demotion. But it was warmer weather in Peninsula. They had a veteran type team. It took the pressure off me.

"Certainly, there were looking for a left hander, they were really depending heavily on Caskey to work in the rotation effectively," Rogers said. "That was the upshoot of his call up. I have been told since that with Caskey, they were looking at him to have a long career. He was a quality left hander. The rotation was getting thin. They were really searching. They needed help."

Caskey recalls that upon arriving in Houston that the weather was almost unbearable.

"It was very hot and muggy outside but it was 70F inside the Astrodome," Caskey said. "It was cool enough to chill the pipe dugout railings. I rested my arm on a railing and it tightened up my forearm."

When Rogers met Mauch at the Astrodome, Mauch told Rogers to take a tour of the ballpark and get to know its intricacies. When I asked Rogers if while he was in Houston, did he think he'd spend the next 12+ seasons with the Expos without going to the minors, he chuckled.

"It's not arrogance. It's the stupidity. I was 21 years old. You never think of going down (to the minors). The vast majority go up and down, more than once. I can't say I wasn't nervous. I'd pitched in two College World Series before some pretty good crowds so that exposure helped me. I can remember (pitching coach) Cal McLish telling me 'You don't have to do anymore than what you got you here. You don't have to be better. What you did in the minors got you to the majors. Don't try to do more than what you are capable of.' "

Rogers made his debut July 18 against the Astros, working solid eight innings in a no-decision.

"Steve pitched his first game, shining brightly," Caskey recalled. "He only needed John Boccabella to call the signals. His pitches were great but he particularly shined with his change-up that John knew when to call."

During that stay in Houston, Caskey had some urgent health problems, not what a prospect wanted to face when he was about to make his MLB debut. So Caskey arranged to have trainer Joe Liscio take him to see a doctor.

"He gave me a penicillin shot for what he called bronchitis," Caskey recalled. "And he said, 'Get in bed because you are close to pneumo-

Montreal Expos photos

Craig Caskey pitched for the Expos in 1973

nia.' I told him that was impossible since we were to leave for Cincinnati the next day. Once we got to Cincinnati, Joe took me to the doctor, who refused to give me another shot. I think it would have knocked it (bronchitis) out but what do I know. He gave me penicillin pills instead with some form of codeine for the cough."

Sicker than a dog, Caskey was asked by Mauch to come on in relief of starter Bill Stoneman in the bottom of the third of the July 19 game which Cox started at second base. Caskey was splendid, throwing one-hit, runless ball in 4.2 innings of work against a top-heavy Reds lineup that included Pete Rose, Dave Concepcion, Joe Morgan and Johnny Bench. Can you imagine Caskey sticking a zero on his resumé in his debut?

"I felt right at home and all my teammates congratulated me," Caskey said.

Caskey was never the same that season. He got banged up in subsequent outings and little did he know it but his last MLB game would be Sept. 30.

"Craig didn't fare as well as I did in my first start," Rogers said.

"My MLB career isn't much to brag about, but if I had stayed true to the debut, I would have been money. I spent a couple of months in the majors, Steve Rogers stayed 12 years," Caskey said. "I didn't get rid of the cold for months. It affected a lot of my outings and my only start in Shea Stadium. I went four innings giving up three hits and two runs. The cold had zapped my energy again and next would come tendonitis.

"In those days, you would get a cortisone shot for tendonitis, which did nothing for me. The issue had shown itself in Venezuela during 1973 winter ball. There were no steps to rehab except rest. I was out for 15 days and then got ripped in my first outing. I'd come off the DL and I basically had a dead arm. They'd say, 'See what you can do.' You'd come off the DL and throw. I fractured my pitching hand punching a steel door. It was ill-advised."

Caskey said it was "stupid" that he had taken his frustrations out on the door but he felt he should have been nursed along because of his tendonitis. Instead, he was rushed into action. Luis Aparicio, the famous shortstop who was his Venezuelan manager that winter, was non too pleased when he saw that Caskey had smashed his hand.

"Luis called me out for messing up my opportunities," Caskey said. "He said, 'What are you doing messing with your career?' " Aparicio took Caskey to see a doctor and then Caskey went home to the Pacific Northwest to heal.

Caskey was a first-round draft choice, 12th overall, out of the University of Puget Sound in Tacoma, Wash., his backyard so-to-speak after his parents moved the family to that state from his birthplace of Visalia, Calif. He was almost embarrassed to say he signed for $2,500. He found out later that other players were getting $25,000 bonuses. Caskey had turned down a $14,000 signing bonus from the Giants several years earlier to remain in school.

Caskey, who called himself a "skinny, little bugger" and a "finesse" pitcher, threw in Single-A in 1972 with West Palm Beach, Fla. and Jamestown, N.Y. Like many school kids, who skip a grade because they were excellent, Caskey was advanced to Triple-A in Peninsula without having to play in Double-A Quebec City. His stint in Peninsula included "three shutout performances" and "even Gene Mauch had to notice."

When the baseball music stopped, Caskey, the one-shot wonder on July 19, 1973, became a window-washer for a brief period before he embarked on a 40-year career as a salesman for Boeing, which has its headquarters in Washington state.

"I bought almost everything on the plane except the engine," Caskey quipped about his job.

Eddie Lopat and Dave Parker

"Gene Mauch sent Eddie Lopat, distinguished MLB player, coach, manager and roving pitching coach to witness my third shutout in a row at Triple-A Newport News. Before the game, Eddie tried to show me how to throw a screwball, without success. We were about done when Dave Parker strolled up, wearing a huge beret and sporting a big-letter murse or man's purse slung over his shoulder, resting on his hip like a saddle bag. Those were a couple of 1970s fashion statements, that were lost on Eddie. Mind you, Eddie had stopped playing in the 1950s, so there were generational norms he thought Dave was messing up. His comment was, 'Look at that. Oh boy, that boy, he'll never make it.' I grinned, thinking this chiseled stud was going to kill it. Dave played 18 years in the majors and had a lifetime batting average of .290. Eddie deserved to have confidence, having pitched, coached and managed in the major leagues, but changes were shaking things up in the '70s. After the game, leading the Peninsula Whips to a shutout victory over the Pirates Triple-A team, Eddie asked, 'What was that one hit you gave up to Parker?' I said, 'I threw him a cut fastball'. To which he said, 'Should have thrown the slider.' Nevertheless, Rogers, Cox and I were headed to Houston to join the Expos."
— *Funny anecdote from Expos prospect Craig Caskey*

Courtesy Charleston Gazette-Mail
Pirates prospect Dave Parker holding uniform of the late Pirates star Roberto Clemente in 1973 when he played for West Virginia's Charleston Charlies.

I arranged an interview with Dave Parker on February 2, 2021 so I could run this above anecdote by him.
"He was trying to make me look bad," Parker said of Lopat. "I didn't really care what opinion people had of me. I was a little more different. I had my own style. I was a trend-setter. I liked beautiful clothes, the saddlebag, bell-bottoms. Don't forget the ear-ring. I had a lot of things I did that people followed. I had the first ear-ring at the major-league level."

Singleton and Torrez

It's cool that Ken Singleton and Mike Torrez remain friends to this day all these years later after the famous Dec. 4, 1974 trade that sent them from the Expos to the Orioles.

Singleton and Torrez hook up each winter in Florida where Singleton says he spends a lot of his time playing golf with Torrez. Singleton's winter home is in North Redington located not far from Torrez's home in Seminole. Their friendship actually began in earnest when they became Expos teammates. Close to 50 years later, they remain close.

Actually on the day of the trade, Singleton and Torrez were together and reminiscing. True fact, according to a column written by Tim Burke and published the next day in the Montreal Gazette. Torrez joked about the trade this way: "Yeah, maybe it's because both of us married Montreal (white) girls."

On the verge of tears, Expos public-relations official Monique Giroux talked to Burke in releasing the news, "What are we going to do? We've lost our two most handsome players on the team."

No question, Singleton and Torrez killed it as Hollywood-handsome dudes.

"When that trade happened many years ago, I knew I was going to a good team," Singleton told me in November of 2020 after I told him about the reaction to the trade when I put an anniversary post on Twitter and Facebook. "During my 10 seasons in Baltimore, we won more games than any other team.

"I also had the good fortune of playing with Eddie Murray, Cal Ripken, Brooks Robinson, Jim Palmer and Reggie Jackson. All Hall of Famers. Not to mention playing for Hall of Fame manager Earl Weaver. Needless to say the trade worked out well for me as I am a proud member of the

Orioles Hall of Fame."

In his dispatch from New Orleans where the trade was made, New York Times sports reporter Joseph Durso had this to say:

"To the public, McNally has been identified with the consistent success of the Orioles on the field since they and the Oakland A's replaced the New York Yankees as the prima donnas of the American League. The 32 year old left hander has pitched in four World Series in the last nine years, has won 20 or more games in four of the last seven and has won 181 times during his 12 seasons in a Baltimore uniform."

McNally and speedy outfielder Rich Coggins were sent to the Expos in exchange for Singleton and Torrez.

"Kenny had a great eye for hitting. He was a pretty good, big guy. If he was a little faster, he would have hit 15-20 points higher," Singleton's teammate Don DeMola said. "He was a solid fielder with a very accurate arm."

There were reports that the Orioles knew of an existing medical condition that Coggins had and dropped him on the unsuspecting Expos.

"Just know he had health problems," recalled Rodger Brulotte, an Expos special assistant back then.

Expos photo
Rich Coggins

The Expos had a choice of taking either Coggins or Al Bumbry and chose Coggins, who did enjoy some success with the Orioles in 1973-74 in a part-time role. Coggins appeared in 113 games for Baltimore in 1973, batting .319 and collecting seven homers and 41 RBI. Then in 1974, he got into 110 games, contributing four homers, 32 RBI and a .243 BA.

Based on those stats, the Expos felt Coggins could contribute at the same level, starting in 1975, at least as a part-timer.

"His arm was terrible. He'd be 50 feet behind second base and he couldn't reach second from the outfield," DeMola said of Coggins. "Plus, he was a big mouth, a real loudmouth like Willie Davis. He had two really big dogs. I forget what kind they were but they stood higher than his waist and his hips."

The Expos lost McNally and Coggins midway through that season, both in June, turning their transaction into a disaster, the worst one ever made in franchise history.

McNally just up and quit June 9 after a 3-6 start to the season and went home to Billings, Montana and Coggins was traded with his dogs to the Yankees on June 15. Unreal. In the space of less than a week, McNally and Coggins were gone. Hrmmph.

Coggins is one guy I would love to talk with. I wanted to get his side of the story so I sent him a postal letter but he never responded.

According to Ian MacDonald of the Gazette in his report from the

**Mike Torrez, the pitcher,
with a bat**

winter meetings in New Orleans, Mc-Nally had requested a swap out of Baltimore. After what transpired, I bet McNally regrets asking for a trade from the Orioles.

"Yes, I asked to be traded," Mc-Nally told reporters. "I told them some clubs that I would like to be traded to and I told them some clubs to which I would refuse to report. There were some clubs that were question marks. Frankly, Montreal was one of the question marks.

"I don't know anything about the team or the town. Our people have spoken to me and the general outlook is good. It's given me new life. The adrenalin is flowing. I felt it would be best for me to make a move, hoping the change of scenery will help.

"I hope that I can do the things that Montreal thinks I can. I hope that I can help."

Foli's arbitration case

Tim Foli wanted $48,000 to play for the Expos in 1974. The Expos countered with an offer of $38,000.

There was an impasse and neither side would budge so they went to the salary-arbitration table. It made history as the first such case involving an Expo. The club won the case. An arbitrator decided Foli would have to play for $38,000. Sounds like cheap money but in those days, it was decent money.

"It was a very professional case," the late Jim Fanning, the Expos GM in that era, told me in an interview in early 1989. "It was my first case and it was the first for Cookie Lazarus, a well known Montreal attorney, who represented Foli."

Foli told me in 1989 that he was never the type of player who had the numbers to convince an arbitrator he should be paid big dollars. In 1973, the season before the hearing, he hit .240 and had two homers and 36 RBI. Foli most certainly wasn't a star player.

"When you get into a hearing, it's big business," Foli told me. "But I still have the greatest respect and admiration for Jim Fanning."

When you get to a hearing, the player and the agent tell the arbitrator about all the good things a player did while the team representatives try to downgrade the player by saying he didn't do this and he didn't do that, blah, blah, blah. Another case that struck Fanning a lot was the one in 1983 when pitcher Bill Gullickson asked for $365,000 and the club countered with $275,000. The club won.

"Bill was very offended," Fanning said. "I felt bad about it, just like I did in the Foli case. I could see Foli starting to boil. I sent Foli a note and I sent Gullickson a note. I told Bill not to let it affect him but he stormed out of there."

The first Expos arbitration case to reach the $1-million plateau came in 1985 and Tim Raines was the player. That year, the Expos had four players go to arbitration. Raines, Bert Roberge and David Palmer won their cases while Bobby Ramos lost.

"In the Raines case, it was the first time in history that both bids were at least $1-million," said Expos vice-president of baseball operations Bill Stoneman, who helped outsider Tal Smith argue the case. "It was also the first arbitration case over $1-million."

Raines asked for $1.2-million while the Expos countered with $1-million. Looking back, could the two sides not have settled at $1.1-million to avoid a hearing? Jeepers cripes.

Larry Landreth's rise to the Expos

Dennis Schulz knew Larry Landreth had the potential to be a major-league pitcher when he was only 12-years-old.

Schulz was the assistant coach to Angie Nigro, who was originally from Landreth's hometown of Stratford, Ontario. Together, as the coaches running the Kitchener, Ont. peewee team, they tried every way to try and beat Landreth's Stratford team. It was an intense rivalry between Stratford and Kitchener.

"At 12 and 13, Larry had the mannerisms of a professional." Schulz said in an interview. "He would walk to the mound with such confidence, take his warm up pitches very deliberately, Then he would grab the rosin bag, put his fingers to the mouth and then appear to wipe them dry. He had the perfect windup, concealed the ball well, a perfect stride, landing in the same spot on every pitch.

"He exuded confidence and glared at the batters, but never smiled or smirked. He was just there to do the best he could. One game in Stratford, he threw a no-hitter against us. Our team had some darn-good hitters but that day, Larry had fantastic control, his fastball was grooving and on the two-strike pitch, the curve was dropping into the strike zone. We didn't stand a chance that day."

When I talked with Denis Flanagan Jr., Landreth's catcher, "a little blond fellow," as Schulz called him, I found out the two of them played some 10 years together on a variety of Stratford teams in the minor-baseball ranks and then for a number of years when they played on Stratford's entries in the Intercounty senior league. Who better to talk with about Landreth than Flanagan.

"I played with Larry from tyke right up to midget," Flanagan said. "He was the centrepiece of the team. He was all heart. He was the hardest throwing pitcher, the most dominant pitcher. We were thankful he was on our team. He had good control for a young pitcher."

Indeed, when you see young tykes and peewees, you're not always sure if they will find the strike zone, even from a short distance because they are small and not that big. But Landreth was something else. There was no surprise he attracted the attention of major-league scouts and eventually signed with the Expos and had cups of tea with them in 1976 and 1977.

"Larry threw around the plate consistently," Flanagan said. "We were good friends growing up on the ball field and away from the ball field. In the winter, I played hockey and he played basketball."

Landreth also got some tutoring from his brother Doug, who was six years older.

"We had many arguments about throwing the ball over the top for a curve," Doug told me. "He said, 'I can't do that.' I wanted him to throw over the top. I tried to tell him the higher the arm, the more action you get. He threw it three-quarters. Then he went to play ball (in the pros) and came back and he said, 'See what I learned? They thought me the curveball over the top.' He changed his mind."

Larry Landreth revealed that Expos roving minor-league pitching coach Larry Bearnarth did attempt in Jamestown, N.Y. to at least

Canadian Baseball Hall of Fame/Expos collection
Larry Landreth in his days with the Expos

show him how to go over the top with the curveball. He didn't entirely buy into the suggestions but came close to it.

"I was not going to go over the top because it gives the pitch away," Landreth told me in an interview. "I basically still threw three-quarters with different grips of it. It was like a slow fastball and a curve. It still had break on it."

Landreth had a bevy of scouts following him throughout southern Ontario and the Expos were the team that convinced him to sign in the days when Canadians were free agents. He remembers a number of Expos bird-dog scouts, who watched him but then he mentioned the Expos brass decided to bring in a "better guy at the end" and that guy was Detroit-based Bill Schudlich, who later did a lot of scouting for the Tigers, and was a Ford Motor Co. employee for close to 40 years in the front office.

Schudlich family photo
Bill Schudlich
signed Landreth

So Landreth and Schudlich agreed on a sign-ing bonus of $8,500 at his parents place in Strat-ford with one stipulation being that he would go to the Instructional league in the fall of 1973.

"That was my first time in pro ball (James-town). I mean, it was kinda a wake-up call. In Canada, I was a big fish in a big pond. There, I was a small fish in a small pond," Landreth was telling me. "There were 40 other pitchers there. Holy cripes, oh my god. I had Walt Hriniak as the manager. He was 5-foot-8 and full of fire. If you didn't play hard, you were going home. That was Walter. But he was a great manager, though."

Landreth really showed the Expos that he meant business the follow-ing year with West Palm Beach when he went 15-7. He kept moving up the ladder, including a 13-9 stint with the American Association champi-on Denver Bears in 1976. Although he had to keep it a secret, he knew during the playoffs that he would be called up to the big leagues by the Expos when the season was over.

Landreth recalled that when he made it to Jarry Park to get his first taste of major-league ball, he was getting his feet wet but at the same time, it wasn't like he wasn't coming to a team he didn't know anything about. He had already played in the minors with many of the Expos on that '76 squad so it made the butterflies easier to accept.

Not long after he reached Montreal, he got the starting assignment on Sept. 16 to pitch against the Cubs and shut them down for six in-nings to get credit for the win on a Thursday afternoon before a minis-cule crowd of 2,877. He allowed only four hits but permitted six bases on balls. Once you're on the mound, Landreth said, the nervousness starts to go away and he remembers at one point when third baseman Larry Parrish came over to have a little chat with him.

"I had roomed with Parrish in Québec City," Landreth said. "He just tried to calm me down. He said, 'I know you are nervous but you can throw. Just throw.' The first guy (Jerry Tabb) gets a single. What the hell? He'd never got a hit off me all year (in Triple-A). I was facing guys like Bill Madlock, who had won a couple of batting championships."

So how does Landreth fare against Madlock? He gives him an 0-for-3.

From there on, Landreth learned that because "you're a Canadian, you couldn't have bad outings. It was kind of tough. If I had a kind of bad outing, I would say, 'What am I going to do now?' "

In many ways, Landreth wishes he had been signed by another team like the Orioles, who called about 10 minutes after he signed with the Expos. He felt other teams may have been more patient with him and give "you more time to develop".

After his wonderful start against the Cubs, Landreth appeared in six more games for the Expos in 1976-77, compiling a 1-4 record and a 6.64 ERA. Little did he know at the time but his win against the Cubs in his MLB debut was the only W of his time in the big leagues. He spent most of the late 1970s in the minors, including stints with other organizations: the Dodgers and Brewers.

At age 24, Landreth decided not to pursue baseball at the pro level following the end of the 1979 season. He quit and came back home to Stratford to play in the Intercounty loop and within a few years, he began a long run of close to 34 years with the Stratford fire department.

"Once you're in the majors, you don't want to play in the minors," Landreth said of his decision not to pursue a baseball career. "I could have played longer but I didn't want to play in the minor leagues."

Denis Brodeur photo/author's collection

Jose Morales was a top notch pinch hitter for the Expos from 1974-77. He was also listed as a catcher and first baseman. He was born in Frederiksted, U.S. Virgin Islands.

Oakland Athletics photo

**Reggie Jackson was pursued by the Expos following the 1976 season
but he signed with the Yankees**

Rudy May loved fishing and scuba diving

Spring training had ended for the Expos at their home base in Daytona Beach, Florida in late March, 1979. Rudy May was flying with his teammates on a plane that would take them to Pittsburgh to start the season against the Pirates.

May's wife and kids took a different route, driving by car from Daytona Beach, heading north to Pittsburgh.

Within days, the May crew met up again in New York where the Expos played the Mets in a short two-game series to close out a five-game road trip to start the season. That road trip concluded with the Expos posting a handsome 4-1 record.

In what was a nice break at the start of the season, the Expos had two off-days on April 12 and 13, so that players could get back to Montreal and get set up in houses and apartments before the home opener on April 14.

May and his wife took turns driving to Montreal and they arrived at some point to their rented house on Montreal's Nuns' Island, an exclusive enclave on the St. Lawrence River as part of the borough of Verdun. May had arranged to rent this house from a Montreal Canadiens hockey legend.

"That's when I met Bob Gainey," May was telling me. "We moved into his house and that's when I found out his wife Cathy and I shared the same birthday, July 18."

On the 14th in the Expos home opener, the Expos beat the Cubs 2-0 to run their record to 5-1. The next morning, May won't forget what happened. He has a story to tell from that day, one he has never told before. And publicly, there has never been anything written about it.

"That's a fact, yeah, man," May was recalling with some hesitance close to 40 years later.

May was driving his wife and kids to Dorval International Airport in suburban Montreal where they would board a plane to fly to California, where the family lived.

"The kids needed to return home to go to school the next day," May was telling me in late 2020.

On his way back from the airport, May decided more or less on the spur of the moment to go fishing underneath the Vaudreuil-Dorion bridge a short distance from the airport before he would head to Olympic Stadium for a game that afternoon against the Mets.

Often, May said he would go fishing the previous year with people such as coach Jim Brewer and pitcher Hal Dues but on this day, he was by himself.

"This is what happens," May told me.

May said he was throwing lines out in the water for "small fish" when a truck stopped on top of the bridge. Somebody asked him if he had fish in his possession or if he had caught any. He replied that he was throwing the fish back in the water. All of a sudden, he noticed a lot of police cars around "every place." Gradually, several cops made their way down to the bank where May was fishing.

"You know you're not allowed to fish here?" one cop asked May.

"No, no, no," May replied. He told the cop he had come to this same spot often in the past. But May didn't realize the spot was all of sudden out of bounds.

"No, you can't fish here. They turned it into a sanctuary Jan. 1 (a few months earlier)," the cop continued. "You're coming with us. What's your name?"

May replied with his name and that he was a pitcher for the Expos. Here he was an American, black, over 6-foot-5 and about to be taken in for questioning.

"They took me. They detained me," May recalled.

May was taken to a nearby police station and kept there for an hour or so. May was trying to figure out how to get out of this mess. He was able to get to a phone at the cop shop and made contact with some people, including some Expos in the clubhouse, notably Gary Carter.

"I'm late. I gotta get going," May kept telling people he talked with. He didn't want to be late for the game or miss the start of the game. Manager Dick Williams was kept abreast of May's predicament. When he got talking with Carter, May said, "Get me out of here. Do what you got to do."

So what happens? Apparently, Expos majority owner Charles Bronfman, upon finding out about May's troubles, maybe from Carter, called the police station or visited the station. May was immediately let go and he found his way to the ballpark about 12:30, much later than usual, but in time for the game. Bronfman told me in late 2020 that he had no recollection of this scenario.

"I didn't know Charles that good. I knew he was the big Seagrams guy. I heard he got me out," May said softly, not entirely happy with what happened.

"How did you know this?" May asked me. I told him one of his friends had informed me.

"If I remember correctly, non-residents weren't required to have a fishing licence and since the law changed, I didn't think it was that big of a deal, that it was a sanctuary and no fishing was allowed," May was explaining decades later.

"I was detained, not handcuffed and I believe I was told I was not arrested. They took me in to get it straightened out. All of a sudden, I was free to go."

Since he was a teenager, May had loved the water, looking at it with his fishing pole in hand. He loved swimming and being down deep below the surface as a diver. When he was 17, he obtained his commercial diver's licence and in a number of off-seasons, he worked for a few companies, fetching about $300 per hour for his expertise.

May shook off the fishing incident and was a giant for the Expos that season, mostly in relief. The Baseball Reference website noted that he appeared in 33 games, seven as a starter. He posted a nifty 10-3 record with a 3.22 ERA. He was one of five left-handed pitchers on the club along with Dan Schatzeder, Ross Grimsley, Bill Lee and Woodie Fryman. That luxury was almost unheard in those days.

This was a team that really opened up a lot of eyes throughout the baseball world that season. After 10 consecutive losing seasons, the Expos finally finished over the .500 mark with a dazzling 95-65 record but it wasn't good enough for a playoff spot.

The Pirates were better and eventually won the World Series. The Expos finished that season at home against the Phillies and as a pending free agent, May didn't see a future with the team. President and general manager John McHale waltzed into the clubhouse.

"The irony of this whole story is that I was going to be a free agent," May said. "I was talking to my agent Dick Moss and he said, 'You're not going to be in Montreal next year.' I said, 'Why do you say that?' He said, 'If they were interested, the Expos would have been trying to negotiate a contract with you by now before other teams would have the opportunity.'

"It's the last game of the season and I'm packing and ready to leave. John McHale comes up to me and says, 'You're packing up everything?' I said, 'I have no reason to leave anything here.' John said, 'Oh, no, we'd love to have you back with the club. What kind of money do you want? I will give you this, a two-year deal.' I said, 'You you can't talk to me. Talk to my agent.' And I walked away."

Shortly after the season ended, May went to the Bahamas to do some fishing. A short time later, May somehow ended up in the Tampa, Florida airport, about to board a plane for home in California. Who should he run into at the airport? Yankees owner George Steinbrenner. No word of a lie.

"George was standing there and I went up to him and said, 'Hey, boss.'"

"Hey, Rudy, where are you going?" Steinbrenner asked May, who had pitched for the Yankees earlier that decade.

So May told Steinbrenner he wasn't likely going back to Montreal so at that point, they started informal contract negotiations. Alexander (Sandy) Manuel, a friend of May's, said May was a "Yankee at heart." May agreed the Yankees were his favourite team "because of Steinbrenner." To this day, May still has the Yankees in his blood.

When May and I agreed on a Facebook phone call for an interview in November, 2020, what team image of him showed up on the screen in the Facebook call? Him with a Yankees cap on. Cool.

As it turns out, May signed a multi-year deal with the Yankees despite McHale's best intentions of keeping him with a similar type deal. May had left the Yankees during the 1976 season following run-ins with manager Billy Martin. May recalled the time Martin took him out of a game and brought in Dick Tidrow to face Rico Carty of the Indians. Carty immediately touched Tidrow for a double but the Yankees still won.

Canadian Baseball Hall of Fame
Rudy May was with Montreal in 1978-79

After the game, May confronted Martin in the manager's office by saying, "You didn't have to take me out of the game!" And Billy went ballistic. He said, 'You so and so. You won't start another game.' He told another player to tell me I was out of the rotation. He couldn't tell me himself. Then a short time later, Dave Pagan was scheduled to pitch a game but he got sick with the flu and I was told to pitch. Billy didn't have the balls to tell me in person."

A few days later on June 15, May was traded to the Orioles. May had joined the Expos in a big trade undertaken at the winter meetings in December, 1977. May, Bryn Smith and Randy Miller were traded to the Expos by the Orioles in exchange for Don Stanhouse, Joe Kerrigan and Gary Roenicke.

May reckons that he was traded to Montreal because Orioles GM

Hank Peters was upset with him diving in the off-season. When he was with the Orioles, May had told an Orioles groundskeeper that he was diving in the off-season. Word got back to Peters and he went "ballistic", according to May. Essentially, he was told to stop diving, as per the Collective Bargaining Agreement and a player's contract.

"No motorcycles, no diving," May told me. "They knocked me out of the starting rotation because I dove. I'd get jobs to work in all my gear during the winter. I'd dive for three hours (per day). That was big, good money. I was told that (diving) was the reason I was traded to Montreal.

"What happened was that my financial advisor had never seen the Basic Agreement. I showed it to him. He says, 'Right here, there are trade clauses in the contract. When you go from one club to another and if the traded club doesn't satisfy the player with those bonus provisions, the player can negate the trade.' "

So the next day, May consulted agent Dick Moss and they approached the Orioles about this contract stipulation. Wanna know what happened? The end result was that the trade to Montreal was accepted but May was awarded bonus money stipulated in his contract, not just for that season but also for the previous two seasons.

"I don't know if we filed a grievance or not but Baltimore paid those bonus provisions," May said. "They said players never exercise that clause but we said we would and they paid those bonus provisions. The information regarding the bonus provisions being due and payable upon the player's trade is in the Basic Agreement, which I have no copy of.

"My contract with the Orioles called for me to receive a bonus of $20,000 in each year of the three-year contract. The addendum said, 'If in the sole judgment of the general manager, the player has made a significant contribution to the club during the course of the championship seasons, the player will receive the sum of $20,000.00 in each of the contract, namely, 1977, 1978 and 1979.' "

Like in 1979, May comprised a 1978 Expos roster that included five southpaws, the others being Fryman, Grimsley, Schatzeder and Darold Knowles. Although this 1978 Expos club was lacklustre and finished at 78-86, it gained considerable notoriety for continuity in the batting order. Williams went with pretty much the same set of players all season, resulting in eight position players producing at least 500 at-bats, which is some kind of record, just like the 1962 Minnesota Twins.

Those eight Expos were Gary Carter, Tony Perez, Dave Cash, Chris Speier, Larry Parrish, Warren Cromartie, Andre Dawson and Ellis Valentine. The eight Twins were Earl Battey, Vic Power, Bernie Allen, Zoilo Versalles, Rich Rollins, Harmon Killebrew, Lenny Green and Bob Allison.

May was one enduring pitcher in the days when pitchers threw late into a game, completing many of them and just plain being a great badass. Not like today when pitchers are coddled and protected by pitch counts.

May threw over 2,600 innings and collected 87 complete games with a pretty respectable ERA of 3.46, including an AL-leading 2.46 ERA with the Yankees in 1979.

May later worked for 20 years as a marketing consultant for the mega giant British Petroleum, buying and selling oil.

It was in 1978 that May ran into a future fishing buddy in Dues, a young man from Dickinson, Texas. They took a liking to each other because they were Nuns' Island neighbours in Montreal.

"We lived next door to one another and did quite a bit of fishing together," May said of Dues.

Dues died suddenly of a heart attack at 66 on Oct. 20, 2020 and it hit home with May.

"That's crazy – 66 and a heart attack. What a surprise," May said. "Too young. That's so sad. What a nice man he was."

Not only was Dues fond of May but especially veteran Expos mainstay Steve Rogers. Dues' wife Harriet told me that her husband truly adored Rogers.

"He really loved Steve Rogers. He was crazy for Steve Rogers," Mrs. Dues said.

Dues was one of those guys you couldn't help but cheer for. He had met Harriet Bishop when he was 15, she was 13. There were childhood sweethearts from Texas. Mrs. Dues told the joke that her father was always involved in baseball but for some reason, he didn't put Hal on his all-star team.

"It was always a running joke," Mrs. Dues said.

Signed for the Expos by Texas-based Red Murff, who had also signed other Expos prospects such as Balor Moore years earlier, Dues spent some time with the Expos farm team in Québec City. The date of Aug. 25, 1977 is the stuff of legends, enough to make one both cry and laugh. A trifecta took place. According to Baseball Reference, Dues didn't actually make his big-league debut until Sept. 9 but Aug. 25 was still a milestone date for him.

"Hal had pitched a really good game that day and they announced in French that I was having a baby in Texas and the fans were clapping," Mrs. Dues recalled. "Hal thought they were cheering for him but it was because I was having a baby.

"Then he was called up to the big leagues after the game. Three good things happened in one day for Hal. It was a wonderful day for him."

Dues bounced back and forth to the majors from the minor leagues because of right-arm problems that went unresolved after unsuccessful Tommy John surgery in California under the knife with the fabled Dr. Frank Jobe. Mrs. Dues revealed that Hal and his hero Rogers had TJ surgery around the same time with Jobe.

"Hal struggled after that for the next few years," his widow said.

71

Dues, not to be embarrassed, decided to retire on his own because of his arm problems because he didn't want anyone in the organization to tell him he was being let go.

"He didn't like the way ballplayers were being released back in the day," his wife said. "He thought it was so disrespectful to see someone released and there is no uniform in his locker. He thought that was horrible and he said it was not going to happen to him.

"Probably the biggest highlight for him with the Expos was when he had one of the lowest ERAs (2.36 in 1978) in the league based on innings pitched (89)."

Knowles was a solid lefty

Canadian Baseball Hall of Fame
Darold Knowles

Darold Knowles only spent one season with the Expos but the lefty was 3-3 in relief with a 2.69 ERA in 1978.

"Gary Carter was probably the best catcher I threw to and I threw to a lot of them," Knowles told me in late 2020. "I remember I rarely shook him off. I enjoyed my time in Montreal baseball-wise. They had an all-star outfield. They really had a good team. Dave Cash paid me a great compliment. He said, 'If you'd stayed with Montreal, we'd won the pennant in '79.

"But it was kind of difficult because we had two small daughters. Language was an issue. There were neighbours we had who didn't speak English. It was a tough time. Living accommodations – we lived in Ste. Adele (tourist town close to an hour north of Montreal). It was a pretty good haul every day (to the ballpark)."

Knowles decided to play out his option and sign with the Cardinals where he finished his 15-season career.

Knowles later spent many years as a pitching coach or as a rehab pitching coach for teams in the minors and majors.

Following the pandemic-marred 2020 season, Knowles shut his baseball career down – at age 78. He had been the Blue Jays rehab pitching coach out of Dunedin, Florida for a number of years.

"It was a kind of a mutual thing," Knowles said. "I spoke with the farm director Gil Kim. I decided to just hang it up. I had no hard feelings. I was very fortunate to live in Dunedin. I had the best of both worlds. I could still put the uniform on and go home every day.

"I used to play a lot of golf. I will take it up again. And my wife has duties for me to do. Luckily, I have good health. My wife makes sure I take my medications."

The whistlin' Alameda Rifle

"Chris, what was the highlight of your time with the Expos, was it the 8-RBI game?" I asked Chris Speier in late 2020.

"No," he told me. His answer had nothing to do with what happened on the field. It was an interesting reply: his experience of living in a small Québec town.

"Actually, the highlight was living in Ste. Adele and being part of that little French community in the Laurentians north of Ste. Sauveur," Speier said. "I lived there full time for five years. Yes, that's probably the highlight of my career with the Expos. It was about an hour from Montreal, four toll booths away."

How about that for a highlight? And did he ever enjoy cross-country skiing in Ste. Adele. Oh, man, it was an enjoyable experience.

"That was something I fell in love with. Oh gosh, yes. It was a great way to stay in shape with the snow and everything," Speier told me. "I ended up cross-country skiing with another guy that worked out at a gym. We really got into it, trails and hills and back country. I was in the best shape of my life. And I found Mont Tremblant: I skied all the way from the bottom to the top."

That's no easy feat cross-country skiing from the bottom of a mountain to the top. Speier asked me if I had ever been to Mont Tremblant, a scenic resort town located about 50 km. from Ste Adele. I told him twice in 1973 with a friend of mine from Renfrew, Ontario, Hank Nieweboeur. He skied and I watched him ski. The scenery was absolutely breath-taking.

"There were other highlights," Speier said. "Most of the them evolve around the team, our making the playoffs (1981) and getting to that point. Those are all highlights, to be able to compete in those situations.

Stratford Beacon-Herald/Stratford-Perth Archives image
**Chris Speier does some cross-country skiing at Olympic Stadium
in April, 1983 under the watchful eye of Scott Sanderson, left,
Charlie Lea, Tim Blackwell, Jerry White, Ray Burris, clubhouse attendant
Tony Araujo and photographer Aussie Whiting at right.**

Hitting for the cycle (July 20, 1978) from an offensive standpoint, that's a big highlight."

Speier is viewed as one of the best shortstops in Expos history. He was not a big run producer but he was solid at his position. Could he fire bullets from short to first? You bet. Thus, the moniker The Alameda Rifle, alluding to his hometown in northern California which is also the birthplace for such fellow baseball alumni as Willie Stargell, Dontrelle Willis and Jimmy Rollins.

Vying with Speier for No. 1 on the all-time Expos shortstop ladder would be his predecessor Tim Foli, Wil Cordero and Orlando Cabrera. People who knew Speier or didn't know him that much looked at him as a very underappreciated, underrated, undervalued player in Expos annals. Neal McClelland, a sports reporter at the Daily Iberian in New Iberia, Louisiana and an Expos fan since 1977, assessed Speier this way: "Criminally understated shortstop."

Speier took over from the volatile Foli in a trade that took place not long after the regular season started in 1977. They merely exchanged positions. The trade in the midst of contract negotiations with the Giants didn't end up with the deal Speier wanted. The Giants figured they were better off trading Speier to get something for him before he became a free agent. That trade happened April 27.

"That whole scenario, it wasn't going to work out," Speier was telling me. "I was going to be a free agent. We were in negotiations with the Giants over a long contract. There were three (MLB) shortstops: Dave Concepcion, Larry Bowa and myself. Those two guys got five-year contracts and I wanted a similar contract. The Giants, at the time, didn't want to do that. With Montreal, we settled on a contract, five years at $200,000 a year."

Speier was an integral part of the Expos' juggernaut that vied for the National East pennant from 1979-83. He was a big part of the team's push to win the second-half title in 1981, allowing the Expos to finally taste post-season play.

In the five-game NLDS the Expos won against the Phillies, Speier went 6-for-15 with four runs and three RBI. He wasn't quite the same in the NLCS but he was still solid at short. He came this-close to getting to the World Series. One of my biggest memories of Speier was him going to his right and snaring a line drive off the bat of Pedro Guerrero and firing to second baseman Rodney Scott at second to complete a double play that ended Game 2 of the 1981 NLCS.

"We had some really good teams. On paper, we were supposed to win but we were never able to get over the hump. That '81 team was the best team I played on," Speier said.

Following the completion of his five-year contract signed in 1977, Speier re-upped with the Expos and signed another contract and all was rosy until the 1983 season when Bill Virdon took over as manager. Speier lost game time under Virdon.

Instead, Virdon went mostly with Bryan Little in 1983 and Little and Angel Salazar in 1984. When I researched the starting lineups at the beginning of 1983, Little started the first five games and Speier got into his first game as a late inning replacement in Game 5. That kind of pattern continued through one and a half seasons, irritating Speier to no end.

Virdon thought Salazar would be as good as fellow Venezuelan Concepcion. Not so. In 1984, Salazar had a terrible season as a starter. In 80 games, his batting average was .155. Sitting on the bench most of the time and watching Salazar and Little was Speier.

"For some reason, Virdon didn't want me as the shortstop," Speier said. "We continually butted heads. We had our disagreements. There was never any chest pumping. He had his mind made up. I didn't have too much control. They never did have a shortstop at the time who could do the things I could do. I was not playing much so they ended up trading me to St. Louis."

That was on Canada Day, 1984. In later years, Virdon admitted he

Stratford Beacon-Herald/Stratford-Perth Archives image
Chris Speier in the on-deck circle for the San Fransisco Giants

handled the whole Speier gig wrong. Speier went on to play for the Cardinals, Cubs and then the Giants again for a three-year span from 1987-89, culminating in his first World Series visit which resulted in Oakland winning it all.

Off the field, Speier can't recall the year exactly but he got into a spirited debate on Montreal radio station CJAD years ago with Dr. Henry Morgantaler, about the pros and cons of abortion. Morgantaler was known for establishing illegal abortion clinics across Canada, some of which were shut down. He challenged the federal and provincial governments to repeal their abortion laws.

Speier had become an activist in the pro-life movement after he converted to Catholicism with his first wife. In the 1990s, Speier had been principal of the independent Ville de Marie Academy in Scottsdale, Arizona. It wasn't accredited by the state nor was it attached to the local diocese but it was still a noteworthy part of his resumé, certainly a breakaway past-time compared to baseball.

In the debate or discussion on CJAD, Speier referred to his opponent as Mr. Morgantaler, not Dr. Morgantaler.

"You can understand my reasoning," Speier told me in an interview. "Doctors using that moniker, they're supposed to be preserving lives. Abortionists don't do that.

"We were on opposite ends of the spectrum. He was pro-abortion. I was totally against it. I've always been pro-life. I still stand by that. It's still a very controversial element now. From my standpoint, I've been an active pro-life proponent."

It was during his second go-around with San Francisco that Speier started to cultivate a relationship with Dusty Baker, who was the team's batting coach. They have remained on the same page for years in an unlikely but cool combination of a black man and a white man. It sure helps that they live not far from each other in Northern California, Speier in Alameda, Baker near Sacramento.

Down the road, when Baker was manager, Speier wasn't far behind as one of his coaches. The 2020 season was Speier's 11th and final season as a Baker understudy.

Speier jokingly made it clear to me that he didn't allow Baker to rib him about the Dodgers beating the Expos in the 1981 NLCS. Baker was an outfielder with the Dodgers, who went on to win the World Series that year.

"Originally, we had such a mutual respect as player vs. player, Dodger vs. Giant," Speier said. "I was out of baseball four to five years and when I got back in, I had the opportunity to start our relationship on a little bit more regular basis.

"Dusty, you know, he's No. 1. He's probably one of the most caring individuals in the game I've met. Baseball is really secondary to him. Everybody loves playing for him. He cares more for the individual."

The manager-coach scenario involving Baker and Speier began in 2007 when Baker was the Cubs skipper. From there, the duo worked together with the Reds and Nationals and the 2020 season with the Astros.

It was a "shock, a tremendous shock" when Baker was hired as a last resort to run the Astros for the 2020 season after A.J. Hinch was suspended for one season over the Astros trash-can scandal. But what was even more shocking to Speier was his own hiring.

"You know when that (Baker) hiring happened, the complete coaching staff was already in place. Dusty inherited that coaching staff. There was really no room on the coaching staff (for Speier)," Speier said. "Dusty asked the owner (Jim Crane). He told him, 'I want to bring in a guy I trust. The manager needs to get someone to get his back. There is a trust in the individual (Speier). I want to bring in a guy I can trust.' It sure worked out for me. I'm just like the extra guy to help out."

So he was given the title of "quality assurance" coach.

"I don't know what the definition is. Tell me what it means," Speier was telling me.

How about the definition be a jack of all trades? That's it. Speier became a multi-tasker. He sat on the bench, helping out wherever he could. And in September, he was pressed into duty as the first base coach when third base coach Gary Pettis was diagnosed with multiple mylema. Speier called it "cancer in the left leg." First-base coach Omar Lopez moved to third and Speier stepped into the coach's box at first.

"Being an infielder, I was working with the infielders, I love the in-game decisions that have to be made as far as defences go, watching young infielders blossom, to try to get them thinking on their own instead of relying on a coach's help. It's very gratifying. I would go through channels, through the infield instructor."

When the Astros were eliminated by the Rays in the 2020 playoffs, Speier retired to spend more time with his grand-children. He was 70. He said it was "time" to pack it in.

What many Expos fans don't know is that Speier's baseball career took him to the Canadian tourist town of Stratford, Ontario in 1969 to play for the Hoods in the Intercounty league, a semi-pro league that had its origins more than 100 years ago. Speier told me the story of how he ended up in southwestern Ontario.

Speier had been attending the University of California at Santa Barbara and the pitching coach there was a guy by the name of Rolf Scheel. So Scheel convinced Speier that it would be worthwhile to accompany him to play in the Intercounty at age 18.

Scheel, 37, was Stratford's manager but he also was a pitcher. It was the first year the Expos started operations in Montreal and it was the first year of operation in the Intercounty for Jack Dominico's now-famous Toronto

Chris Speier when he played for the Stratford Hoods in this Stratford Beacon-Herald/Stratford-Perth Archives image.

Maple Leafs.

"There were a lot of older guys in the league, former minor-league players so it was a good step up," Speier said in an interview. "I was looking to play somewhere in the summer. I had made the decision not to go back to Santa Barbara.

"Three years of college ball wasn't going to help me. I had a good year as a freshman. I don't remember what I did offensive wise in Stratford."

Speier must have done something right because the Alameda Rifle was selected that year to the Intercounty's first all-star team at shortstop. Intercounty statistician Herb Morell relayed Speier's stats. They were impressive.

While it was common that some import players would leave an Intercounty team before the end of each season to return to school in the U.S., Speier played the full slate of 28 regular-season games with Stratford that season, batting .320, which was second on the team to Steve Kyle's .323.

Speier led the Hoods with 130 plate appearances, 33 hits, 26 runs and 25 walks. He had one homer and 12 RBI.

In the playoffs, Speier played all three series his team was in, appearing in all 19 games. In the championship series, the London Pontiacs beat Speier's Hoods 4-3. The seventh game was played Sept. 29 when London won 7-5. In the last four games of the final, Speier collected seven hits.

"Chris whistled all the time. He was a whistler. It was unique," recalled Arden Eddie, who played for the Pontiacs as part of a long-long run as a player. "That was his way of chattering, general infield chatter. That kind of thing, you remember. In 37 years of playing in the Intercounty, I don't recall anybody else whistling once.

"We knew Chris was going places. You could tell he was head and shoulders above anyone. He was that good. He stood out. He had something different from other people. We knew that's why he signed. There was no surprise with that. He had that special whatever it was. I didn't have what he had."

Eddie's teammate Barry Boughner seconded the motion about the whistling on the part of Speier, a ritual that was quite annoying to those on the field. Eddie said when he got into the batter's box that he could block out any noise, including Speier's antics.

"We all remember Chris," Boughner said. "There was one thing he did when he was playing shortstop that drove everyone nuts – he whistled very loudly and non-stop for the entire amount of time that his team was on the field. All you could hear all game long was Chris whistling.

"Chris was a very good hitter but what impressed me most of all was his fielding ability. You couldn't help but notice how good a shortstop he was. Chris was like a human vacuum cleaner at shortstop. He had great

Canadian Baseball Hall of Fame   Canadian Baseball Hall of Fame   Houston Astros photo   Danny Gallagher photo

Chris Speier as he has looked over the years. He began his MLB career in 1971 and ended it in 2020

hands and a very strong throwing arm, especially when he had to go deep into the hole between third and short," Boughner said.

"It was a funny situation in Stratford," Speier said. "No. 1, they gave me a family that took me in so I had a place to stay. Then they also got a job for me during the day with all the games played at night.

"I started out in a food-supply warehouse that teaches you how to fill up the carts. For me, it was kind of tedious and boring so I asked, 'Is there anything else?' I was told they had a job for me out in the train area where you had to load up railroad cars. 'Yeah, I will try that.' It ended up we loaded these rail cars with bathtubs. Two of us had to load and unload the cars. Oh my god, that lasted four days. I was worn out."

So Speier finished out the season, hanging out at the ball park all day at less strenuous work, taking care of the infield and mowing the grass, "whatever work had to be done." Scheel looked after the ball diamond and often during the day, he would hit fungos to Speier at short and he would throw BP to Speier from the pitching machine.

That experience with lifting heavy bathtubs didn't help his back and for many years, he has had problems with his back.

"I remember my back would go out every once in a while. I'd be incapacitated and it would hurt when I would swing," Speier said. "So to make it easier to swing, I'd turn around in the box and bat left a few times. They (opposition) thought I was trying to show them up and they threw at me a couple of times."

Watching Speier many times that season in Ontario was Giants area bird-dog Herman Hannah, who was based out of Detroit. Hannah met up with Speier on a few visits and wrote Speier up in a report he sent to his Giants' superiors.

One of Speier's teammates, Ron Earl, a shortstop, had transferred to Stratford from Kingston, Ont. in his job with Household Finance and was ready to continue his senior baseball career after 10 years or so in Kingston. Earl showed up at his first Hoods' practice and was told that there was a new shortstop in camp and you "won't beat him out at shortstop."

So Earl was introduced to Scheel, his new manager.

"What position do you like to play?" Scheel asked Earl.

Realizing that Speier was taking over at short and even though "I never played second base before", Earl decided to answer this way: "Second base" and so that was the way Earl eased his way onto the team. Scheel told Earl to get changed into his uniform and when he came onto the field, Earl saw Scheel hitting balls to Speier at short.

"Oh," Earl said, in getting confirmation that Speier indeed would be playing short and that's all there was to it. Eventually, because of an arm injury, Earl was shifted to first base.

"Chris was a great teammate," Earl told me in an interview. "He was really good for an 18-year-old kid. Very mature. All he wanted to do was win. He was confident. He knew what he was doing. Never to this day have I seen such a strong arm and the way he could throw the baseball.

"He made a lot of errors because he got to balls that nobody else could and tried to throw runners out. He could throw the ball so hard. I remember one time a runner just moseyed on down to first thinking he had a single but Chris tracked down the ball and threw him out by three feet. The guy couldn't believe that he got to the ball.

"There was one time he picked up a high-hopper near the mound and threw it on the run and bounced it in front of me and it went past me. He comes up to me on the bench and fired his glove down and said, 'Get in front of the effin ball'. I looked back at him and said, 'If I had blocked it, it would have gone through me.' He said, 'I was just kidding. I know it would have killed you.' "

As for Speier's whistling, Earl said, "That was his trademark. I'd just say he did that to keep everybody aware."

Down the road when Earl and some friends would go to Montreal to see Expos games, Speier gladly put tickets away for them.

Several months after he returned from Stratford, Speier played part of that winter in the San Francisco-based Peninsula league which was sponsored by major-league teams. In January of 1970, the Giants, on Hannah's recommendation, drafted Speier. He spent the 1970 season with the Giants' Double-A Amarillo team in the Texas league and by the following season, he was in the majors with the Giants and helped them win the NL West title.

"Chris played only one season in the minors in 1970," Eddie remembered with great admiration.

Just like he did in Stratford when he literally forced his way into the shortstop role for the Hoods, brushing Earl aside, Speier did much the same thing in San Fran, taking the shortstop role away from incumbent Hal Lanier. Imagine this brash rookie coming in and telling manager Charlie Fox that he wanted shortstop. What did Lanier do? He agreed to go and play second like Earl agreed to do in Stratford.

Speier went on to play 19 seasons in the majors, including coveted time as a Giants' teammate of Juan Marichal, Willie Mays and Willie McCovey. A shiny example of how a guy travelled from California to play in the Intercounty with Stratford and made his way to the majors.

I ran into Speier during spring training in 2017 in West Palm Beach and again at Exposfest in Montreal in 2018. I remarked to myself how he stayed in such great shape. For years, he was always a "gym rat" kind of guy and would run up and down stadium steps at home or on the road, both as a player and as a coach. A few years ago, he stopped the running, partly due to knee problems.

In our phone chat in October, 2020, I complimented Speier on staying slim the same way as former teammate Steve Rogers.

"What do you do to stay in shape?" I asked Speier.

Juanita Moore photo

Chris Speier, at right, poses with Grant Jackson at Expos Camera Day in 1981

"No. 1, I gave up alcohol," he revealed. "That helped. It's sad but I'm a recovering alcoholic. It was definitely a problem. I gave it up in 2000 (despite some relapses). I did soft liquor, hard liquor, you can put anything in there. I liked scotch. It's not a good combination. If that's part of your story, I am fine with it."

Chris, thanks a lot for giving me such a great story on your life.

Odd case involving Tito Fuentes

One of the more controversial, salary-arbitration cases involving the Expos centered around a player, who never put on a uniform on for the team in regular-season play.

His name was Tito Fuentes. Remember him? He was one of the last baseball players signed directly out of Cuba before the U.S. implemented an embargo against the Caribbean country as baseball-loving Fidel Castro was taking over power.

Fuentes was an infielder signed by the San Francisco Giants in 1962 and who went on to play 8+ seasons with the west-coast club before moving on to suit up for the Padres and Tigers prior to a trade to Montreal. He was one of those rare players back in the day who played with style and flair.

In his book The Bronx Zoo, Sparky Lyle called Fuentes "one of the most renowned hot dogs in baseball history." There was a reason behind that. Fuentes often wore headbands, sometimes on the front of his baseball cap. When he came up to the plate from the on-deck circle, he was known to hold the bat by the barrel, tap-handle it off the plate, flip it into the air and grab it by the handle.

The staid baseball establishment didn't appreciate this kind of behaviour and Fuentes didn't endear himself to opposing pitchers. Often, he would receive chin music and hit the dirt.

In 1977, in his only season with Detroit, he batted a career-best .309 with 190 hits and five homers and 51 RBI in 615 at-bats as the team's everyday second baseman. What a season so that winter, Fuentes and his agent Dick Moss asked the Tigers for a $135,000 salary, compared to the $91,000 stipend he earned in 1977.

Outraged, the Tigers decided to get rid of him and sold him to the

Fernand Lapierre photo

Expos general manager Jim Fanning, waving, poses here in the 1970s with Expos public-address announcer Claude Mouton in the golf cart and brothers Charlemagne and Paul Beaudry, who were Expos minority shareholders.

Expos on Jan. 30, 1978 for cash – Fuentes told me in 1988 that it was for $100.

Once Fuentes became Expos property less than a month prior to spring training, he wanted more money than what he asked the Tigers for. Although the Expos and other sources at the time had no records to confirm it, Fuentes told me that he requested $157,000. He said he was offered $135,000, which was the figure he requested in his standoff with the Tigers. The arbitrator ruled in favour of the Expos.

"It was a bit strange dealing with a guy who never picked up a ball for you," said then Expos executive Jim Fanning, who argued the case for the team. "After the hearing, after all of the things that were said and refuted, I was like a whipped dog, who'd pulled a dogsled all across Canada. It was a tough session of about five hours.

"I was all alone. Dick Moss argued the case for Fuentes. He's a tough agent. But I beat him. He took a lot of razzing. I remember him coming to the hearing and asking where (general manager) Charlie Fox was. 'He's not here,' I told him. 'Oh, that's too bad,' he said. Then he brought in about seven or eight young attorneys in behind him, almost as if to intimidate me.

"Near the end of the hearing, Moss compared Fuentes to a Hall of Famer and when he said that, I summed up by saying that of all the terribly ridiculous things said that day, that statement was the ultimate."

Fuentes said that the arbitrator told him outright at the hearing that he was earning too much money.

"He was a very old man. He was jealous of the players because he didn't make that kind of money," Fuentes said about the arbitrator.

Fuentes and Moss filed a grievance, saying the hearing was conducted unfairly. The grievance was dismissed. That wasn't the end of the story. The Expos won the case but they were pissed because Fanning was subjected to a five-hour hearing and they were pissed that the grievance was filed. Fanning passed this news on to Fox and president John McHale, who were not too pleased with Fuentes and Moss.

So when Fuentes reported to spring training in Daytona Beach, Fla., the Expos had it in for him and he was treated shabbily, he said.

"I played one game during spring training," Fuentes said. "I was coming off my best year of my career and Fox said the team wanted me only as an utility player. I didn't want to do that. So Fox said, 'Okay, let's see how good you are. Let's see if anyone in baseball will pick you up.' I was blackballed by the Expos. I was released and nobody picked me up.

"I ended up playing in Mexico but later in the season, Charley Finley, the owner in Oakland, asked me to come and DH (he had only 43 AB)."

After a career season in 1977, it was hard to fathom that the Expos just discarded him. Blackballed? It's the same theory Bill Lee has held since he was released by the Expos in May, 1982, never to play another MLB game. Fanning told me in 1988 that Fuentes was finished because his skills had deteriorated.

Thankfully, Fuentes wasn't out-and-out blackballed because his first team, the Giants, has employed him as a Spanish language broadcaster for more than 30 years. As we went to press, he was back at the microphone for the 2021 season.

Battlin' Bad Billy

Rudy May and many other major-leaguers had problems with Billy Martin as a manager. There were others who accepted him for who he was because he was a winner.

Ron LeFlore, a one-season wonder with the Expos in 1980, played for Martin with the Tigers in 1978 and was indebted to Martin because Martin rescued him from prison and had the troubled kid signed by the Tigers.

Martin for all kinds of different reasons got into trouble, whether it was with players like May, Reggie Jackson, whoever or with people he had met in a bar. Billy had a drinking problem for sure even though he was very much the toast of New York when he was with the Yankees.

Battlin' Bad Billy, for the controversy that he stirred up, somehow had me as an admirer mainly because many of the teams he managed were winners.

On Oct. 10, 1979, Martin got into trouble at a bar in Minneapolis, Minnesota. At the Hotel de France, Billy was getting bad vibes from someone later identified as Joseph Cooper, a marshmallow salesman. Martin claimed the guy was taunting him, saying he shouldn't have won the American League manager of the year award.

The salesman, probably under the influence of alcohol, felt the award should have gone to someone like Earl Weaver of the Orioles. Martin apparently also razzed the marshmallow salesman about his profession.

The guy wanted to fight Martin. Foolish as he was on occasion, Martin agreed to a fight about a half an hour later. Martin apparently hit the guy with a right fist and the guy fell down. Word about this incident got back to Yankees owner George Steinbrenner and the bombastic owner fired Martin a few days later.

Martin was fired for that episode but he could just as easily have been fired a month before that over an incident I witnessed at Toronto's Westbury Hotel, one of my all-time favourite watering holes at 475 Yonge St. on the east side. It later became known as the Courtyard Marriott and other names but sadly, the space was recently taken over by condo towers.

The Westbury was named after the Knott Westbury Hotels in London, England and New York. It was a go-to place on the Yonge St. strip, a place for people-watching, a place to be seen, a place to check out women and see if any familiar faces were there and of course, have a cocktail or two, and sometimes dancing was available to the tunes of a piano player.

Martin could have been fired or at least there would have been publicity over it if the Ottawa Journal, my employer at the time, had taken my account of an episode involving Martin and another bar customer on Friday, Sept. 21, 1979. This is a story I have never told before, a story I have never publicized until now.

I have this all detailed on record in a story draft that was last spun out on 88 lines on a teletype printer on April 1, 1986 in the newsroom at the Regina Leader-Post where I worked from 1984-88. So on Nov. 22, 2020, I started typing the details of this story for this book.

I was on holidays that day in 1979 and I was in Toronto to see the Yankees play the Blue Jays that night. Tom Underwood (9-16) got the win over Ron Guidry (17-8) as the Jays won 3-2. When the game was over, I made my way from Exhibition Stadium to the Westbury on Yonge St. about midnight. I walked over to the far end of the bar in Beaton's Lounge and waited for a bartender to serve me.

As I was waiting for the bartender to come over, I looked around and lo and behold, I saw Billy. What a surprise and he was only a few feet away. Never did I expect to run across him, except maybe in the Yankees clubhouse or on the field before a game during batting practice. I never made an attempt to introduce myself. I just figured I would just leave him alone and not bother him.

Yet, there he was in the flesh, having a few drinks and really enjoying himself. There was a Yankees entourage of three with Martin and two of them were familiar faces to me: Mickey Morabito, the Yankees public relations director, and Charlie Lau, the famous hitting guru. I didn't know the fourth man. I can't remember if the Yankees were staying at the Westbury. Not sure.

Several stools away, a customer, unknown to Martin, started complaining to the bartender that his bar bill was a bit too high. The bartender said his bill was correct. The customer continued to complain. Then Billy intervened in an attempt to clear up the squabble over the bill. Martin offered to give the complainer the money in U.S. funds needed to cover the bill.

"Here," Billy said, "take this money and pay the bill."

The guy refused Billy's offer and Billy took exception to the guy refusing him. Oh shoot. The guy then started complaining about what Billy was saying to him and both got off their stools and began to fight.

Lau, Morabito and Co. tried to hold Billy back but he broke out of their reach and started fighting with the whiner. The guy kicked Billy and Billy responded with a few punches. The fight was short-lived and the two combatants headed to the street to avoid any further controversy or possible publicity.

Witnessing this, I gathered it to be a good story for the Ottawa Journal. When I went back to my hotel room at the Strathcona Hotel near the Royal York Hotel, I weighed the pros and cons of whether I should call the Journal and offer the story. Journalists often look the other way when these kinds of things happen. There's the old expression that says, "What happens in a bar stays in the bar." And there's the expression, "What you saw you didn't see."

I checked with the Metropolitan Toronto police department to see if charges were laid. I was told no. I decided to call the Journal and talked to deskman Mike Pasternak. He asked me if any charges were laid and I said no. He felt that no story should be written. Pasternak put me onto sports editor Gerald Redmond.

"I don't think we should do a story," Redmond told me. "If we do something, the papers in Toronto (and New York) will pick up the story and Martin will be in trouble. Martin is in enough trouble already."

I felt disappointed with the decision not to take the story. It was poor judgment. Here was a great story to get the Journal a big scoop and it was all turned down. To this day, I don't think any of the Toronto and New York media ever heard of this incident.

When Martin was fired less than three weeks later over the episode involving the marshmallow salesman, I saw Redmond downstairs in the newspaper's composing room and I told him that we could have had Martin fired weeks earlier. He had nothing to say. I never held a grudge against Gerald. He was a great man, a great writer and a great drinking buddy.

Schatzeder for LeFlore

Ron LeFlore was in the middle of shaving his 5-oclock shadow when a phone call came so he got his then girl friend, Sara, to speak to Tigers vice-president Bill Lajoie.

"It's important," Lajoie told LeFlore's girlfriend. "If Ron can't come to the phone, then I'll tell you, Sara. We've traded Ron to Montreal," Lajoie continued.

"Oh, my God," Sara exclaimed.

A few seconds later, LeFlore was on the phone.

"Ron, I have some news for you. We've traded your contract to Montreal."

"Who did you get?" LeFlore asked.

"Dan Schatzeder, a left-handed pitcher."

"Straight up?"

"Yes."

Then there was silence. You could hear a pin drop.

In the exchange as it was parlayed by LeFlore and his girlfriend to a Detroit reporter, Lajoie told LeFlore, "Ron, you know my personal feelings concerning you. However, this is a business deal and I'm sure you understand that. We were able to get a left-handed pitcher, who was the leading earned-run man among National League pitchers."

There was more dead air.

"Okay," LeFlore said, "That's it. I wish you and the ball club all the luck in the world, Bill."

LeFlore later told a Detroit reporter that he was "crushed" by the trade.

"I never thought it would happen," LeFlore said. "In a way, it hasn't sunk in yet. I devoted everything I had to this town. Detroit is my home.

Now I'm gone."

LeFlore had spent six seasons with the Tigers and was heading north to Montreal for his seventh season with a team that almost won the National League East in 1979.

Schatzeder was a key component of the Expos drive but the team was stalled at the end by the Pittsburgh Pirates.

Some baseball folks and media were of the opinion that LeFlore's acquisition might have handed the Expos the 1980 pennant. The headline in Ontario's Ottawa Journal, a newspaper I worked for two hours west of Montreal, declared, "LeFlore now, pennant later?"

Tigers manager Sparky Anderson said LeFlore would not be missed if rookie Kirk Gibson comes along quickly.

"I think we have a good replacement for LeFlore in Gibson. He's 6-feet, 220 pounds and he's the fastest man in the league next to Willie Wilson."

One reporter who wrote a story on the trade from the winter meetings, eloquently wrote this: "Gibson is a 22-year-old outfielder who is built like Pike's Peak and moves faster than inflation. Anderson saw in him the embodiment of Johnny Bench and Pete Rose both."

Expos GM John McHale reasoned that the two clubs involved in the trade weren't of the same ilk.

"Do you see our situation is a bit different than the Tigers?' They are still building but we are committed to a winner," McHale said at the time.

Anderson was happy to get a second left-hander for his rotation, a commodity he had sought since he became Tigers skipper several years earlier.

"Now, when we go into a three-game series, I can throw Jack Morris one day and Schatzeder the next. This is going to be just all right with me," Anderson said. "There is no question he will be our No. 2 starter. Last year, we had Morris and then it dropped off to nothing."

Schatzeder, like LeFlore, was also floored by the trade. He enjoyed his stint with the Expos after being drafted out of the University of Denver. All of a sudden, he was going to a new team. The story about Schatzeder is "two different stories", as he put it, because he had two different stints with the Expos.

"I was shocked when I got traded to Detroit. It was the first time I got traded," Schatzeder told me in September of 2020. "Know what, it was not easy, the way it came down. It was rough when I got the phone call. I realized it was a business, that I was expendable but I still didn't like it. It was a rough winter.

"It's the first time you get traded so it was a wake-up call. It went back to John (McHale). He was always fair to me. He was just trying to improve the team. The Expos were looking for a solid lead-off hitter, they were trying to put the puzzle piece together to get to the next level."

Schatzeder had made his MLB debut as a September call-up in

Photos courtesy Detroit Tigers

Ron LeFlore spent six seasons with the Tigers before he was acquired by the Expos at the winter meetings in December, 1979

1977 after stints that summer with Double-A Québec City and Triple-A Denver. It was in Denver that manager Doc Edwards had told him long before his call-up in convincing fashion like a physic that "You are going to the big leagues."

"It was the first time a coach or manager had actually said that to me. I told him, 'Thanks for telling me that,' " Schatzeder said. Sure enough, two months later, he got the call to the Big Show.

CBHOF collection
Dan Schatzeder

"We were playing in Denver at the time. It was pretty cool because I played university ball there," Schatzeder said. "My biggest thrill getting called up was just walking into the clubhouse in Montreal. Being in the clubhouse for the first time was a big thrill. I remember seeing Del Unser. He was obviously a big kid.

"I remember my first game. The bullpen, a trailer, was down the right-field line. Norm Sherry was the bullpen coach," Schatzeder was saying. "Jackie Brown, a veteran, was facing the Astros. He walked the first guy, walked the second guy. The phone rings and Norm says for me to warm up. Brown gives up another walk and the bases are loaded. Bob Watson comes up and hits a grand slam."

Holy shoot. Brown is out of the game and Schatzeder makes his big-league debut. So he walks across the white line to the rubber, taking in all the sights and sounds of Olympic Stadium.

"There is no pressure on me. I get to the mound and Gary Carter says, 'Don't be looking around the stadium like that. Focus on the glove.' My first pitching coach with Montreal was Jim Brewer. He was like a father to me. He took me under his wing. I remember him as a great coach, the biggest influence on me as a pitcher.

"When I first came up, I was a young star," Schatzeder said. "I had a couple of good years, mostly as a starter. They had guys like Tony Perez, Gary Carter, Steve Rogers, Andre Dawson, a lot of veteran players. I remember watching everybody and how they would act. I was trying to learn from everyone.

"In 1979, we lost out to the Pirates. We dominated the rest of the league. If there had been a wild card, we would have been in."

So what he did from 1977-79 sure impressed the Tigers. Just what Anderson expected, Schatzeder was reasonably good as a starter in 1980 with a 11-13 record and a 4.02 ERA while LeFlore was exceptional in his one and only season with the Expos.

LeFlore stole 97 bases, establishing a franchise record that was never broken.

In 1981, Schatzeder was sporadic with a 6-8 record with a 5.32 ERA in Detroit. Almost two years to the day he was traded by the Expos to the Tigers, he was swapped to the Giants. In 1982, he started off poorly with the Giants and was optioned to Triple-A Phoenix. While languishing in the heat of the desert, Schatzeder wondered if he would ever get back to the big leagues.

"John McHale was one guy to have faith in you," Schatzeder said. "He was a man as far as I'm concerned. He gave me another chance. He brought me back. I was glad to get back to Montreal. I had a few more good years."

That trade was made June 15, 1982 and he went on to pitch for the Expos until 1986.

"When I came back, they still had a good young team, Carter, Dawson, Raines, the mainstays were still there," Schatzeder said. "Tim Wallach and I hung out a lot, Terry Francona, Scott Sanderson. And I met Jeff Reardon. We'd hang out in the bullpen beyond last field, which was a trailer back then, where you got to know everybody."

Schatzeder had a few stories to tell, including the time Bill Virdon called him over.

"It's spring training and managers like to walk around. Bill liked to hit fungos to the outfielders," Schatzeder said.

"Schatz, come over here. I want you to shag balls with me," Virdon said.

"So Tim Raines is out in left field, about 150 feet away from Bill and Bill is smoking balls at Raines, one-hoppers. He was hitting rockets at him," Schatzeder said, chuckling. "I was catching the balls. Raines must have been saying, 'What's going on here?' "

When I mentioned to Schatzeder that one reporter years ago referred to him as a "stylish pitcher" because of his delivery, it was his chance to tell me a story about hitting Andy Van Slyke of the Cardinals on Sept. 26, 1983, although he claimed his delivery was unintentional.

"It was in St. Louis. Bob Forsch, their pitcher, had been telling people he was going to hit Gary Carter the first time out," Schatzeder said. "So he plunked him in the ribs. So the umpire, Harry Wendelstedt, sent Gary to first base. So Wendelstedt came out to both teams and said, 'Enough of that stuff.' "

Meaning if another pitcher hits somebody, then that pitcher would get heaved. In the sixth inning, Schatzeder was called on to relieve Steve Rogers.

"So Van Slyke is up for them, he's a lefty and I'm a lefty. The first pitch, I threw as hard as I could. The ball got away from me," Schatzeder said. "It towered up and hit the tip of his helmet and the helmet goes flying. He goes down and the umpire said to me, 'You're out of the game.' I was gone after one pitch. I was thrown out.

Expos who returned after switching teams

Tim Blackwell
Gary Carter
Wil Cordero
Jim Dwyer
Joey Eischen
Cliff Floyd
Tom Foley
Woodie Fryman
Andres Galarraga
Wilton Guerrero
Greg A. Harris
Bob James
Wallace Johnson
Andy McGaffigan
Dale Murray
Curtis Pride
Tim Raines
Bobby Ramos
Henry Rodriguez
Mel Rojas
Dan Schatzeder
Rodney Scott
Tony Scott
Dan Smith
Rusty Staub
Dave Tomlin
Tom Walker
Lenny Webster
Jerry White

Note: Lenny Webster came back a third time

CBHOF Collection
Lenny Webster

"Virdon was coming out. I thought he would be pissed at me because I was gone after one pitch. He had his hand out and had a big smile on his face. He said, 'Good job.' He liked that I went up and in on him."

A check of the boxscore from that game showed that both Schatzeder and Virdon were ejected for "Intentional HBP".

What some people don't remember is that Schatzeder was what you called a "good hitting pitcher." He was solid as a hitter at the U of D. His lifetime average in the majors was a pretty impressive .240 (58-for-242) with five homers, including two in 1985. In a combo season in 1986 with the Expos and Phillies, he hit .385 (10-for-26). Five of those 10 hits were pinch-hit jobs, the most in the majors by a pitcher since Don Newcombe in 1959.

"I enjoyed hitting. I hate the DH," he said. "That was the ball player in me, the hitter. Bob Forsch was a good hitting pitcher, too. I played outfield in college. I was all-district. I had a great arm, good speed and I was good at stealing bases. But pitching was the way to the big leagues.

"1979 would have to have been my best season. It was a real good year for me. I got a chance to start. I was not a ground-ball pitcher. I gave up fly balls. It was great to pitch at Olympic Stadium. We had the outfielders to run balls down. I'd say to Raines, 'Get ready.'"

Your all-time favourite game that stands out, Dan?

"I had some really good moments," he said. "I'm from Chicago. I grew up in Chicago, a White Sox fan, a member of the White Sox Fan Club. In 1984 in Montreal, I started a game (Aug. 9) against Dennis Eckersley. We won 1-0. I pitched 10 innings. It was my best game as a starter and it was against the Cubs."

In a game that took only 2:22 to play, Schatzeder spun a four-hitter. A game never to be forgotten.

Thank you for the memories, Schatz.

LeFlore's wonderful season in 1980

I lucked out when I sent Ron LeFlore a postal letter to a Florida address where I believed he resided. Almost immediately upon receiving the letter, he called me. It was the same strategy I used in the case of Schatzeder. I wrote Schatz a nice, typed-up letter and he phoned me.

As for the trade from Detroit to Montreal, LeFlore said it wasn't a business transaction per se. It was more than just that in his eyes. Tigers president and GM Jim Campbell and Expos president and GM John McHale had a special connection. LeFlore knew about this.

Campbell and McHale had joined the Tigers organization almost simultaneously in the late 1940s in minor-league executive roles. When McHale became the Tigers GM in 1957, Campbell became the major-league team's business manager.

So 23 years later, LeFlore figured it was time for Campbell to help McHale out by agreeing to the trade sending him to Montreal. In fact, McHale had done at least one other trade with Detroit prior to the Schatzeder-for-LeFlore deal. In 1974, the Expos acquired Woodie Fryman from Detroit.

"It was payback for Campbell," LeFlore said. "John gave him a job. John said, 'Jim, I hired you. I need a player. I need a lead-off hitter (LeFlore).' Transactions like that happen. It's a little boys network."

When our interview ended, we hung up. But LeFlore had forgotten something so he called me back with more information about the trade from Detroit.

"Somebody dumped a load of horseshit in front of the Tigers office to protest the trade," LeFlore said. And we both started laughing.

"Really?" I asked in astonishment.

LeFlore enjoyed a tremendous season with a franchise-record 97 stolen bases as the Expos came this-close to reaching the playoffs for the first time. LeFlore was like a cherry blossom, whose beautiful season was carved in its brief existence. One could argue it was the biggest one-season accomplishment by a player in Expos history.

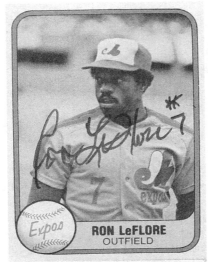

RON LeFLORE
OUTFIELD

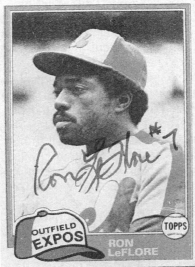

Fleer cards signed by Ron LeFlore
for the author

LeFlore was denied at least 100 stolen bases when he broke his left wrist Sept. 11 because he couldn't play in the everyday lineup.

"I would've had over 100 if I hadn't broken my wrist. I was running for a towering fly ball hit by Dave Kingman in foul territory and I got too close to the wall," LeFlore explained. "I couldn't get stopped in time. It scalped the bone on my wrist. I felt I had a pretty good jump, I saw I was getting too close to the wall. I threw my arms out. I stayed in the game. I had to wrap my hand and fingers around the bat. I hit a double off Bruce Sutter."

Imagine the memories 40 years later. LeFlore was replaced for the ninth inning and he didn't start a game the remainder of the season. He didn't go on the disabled list and did some base running.

Despite the injury, LeFlore actually called up manager Dick Williams one day to say that he wanted to be back in the starting lineup instead of just pinch-running, as he said in an interview with Montreal broadcaster Ted Tevan many years later.

"That's what I did," LeFlore told Tevan. "I told him, I said, 'Dick I want to waive my insurance, right? I want to go out on the field.' I had taken the cast off to where I could grip the bat and all I had to do is lay some glove on the hill and I was able to put the glove over my hand and I was told by John McHale that he wasn't going to risk the chance of my career and I said I didn't care about my career. I wanted to take Montreal to the World Series.

"You know, and if I could have played, I would have been able to hit the ball and I would have been able to steal bases. We would have been able to win the pennant. I was just turned down by the doctor (Bob Brodrick). I mean the doctor knows best, I guess, but there are times as a competitive player, you want to go out and do whatever you can to help the team.

"And I thought that whatever I did on the field if it wasn't 100%, it was going to be better than not having someone to do it at all," LeFlore said in his chat with Tevan. "And I wanted to risk that chance of possibly having a fused wrist where I would never be able to bend again to go out to try to help the baseball team win the pennant that year."

With LeFlore in the lineup, the Expos could have beaten the Phillies out at the end.

Hitting out of the lead-off spot upon his arrival, LeFlore had what would appear to be low numbers of four homers and 39 RBI. And he only batted .257, which was down considerably from his lifetime average which he knew off-by-heart as .288.

But his speed made him a threat on the basepaths along with Rodney Scott, who swiped 63 bags. Aside from his 97 stolen bases, he got caught stealing 19 times.

"He played like a good back in football," his 1980 teammate Larry Parrish told me in late 2020. "He was really fast but was big and thick. He slid late into bags with a pop-up slide and was big enough he moved shortstops and second basemen.

"Funny when he got rolling, he ran by balls in the outfield. I remember watching some fly balls and wondering if he could get there then start yelling 'Whoa' because he was going to run by it."

"If I hadn't broken my wrist, I would have over 100 stolen bases to beat Rickey Henderson's 100," LeFlore told me.

As a big admirer of LeFlore, Expos fan and Saskatoon, Saskatche-

Some ugly injuries in Expos history

Player	Date	Injury
Ellis Valentine	May 30, 1980	Hit by a pitch on left cheekbone
Ron LeFlore	Sept. 15, 1980	Broke left wrist chasing fly ball
Tim Raines	Sept. 13, 1981	Fractured right hand sliding into 2B
Terry Francona	June 16, 1982	Wrecked right knee crashing into OF wall
Terry Francona	June 14, 1984	Wrecked left knee trying to elude tag
Mike Fitzgerald	Aug. 1, 1986	Smashed middle finger on right hand
Hubie Brooks	Aug. 1, 1986	Tore ligaments, chipped bone in left thumb
Moises Alou	Sept. 16, 1993	Wrecked left leg when cleats caught in turf
Cliff Floyd	May 15, 1995	Wrecked right wrist in collision at first base
Rondell White	April 27, 1996	Bruised spleen & kidney chasing fly ball

Author's memories with help from trainer Ron McClain, dates from Baseball Reference

wan journalist Don Rice had some interesting nuggets about LeFlore's season.

"He got caught stealing twice before he got his first stolen base for the Expos – in his fourth game," said Rice, who has worked at the Star-Phoenix newspaper for close to 12 years. "He had six stolen bases and scored four runs in eight appearances after that horrible injury. On Aug. 4, he stole home. That was such an exciting play.

"Officially, they called it a balk but I count it as one of his 98 stolen bases. Dave Van Horne called it a steal at the time in the play by play. I don't remember the video of the play but I had always thought it was a stolen base until I looked it up years later. If I ever found video of that steal, I would be euphoric to actually see it.

"I couldn't believe it when my brother Murray told me that day that Ron LeFlore had stolen home. At that time, I was probably not even aware that a steal of home in that level of baseball was even possible. I incredulously asked how LeFlore could have done that? My brother said that LeFlore just took off for home and the pitcher threw the ball away.

"I couldn't stop laughing about it and admiring the accomplishment," Rice said. "The memory of what my brother told me always stayed with me, that somebody could pull that off. Since then, I've realized that it does happen, but a straight steal of home is one of the rarest and most exciting feats in baseball.

"Although I had always loved LeFlore since he became an Expo, I think hearing about that steal of home was the moment that sealed him as my favourite player. The fact that he still maintains the all-time Expos single-season stolen base mark with 97 has always stood out as a point of admiration for me as well."

Four days later following that balk/stolen base scenario, another momentous occasion for LeFlore came along.

"I stole four bases in only one game in Chicago. I stole second and third twice," LeFlore recalled.

"It happened 8/8/80. That's one of my favourite games," Rice pointed out. "He took himself out of that game early so he could be fresh for the doubleheader the next game.

"One neat thing I found was that there was only game where LeFlore and Raines got a stolen base in the same game – Oct. 4. It happened in the same inning. LeFlore was on third when he stole a base earlier when Raines came in to pinch run and stole second. It was almost like the passing of the guard from one stolen base champion to the other, although nobody would have thought of it that way at the time."

True, there was no way of knowing then that LeFlore would not return for the 1981 season.

"The story behind the 96th and 97th stolen bases – he told pinch hitter Larry Parrish ahead of time not to swing so he could steal two bases and beat Omar Moreno by one stolen base for the NL championship,"

Rice continued.

"LeFlore had possibly his best game for the Expos for June 18 in Los Angeles. He was 3-for-5 with three runs, three RBI and he stole home as part of a double steal with Andre Dawson."

The issue of stolen bases was something LeFlore broached when he consented to what turned out to be a controversial interview with Sport magazine during the 1980 season. LeFlore's tenure with the Expos lasted one season because some teammates didn't take a liking to him because of the magazine fiasco and he also caught up in the wrong crowd by doing drugs. It's long been thought that Montreal resident Bobby White supplied LeFlore, Ellis Valentine and others with drugs.

LeFlore was perturbed that he wasn't named to the mid-summer all-star game in 1980 and let it be known in the popular monthly publication.

"I guess I spoke at a time when I shouldn't have," LeFlore said in the interview with me. "I wasn't picked to the all-star team. I had 50 stolen bases at the all-star break. I was just upset.

"I made a statement that there were rednecks on the team, mostly southern players. It didn't really mean anything. It was taken out of context so much. I got a letter from the commissioner's office and Bowie Kuhn asked me to apologize."

Controversy aside, LeFlore said the '80 Expos squad was the best he ever played on.

"We had an awesome, phenomenal team," No. 7 said. "We were better than Philadelphia. We just had a solid team, we had a great pitching staff, we could run, we had three guys that could run (him, Scott and Dawson). Most teams couldn't afford that luxury. All the guys were good guys. The camaraderie was really good. I was really close with Rodney, Ellis Valentine and Gary Carter."

It was said that LeFlore and Valentine were into drugs that season and LeFlore admitted that he indeed did the stuff. I was half expecting LeFlore, a former prison inmate, would get mad at me for broaching the issue but he didn't.

Two years prior to his season with Montreal, LeFlore was the centre of attention in One in a Million: The Ron LeFlore Story, a made-for-TV biographical sports drama. LeVar Burton played him in the film and former Tigers manager Billy Martin, who discovered LeFlore in prison, played himself.

"I'm not going to deny it," LeFlore told me about his drug use. "It wasn't just the Expos. Everybody in the league was doing it. When Ken Burns did a documentary, he had a picture of me in my Expos uniform. It (drugs) got bad one time. They put me in rehab. That was 1986. I was in detox for seven days. That was enough."

His wife laid down the law and said it was either drugs or her. LeFlore decided having his wife was more important than drugs. He chose his wife. But looking back at the drug situation that affected him and the Expos and the game in general, LeFlore said many players were into "greenies, uppers and amphetamines."

It's been said that LeFlore would be one of the first players out of the clubhouse so he could chase women in downtown Montreal bars.

"When LeFlore wasn't on the field or at the park, he was chasing women on Crescent St.," joked Victor Cupidio, a long time Expos fan.

LeFlore told me he was one of the last to leave the clubhouse. He admitted to "partying on Crescent Street" and spending considerable time at Sir Winston Churchill Pub where he would enjoy drinking Crown Royal or Molson Ex.

"Sometimes, I'd go to the Laurentian Mountains and have a good time away from telephones," LeFlore said.

LeFlore said he hasn't drank "in a long time", telling me that he has "no liquor at my house and I don't buy it at the store."

When LeFlore and the Expos parted ways following the '80 season, mostly because of that Sport magazine article, he signed with the White Sox and played on the South Side for two seasons before being dropped early in the 1983 season over drugs and weapons charges. He never played in the majors again.

LeFlore's agent Ken Fishkin said the Yankees were also a serious suitor for his client. Fishkin even went to New York to meet with owner George Steinbrenner.

"I don't remember Montreal making a great effort to sign Ron," Fishkin said. "I went to New York to meet with George Steinbrenner and then I went to Comiskey Park in Chicago to meet with the White Sox. I met with Bill Veeck. He was quite the character. And Roland Hemond was the GM.

"Veeck liked Ron's speed, his energy, his hitting ability. He could run, that's for sure. He could steal bases, he could hit. He was pretty good. He was always a great guy. I always enjoyed being with him. He was a lot of fun. He was his own man. He was always an adventure."

When I mentioned Fishkin to LeFlore, LeFlore wasn't happy. LeFlore called Fishkin a "scoundrel" when it could have called him an asshole or a son of a bitch.

"He was my power of attorney and he told $200,000 from me," LeFlore said.

When I brought up this alleged theft of money, Fishkin confirmed that as the player's agent, he was the power of attorney. He neither confirmed nor denied that he took the money. Instead, his reply to me was this: "I'm surprised and shocked that he would even say that."

LeFlore attempted to get back into the majors in some capacity by managing in a number of independent leagues, including the Frontier and the Canadian league.

In 2003, he came to Rice's home city of Saskatoon to be manager of a team in a league being started by Canadian legend Fergie Jenkins, whom LeFlore was "pretty close" to over the years. After spending a few weeks in Saskatoon, his wife Emily issued him another ultimatum: me or baseball.

LeFlore chose Emily and returned home to Florida despite his team sporting a 7-1 record. True. But there was a big reason LeFlore went home: Emily was undergoing major surgery. He was showing love and support for his wife. Just like in 1986, his wife issued the ultimatum.

In 2010, LeFlore began experiencing problems with his right leg, more specifically his right foot. First he told me he had the little toe removed and then the toe next to it. And the third amputation saw him lose the leg from just below the knee. Shoot. Emily told one interviewer that there were several times when LeFlore almost died.

Officially, it was called arterial vascular disease. He said, "I mean the circulation got bad" and the theory and assumption is that his lifelong passion for smoking cigarettes somehow led to the loss of his leg. The nicotine may have been part of the problem but he offered additional reasoning.

When people may have suggested his trade to the Expos was a business deal, he preferred to say that Campbell owed McHale a favour.

So rather than accept that cigarettes were the main cause of his leg problems, he preferred to reason that something more sinister and revealing from his playing days was also at stake. When he slid into second or third base, his right leg, he said, was the leg used mostly when he slid in and popped up again on the bag. Over the long run, wear and tear, he said, would cause problems within his body.

"When I would steal second base, I would make contact with my right leg," LeFlore explained. "Athletically, running isn't a normal activity. People don't realize that. People running left and turning left on the field, left hand turns and right leg put pressure on the right leg," LeFlore said. "Being an athlete, you damage your joints."

Unbeknownst to many people is that LeFlore told me he's of Native American descent from a tribe originating in Louisiana. LeFlore looks like it's a French name but not so. And LeFlore shot down an online report that said he was fluently Polish. No way.

LeFlore also talked about his time as a baggage handler in the 1980s.
"It was good money. I worked for Eastern Airlines out of the airport in Sarasota, Florida," LeFlore said. "A lot of New Yorkers. They'd tip $50 a bag. If you had two bags, they'd tip another $50. So that would be $100. I did it for two years."

LeFlore also recalls the time in Montreal when a famous duo came into the clubhouse.

"I remember that Pierre Trudeau, the Prime Minsiter, was in the clubhouse after the game with this two kids. The Prime Minister now (Justin) was just a kid then," LeFlore said.

Photo supplied by Mike Enos

Expos conditioning coach Ed Enos, left, and Expos third baseman Larry Parrish, right, had the privilege of posing with Yankees great Joe DiMaggio at a banquet in Montreal back in the day.

Rogers had outstanding 1982 season

What happened on Oct. 19, 1981 didn't faze Steve Rogers when he returned to the mound the following season.

Sure the disappointment was there but Rogers cleaned out his brain of thoughts and enjoyed the Season of Seasons in 1982.

He came within a win of reaching the 20-win plateau. He went 19-8 with a stingy ERA of 2.40.

"Remarkable that Steve Rogers had one of the best years of his career in 1982 after the devastating loss he suffered on Blue Monday the year before," said Dave Fineberg, a broadcaster in Canada's Maritime province of Nova Scotia. "What a testament, not just to his character but to the human spirit that it is possible to excel after such a soul-crushing setback."

When I relayed Fineberg's thoughts that were posted on Facebook in late September of 2020, Rogers totally disagreed when he sent me an email.

"That statement is most definitely by a person who never played a sport at a high level and who is now a huge fan of the game," Rogers said. "His soul may have been crushed but as I stood in my locker and repeated my explanation that day in Montreal, my soul was anything **but** crushed.

"I did not have the learned ability to control my adrenalin in a situation I had never been in before and it resulted in multiple bad pitches that inning. As soon as the adrenalin was gone, I painted (Pedro) Guerrero with four pitches. I did not handle a situation which requires a learned mind set.

"So while the person who offered that critique of not only my 1982 season but of Blue Monday was trying to be kind, it highlights his lack of

Steve Rogers has been wearing a moustache non-stop since late in 1976. That's about 45 years. "No facial hair and/or sideburns below the ear was Gene Mauch /Expos policy from day one," Rogers said. "The move to Olympic Stadium and Dick Williams ushered in the relaxed grooming requirements." Rogers plans to continue working for the MLBPA until further notice because of the pandemic in his role as special assistant, player benefits and career development program.

MLBPA photo

understanding. Sorry for being a less than grateful 70-year-old man but if he had said those words to me in conversation I would thank them and bite my tongue. Come to think of it being remembered for "anything" 40+ years later is pretty cool."

Rogers was a workhorse for the Expos going back to his first season in 1973. He gave it all he could for 12 seasons, the only player of longevity with the franchise to spend his entire career with the Expos.

Remember the lyrics of Carole King's song? "Doesn't anybody stay in one place anymore?" Rogers did stay in one place despite a contentious relationship with manager Dick Williams, who for some strange reason, didn't like him.

As Ken Fidlin wrote in the Ottawa Journal in December of 1979: "Rogers makes no secret of his enmity for Williams and there has been and still is speculation he'll be dealt away before the winter is out." When Fidlin broached this topic with GM John McHale, the Expos executive replied, "It is common knowledge that Dick doesn't really care how people feel toward him. He's not running for office, you know."

Chris Kazanas, when he thinks of Rogers, has only negative thoughts.

"Can't hear that name without thinking of Blue Monday," Kazanas said. "Not his fault but he will forever be associated with that one at-bat."

In another Facebook post, Bob Gray said this: "Sooner or later your number comes up. This was the year when it was our turn, and we finally beat the Phillies. Mike Schmidt didn't break our hearts. Stanley Bahnsen had finally left. We had no real inkling that Blue Monday was around the corner and would haunt us forever."

All these years later, Ray Burris said he wanted to continue pitching in the ninth inning of Game 5 but Fanning went with Rogers. Burris went into the on-deck circle in the bottom of the eighth inning with a

West Palm Beach Expos photo

This is an unusual, casual photo taken in West Palm Beach during spring training in 1981. You would think that it is supposed to be a photo of the Expos' MLB squad but it isn't, as the author found out. David Palmer said it's a West Palm Beach Expos Alumni photo. Front row, left to right: Pat Scanlon, Jerry White, Tim Raines and Steve Ratzer. Middle row: Gary Carter, Anthony Johnson, Bobby Ramos, Larry Parrish, Dave Hostetler and Ellis Valentine. Back row: manager Felipe Alou, Hal Dues, Bill Gullickson, Bob James, David Palmer, Scott Sanderson, Tom Wieghaus, Brad Mills and Kevin Mendon. It should be noted that Mendon is the only person in this photo, who never made it to the majors. It was Palmer who IDed Mendon for me. Guys like Tim Wallach, Steve Rogers and Warren Cromartie are not in the photo because they didn't play minor-league ball in West Palm.

huge winter coat on but he was called back to the dugout in favour of pinch-hitter Tim Wallach.

"It was a special day in a lot of our hearts," Burris told me in 2020 about Blue Monday. "It was a kind of a crazy year. We had the strike. We had some great talent, the speed, starters to relievers, bench players, part-time players. We were in a position to get to a place where we wanted to be but it didn't propel us into the final event, the World Series.

"It was a great opportunity for me in the post-season in my career to go and perform like I did. It was very gratifying. What was more gratifying was to show my teammates the type of pitcher I was on that stage. They made the best decision to give me the ball on this day.

"What I want to say is that Steve Rogers was a helluva pitcher, a helluva man, he did a helluva job. I don't want fans to put the blame on him. Unfortunately, he got a pitch up that he (Monday) could hit and he put it out of the ballpark."

Burris and Fernando Valenzuela went head to head for eight innings, allowing only one run each, prompting Burris to say this about the lack of offence in the game: "On both sides of the ball, good pitching will slow great offences."

Without Rogers, the Expos don't make the NLCS because he out-duelled Steve Carlton of the Phillies twice in the NL East series to allow the Expos to advance. Rogers also won Game 3 of the NLCS, which was highlighted by Jerry White's electrifying, three-run homer which he pulled into the left-field stands.

"No doubt about it, White's shot over the left-field fence gave me the biggest thrill I ever experienced at Olympic Stadium," Pierre Miquelon of Montreal said in response to my 2020 Facebook post on the 39th anniversary of that game.

"Not only was that my greatest memory of the Expos but also one of the best of my dad," Andrew Smith of Montreal added. "I was 13 and he came home from work early that Friday. He asked me if I'd done my homework. It was a Friday. It would have been a miracle if I'd done it by Sunday night.

"So he told me I'd better get it done if I wanted to go to the game that night. We had one of his biggest client's seats (Gerry O'Donnell, King of the Movers), 10 rows behind home plate. Warren Cromartie's mom was sitting in front of us along with a lot of the Expos' wives. I will always remember the micro-second of silence that gripped the Big O just as White's home run cleared the fence and the euphoria that followed."

Nova Scotia resident John Murray had this to say, "I was sitting down the third-base line in the lower deck when the ball sailed over the left-field wall. I thought the Big O was going to explode. There was no French or English that night. The greatest day I ever had at a ballpark."

The win gave the Expos a 2-1 lead in the best-of-five series and it should been the impetus for the Expos to polish off the Dodgers the next day. But the next day, it was a downer as the Dodgers won 7-1, setting the stage for Game 5 on a Sunday. But inclement weather and some questionable strategy by Expos manager Jim Fanning involving the meteorologist sure added to the conspiracy theories.

Fanning wanted the game postponed so that Burris would have four days rest to pitch the next day. But that also meant Valenzuela would have the same rest for the Dodgers. Fanning and Expos front-office assistant Rodger Brulotte concocted a scenario where NL president Chub Feeney would be advised that the weather wasn't going to improve. But the rain did stop by that time, although many players had left Olympic Stadium.

"Bad karma brought on by Jim Fanning," Bobby Jasmin, an Expos

Del Rice photo

Manager Jim Fanning has his arm around Expos fan Don Rice and next to Don is his brother Murray during Camera Day at an Expos game in 1981. In front are Expos player, Pat Rooney and coaches Steve Boros and Ozzie Virgil.

scorekeeper, said in a Facebook post. Jasmin was privy to what was going on between Fanning, Brulotte, the meteorologist and Feeney. "Had he (Fanning) let destiny take its course, we would have played Sunday night but n-o-o," Jasmin said. "As the meteorologist was telling me on the phone around 5-6 o'clock that it was going to stop raining and we were clear for the night, I was about to turn around to tell that to Feeney."

At that very moment, fate struck. Brulotte appeared and told Jasmin to ask the meteorologist to tell Feeney that it would rain all night. Imagine. The exact opposite.

"I reluctantly did as asked. The meteorologist said what I told him to say to Feeney and the rest is history," Jasmin said. "What happened is exactly what my parents brought me up to believe: don't fuck around, fuck straight. Fanning had the bright idea to give Rogers an extra day off

109

in case he needed him the next day."

If that fifth game had been played on the Sunday, there would have been no Blue Monday. Cromartie could be seen in one photo from Oct. 18, 1981, looking up to the sky and praying for the rain to stop so that the game could be played that day, so that they wouldn't have to face Fernando with four days rest the next day.

All these years later, White volunteers to lament the fact that he swung at the first pitch against Bob Welch for the last out of the 1981 NLCS. After seeing two consecutive batters reach base with walks, White wonders why he didn't take a pitch to make Welch work.

After the devastating loss in Game 5, there was much gnashing of teeth. The Expos had come this-close to the World Series to be played against the Yankees.

White recalled that he went home once he left the ballpark. He didn't go to a bar to drown his sorrows with the drinkers on the team. White and Dawson weren't drinkers.

"I would drink chocolate milk," White said.

"Maybe some ginger ale," Dawson said.

Blue Monday

"I was there. You could have heard a pin drop when Monday homered.

—Jim Provost

"I was in Cégep (college) that day. I had a Philosophy class scheduled at the same time as the beginning of the game. Obviously, I skipped class to watch the game with friends in our student lounge. So, we turned on the TV set and grabbed some chairs at random. I sat beside a beautiful girl and after the game, we started to chat. We chatted until early evening. We went out a few times and we got married (in 1985). All that to say, thanks to your beloved Expos and Rick Monday for that unforgettable afternoon."

—Serge Bruno

"I was 11 and crestfallen. My dad told me to cheer up and that there would be better days. In 1994, I decided he was right and I bought tickets to a late-season game and made arrangements to stay at a friend's house for the weekend. As I drove from Toronto to Montreal, they cancelled the season. Not sure which memory hurts more."

—Brent McCain

"Ray Burris pitched an excellent game. I've read over the years that it was Steve Rogers who suggested to Fanning that he go in. But we had an excellent reliever in Jeff Reardon. Was he not ready? I guess we'll never know the real reason but I was at that game and I can tell you that no one amid the thousands of people who were coming home on the Metro that day was talking. We were all too afraid we'd burst out crying. And what was there to say anyway?"

—Dolores Huard

"Blue Monday proved what a cruel mistress baseball could be. Was I disappointed? Of course, but I thought there'd be other days. Those days that never came. The loss of the season in 1994 was different. It just embittered me toward MLB. Blue Monday cut like a knife."

—Eric Hansen

"Was listening on the radio at work – crushed my spirit."

—Gordon McFee

"I was at the game. Miserable, cold and wet day. And then Blue Monday happened."

—Dave Marchant

"I was there. I'll never forget Rick Monday's home run. The sinking feeling was overwhelming,"

—Keir Cutler

"A classic NLCS game. I was in the fifth grade. That game was to be played on Sunday but in Montreal, it was a wintery mix. Vin Scully had reported it was 85 degrees in the San Fernando Valley so it was Monday. Luckily, we got to watch the game at school."

—Eric Easterling

"Wrote an exam, watched the game at Oliver's Pub at Carleton University (Ottawa). After Bob Welch got the final out, I ran off to write my second exam through clouded eyes. So close."

—Richard Voss

"The irony of a guy named Monday (Rick Monday) ending the Expos only playoff appearance on a Monday wearing Dodger Blue is the stuff that lingers forever in baseball lore."

—Jamie Bramburger

"I cried all the way home on the school bus."

—Michele Gervais

"I took off work for the playoffs and had to go back to work on that Monday. I was a waste that day and my boss let me watch the game. Ironic, the game was on Monday and the GWHR was hit by Rick Monday."

—George Pobedinsky

Arkansas Train

He was known as the Arkansas Train, a brute of a specimen with impressive hitting credentials in the minors but he just couldn't cut it in the majors.

Such was the career of Roy Johnson, a 6-foot-4, 205-pound outfielder, who showed the promise of a phenom when selected by the Expos in the fifth round of the 1980 amateur draft out of Tennessee State University.

"He was a heckuva prospect with a world of talent," recalled Jim Fanning, a former field manager, general manager and jack of all trades for the Expos. "When he joined us in 1982, we all felt strongly about him but it's just that the talent wasn't displayed for us or any other team in the majors."

After hitting an eye-catching .361 with 90 RBI in the first half of the 1982 Triple-A season in Wichita, Kansas, Johnson was called up by the Expos on July 3 of that year but he never produced.

Johnson played parts of three seasons with the Expos with an overall batting average of .171 (12-for-60) – not the kind of production that would keep him in the major leagues.

It didn't help either that during much of his time in Montreal, the Expos outfield was stacked with Warren Cromartie, Tim Raines and Andre Dawson.

"In one game, he hit a rocket off the wall for a double at Wrigley Field in Chicago," Fanning told me. "Then leading up to his next at-bat, Doug Flynn had made an out and fired his helmet into the dugout. The helmet came back and hit Johnson in the face and it appeared to affect his vision. I took him out of the game before his at-bat because he wouldn't tell me one way or another if it affected him."

Johnson also had his demons. In 1985, when he was back in the minors, he found out Fanning was on a scouting mission in the U.S. so he asked Fanning if he would meet him for breakfast the next morning.

"He was very troubled," Fanning recalled. When Johnson was asked what was wrong, the player replied, "Drugs."

Fanning never asked Johnson what drugs he was using but feeling sorry for the outfielder, he immediately arranged for Johnson to be admitted to the Betty Ford clinic in California.

Canadian Baseball Hall of Fame
Roy Johnson

"He said he really needed help," Fanning said. "Even though he was in trouble and had his problems, I loved him. He was very humble and personable."

In December of 1985, the Chicago White Sox selected Johnson in the Rule V draft but he never played in the majors again, although he toiled for a few seasons in the Oakland Athletics' farm system.

Johnson then proceeded to carve out a productive career in the Mexican league. He clobbered 114 homers for the Pirates de Campeche of the Mexican league and later became their hitting coach.

Johnson, at one time, shared the Mexican league record for most home runs in one game with four, making him one of the most powerful, foreign-born hitters to play in Mexico.

"Johnson's was almost a tragic life," former Expos PR specialist Rich Griffin wrote in his Toronto Star blog in April, 2009. "The reason I remember Johnson so vividly and so fondly is that he was physically intimidating, but personally gentle, humble and naive.

"He was a lost soul with very little family support in Chicago, which made it difficult to go home in the off-season. That led to lingering problems with drugs. These were the days when organizations treated many of their young players that found trouble like family.

"The players, in turn, did not turn to their agents for help as they do today. It was a much closer relationship, so when the Expos realized Johnson was struggling, they tried to help him out."

Griffin recalled that the late John McHale, the president and GM at the time, lived in the West Palm Beach area. Instead of sending Johnson back home where he "might drift and hang with a bad crowd", McHale found him an apartment near the spring training site and gave him a job on the construction of the Expos' new minor-league complex.

"The first Christmas Johnson was in town, the late Patty McHale, a marvelous woman and the conscience of the organization, made sure that Roy was invited over for the family's Christmas dinner. Johnson was truly touched," Griffin wrote.

Invariably, Griffin had some memorable Johnson stories, "stemming from his unique circumstances." Griffin mentioned that one time, Johnson saw a basketball court on the other side of a chain link fence.

"He went back to his apartment, got a ball and climbed the fence to shoot some hoops. As he went to climb the fence after he was done, some guys in white jackets came running over to stop him," Griffin wrote. "He had trouble talking his way out of the psychiatric asylum."

As Griffin continued his story, he said that one day at spring training, Johnson failed to show up for work. Travelling secretary Peter Durso received a call from the Lake Worth police. Johnson was in jail.

"It seemed that he was doing his laundry at a laundromat the night before. He threw his stuff in the dryer and stepped out onto the mean streets of Lake Worth for some fresh air," Griffin wrote. "He started to chat up a young woman on the sidewalk. It turned out she was an undercover cop. His attempt at pleasantries turned into a night in the slammer as his laundry continued to spin dry."

Griffin's favourite story, though, was the late Larry Bearnarth's re-telling of the three Johnsons. Bearnarth was managing the AA-Memphis Chicks in 1981. As best Griffin could recall, Bear had Roy Johnson on first, Wallace Johnson on second and Anthony Johnson batting.

As Griffin told the story, Anthony smoked a drive in the air down to the left field corner. Wallace went half way to third. Roy went to second and stopped to make sure the ball dropped in. Anthony broke from the batter's box. In the gloom, the ball looked like it was caught, but it dropped in on the track.

Wallace headed back to second, Roy headed back to first where he was passed by Anthony cruising into second. Wallace saw Anthony as he came back to second, then turned and headed to third where he beat the throw. Somehow the batter was on second and the runner was on first. The bases were loaded.

The opposing manager was screaming. As Bearnarth recalled the conversation, it went something like this, according to Griffin:

Umpire: Who's on second?
Bearnarth: Johnson
Umpire: Who is supposed to be on second?
Bearnarth: Johnson.
Umpire: Who's on first?
Bearnarth: Johnson
Umpire: Who is supposed to be on first?
Bearnarth: Johnson
Umpire: Play Ball

Wood Peach No. 1 and Wood Peach No. 2

It was a cool combination of a black man and a white man enjoying a wonderful friendship, not just in the clubhouse or at the ballpark but also away from the game.

Ray Burris and Woodie Fryman. Whenever Burris and Fryman were on a road trip to Cincinnati, Fryman always invited Burris to drive across the border to his Kentucky home to be with his family for a day and then drive back to Riverfront Stadium later in the day.

"Woodie and I were like brothers," Burris was saying in an interview. "We were very close. We spent a lot of time together, talking baseball day in and day out. It was remarkable to have him as a teammate. What I learned from Woodie was playing the game and pitching, reading pitchers. It was a constant flow of information that he brought to my attention."

Fryman was a much loved teammate with the Expos. He was a laid back kind of guy from a town in the American midwest, a farmer who specialized in tobacco and dairy cattle. He even got on a stool to milk the cows in a contest before an Expos game way back when.

Burris and Fryman first got to know each other when they pitched for the Cubs in 1978 and when Burris left to go elsewhere he feels Fryman suggested to Expos GM John McHale that he acquire Burris for the Expos. So Burris and Fryman hooked up again with the Expos from 1981-84.

"I think Woodie had a say-so in signing me. He never told me but I'm guess-timating off the top of my head that John McHale asked him or some of the players about me," Burris said. "Woodie was a very good judge of talent and character. He would have been a good manager. The thing I would ask him a lot of times, 'What do I need to get better?'

Canadian Baseball Hall of Fame
Ray Burris

Canadian Baseball Hall of Fame
Woodie Fryman

And he would give me his feedback.

"To show how tough he was, he had bone spurs in his left elbow. He'd be sleeping or eating and his arm would be stuck out like at a right angle and he'd take his right arm and move that bone spur around. Most people don't know that, that he was tough as nails. You don't make players like that."

Fryman enjoyed two different tours with Montreal: from 1973-76 and then again from 1978-84. His acquisition from the Tigers on Dec. 4, 1974 coincided with another trade the Expos made the same day. The other trade saw the Expos pull off a shocker: they gave up star outfielder Ken Singleton and pitcher Mike Torrez to the Orioles in exchange for veteran pitcher Dave McNally, outfielder Rich Coggins and infielder Bill Kirkpatrick. You know how that trade turned out.

Fryman was re-acquired by the Expos on June 9, 1978 from the Cubs for a player to be named later and he remained with Montreal until he decided to pack it in because of elbow problems halfway through the 1983 season. He never played in the majors again but the Burris-Fryman friendship continued.

Fryman died of Alzheimer's in 1995.

"It was a very special friendship and still is, even though he's gone," Burris said. "He's always in my heart as a friend, teammate. He'd do anything in the world for you. He had a heart of gold. When he passed away, his family asked me to write an eulogy for the service. I was very honoured to do that. His wife Phyllis knew what he meant to me.

"He loved to eat and I loved to eat. We had nicknames given us by Warren Cromartie: Wood Peach No. 1. Wood Peach No. 2."

Del Rice photo
Ruby Rice enjoyed Camera Day in
September, 1981 with Woodie Fryman

Carter's visit to my native Renfrew, Ontario

In the second half of the winter of 1980-81, Gary Carter took his popularity to various parts of Canada for speaking engagements, including Halifax, Thunder Bay, Toronto and Edmonton.

And then there was Renfrew, Ontario where I was born on Boxing Day in 1950. Carter made his way there on Jan. 27, 1981 for a $25-per-plate fund-raising event in support of a new baseball facility called Ma-Te-Way.

Renfrew was a coup on Carter's list of communities to visit. It was and still is a town of about 8,000 people, compared to the cities that he would visit in Canada. Banquet organizers, especially Billy Butson, somehow convinced Carter to come to their small town, which at the time, was a bustling factory metropolis with Blue Bell and Wrangler the cornerstones.

Like me, famous NHL player Ted Lindsay was born in Renfrew – in 1925, although he didn't hang around long. He was four when he left to accompany his parents to Kirkland Lake, Ontario.

Renfrew is also the birthplace of the NHA, the forerunner of the NHL. Renfrew even has its own little NHL museum that people can visit to see artifacts and memorabilia affiliated with its connection to the NHL.

The museum's very existence is completely ignored by the NHL. I've tried several times to get commissioner Gary Bettman to come to Renfrew to visit the museum. I even wrote a personal letter to Bettman at his office in New York but those attempts have been rebuffed by the suits in New York and Toronto.

The Renfrew Millionaires were a professional hockey team that would attract national attention to the small timber town in 1910 and 1911. The creation of railroad contractor and town founder, M. J.

Angela McEachen photo   *Ilse Vooght photo*   *Wanda Blimkie, Renfrew Mercury*

When Gary Carter visited Renfrew, Ontario January 27, 1981, it atttracted a large crowd. In photo, left, he shakes hands with another great catcher, John McEachen of Douglas, one of the all-time great players in the Ottawa Valley. Gary Carter is shown appearing with Paula Vooght and her brother James. Carter was presented with an Indigenous headdress.

Ma-Te-Way Baseball '81

Fund Raising Dinner

featuring

Gary Carter
of Montreal Expos

Valley Motor Hotel

Tuesday, January 27, 1981

Supplied image

Invitation for dinner

O'Brien and his son Ambrose, the Renfrew Millionaires were originally called the Renfrew Creamery Kings. Dreaming of having their hockey team win the Stanley Cup, the O'Briens fought to have the team recognized by the Eastern Canadian Hockey Association, which would later become the Canadian Hockey Association (CHA).

After numerous rejections and snubs, the O'Briens finally created their own League, and called it the National Hockey Association (NHA). M.J. financed four teams in the League: the Renfrew Creamery Kings which became the Renfrew Millionaires, Cobalt, Haileybury and Les Canadiens de Montreal.

Carter's visit to Renfrew was at the height of Cartermania and Renfrew was chosen as a spot to give kids and adults the thrill of a lifetime. Carter had just completed his sixth season with the Expos and it was a splendid one indeed. He hit .264, belted 29 homers and drove in 101 runs during the regular season of 1981 when the Expos made it to post-season play for the first time.

Carter brought along about 200 postcards of his headshot to Renfrew and went to the Legion auditorium where he was besieged by autograph seekers and young girls wanting to plant kisses on his handsome face.

Robbie Ingram, as the Mercury reporter Wanda Blimkie said, "chose his spot with care, about one inch from Carter's chair and stayed tucked almost under his arm throughout the entire autograph session."

Jack Vooght, my Renfrew Red Sox teammate from 1971-75, and his wife Ilse brought along their kids, James and Paula. Those kids were the envy of many when they managed to manoeuvre their way in to sit on Carter's lap while their mother snapped photos.

Carter was asked all the usual questions regarding batting average, training, top pitchers, tough teams to beat, draft choices and how fast he could throw. Carter let it be known that he could throw the ball about 98 m.p.h.

Some boys brought baseballs and even catchers' mitts to have them signed by the heartthrob. One lad gave Carter a hockey puck. At the banquet, the emcee was Ottawa Citizen sports reporter Bob Ferguson and over the course of the evening, Carter was presented with an Indian head-dress.

Invariably, it was a visit that saw the veteran Expos catcher continue to make noise about wanting a new contract from the Expos.

Finding out that Carter was going to be in Renfrew, I took a day off from my short-term contract job with CBC Radio in Sudbury, Ont. to pen a freelance piece for Toronto's Globe and Mail newspaper. Bill Catalano, the radio station's news director, knew why I was going to Renfrew and he wasn't that pleased that I was writing for the Globe and Mail, although he never said anything to me.

I knew what I wanted to talk to Carter about: his contract. It was the first time I had ever met Carter but not the last as I would see him many times later during my time as an Expos beat writer, either at his foundation office in West Palm Beach, Florida or during the 1992 season when he returned for his final MLB season.

As we stood in cold weather outside the Renfrew Legion where he was to make one of several appearances that day, Carter said he was hopeful the Expos would renegotiate his $300,000 U.S. a year contract before spring training would end a few months later.

"I'm looked at as the best catcher in baseball," Carter told me for my story, "so it would be a benefit for the Expos to upgrade the contract. We've had a couple of meetings with the Expos so far about renegotiating the contract and they've made an offer but it wasn't equivalent to what free agents are getting."

The Kid was referring to contracts signed by Ted Simmons of the Milwaukee Brewers and Darrell Porter of the St. Louis Cardinals – Simmons for $800,000 a year and Porter for $700,000.

"But I'm willing to finish out the final two years of my contract," Carter said. "I will honour that contract. Right now, all I'm interested in is bringing a championship to Montreal.

"I'm happy in Montreal and I'd like to finish my career in Montreal but if the Expos procrastinate enough, maybe I'll have to think about playing elsewhere.

"John McHale always said that he wanted to renegotiate Larry Parrish's contract and my contract. He renegotiated Larry's contract but not mine. Dave Roberts is making more money than me and he's just a backup to Alan Ashby in Houston."

Gavin Murphy, who attended the Renfrew banquet as a reporter for the nearby Eganville Leader weekly paper, also had a long chat with Carter about his differences with the Expos.

"He has two years remaining on his present contract and unless the Expos come up with more money, Gary makes no bones about the fact that he will test the free-agent market," Murphy wrote in his story.

"I'm not going to squabble with them," Carter said of Expos management. "I'm going to play hard to win the championship. My No. 1 goal is to bring a championship to Montreal. I enjoy playing for the Expos. I really believe we have one of the better pitching staffs in baseball. I feel this is the year. We're right there. The ball club we have now is capable of being champs.

"I'll honour my contract and we'll go from there. This is the only organization I have played for. But thank God for the free-agent market. I'd like to finish my career in Montreal. I'm the best public-relations guy the Expos could ask for. It boils down to whether or not they are willing to dig into their pockets. You don't know what's going to lie in the future."

Carter pointed out that Roberts and journeymen catchers such as Milt May and Gene Tenace were making more money than him.

Carter said a salary of $700,000 to $800,000 a year is "only fair."

When I contacted Murphy about his encounter with Carter, Murphy recalled it vividly.

"Good grief that is nearly 40 years ago, but I remember it well. It was a cold winter night in Renfrew," Murphy said. "I seem to recall that Carter was a great guy, God-fearing with huge hands. He also wanted more money, pointing out he was making less than some back-ups. I remember doing a full Q/A interview with him that appeared in the paper. I sent it to him and he sent back a thank you note. Nice."

Nudge forward to spring training in West Palm Beach, several months later. Expos GM John McHale continued to negotiate a new contract for Carter with his agent Dick Moss. But a new deal wasn't consummated for several years.

"Carter went for the jugular," said Vic Cupidio of Burlington, Ontario, who would often go to spring training and sit behind home plate where he would see Expos majority owner Charles Bronfman.

Cupidio would often see McHale coming to Bronfman during a number of spring-training games and giving him updates about the negotiations. Cupidio could see Bronfman just seething and shaking his head as he puffed on his pipe, especially when the contract was done.

Initially, the deal was proposed for eight years and $16-million but it was reduced to seven years and $15 million. It was a deal Bronfman didn't want at any cost but he signed off on it very reluctantly.

Even when Carter returned to the Expos via a waiver claim from the Los Angeles Dodgers in November, 1991, the contract negotiations were again contentious. Vice-president Bill Stoneman was pretty stringent about offering a set fee of $500,000, a figure Carter flatly rejected.

There was talk from Carter's camp that he would not sign a contract if Stoneman didn't up the ante. In the end, Stoneman saved the day by offering Carter incentives that would bump the fee up thousands of dollars more.

I remember attending the winter meetings at the Fontainebleau Hotel in Miami in December, 1991 and being in a suite where Expos official Richard Morency talked about the team's negotiations and then Carter's agent Dick Moss talked in defence of his client in the Expos suite, no less. Weird.

In anticipation of Carter not agreeing to terms, the Expos were in talks with the Angels to obtain Lance Parrish and they even chatted with the Tigers about Rich Rowland.

Just think, if Carter hadn't signed with the Expos, there would have been no fairy-tale ending to his MLB career on Sept. 27, 1992 when he launched a double over the head of former teammate Andre Dawson.

Carter's contract was "obstreperous"

Murray Cook, newly hired by team president John McHale, had barely taken over as Expos general manager when majority owner Charles Bronfman sidled up to him at his office in Montreal and asked him to do him a favour.

Cook was being saddled with a huge request.

"That was the first time I had ever met Charles," Cook told me. "He said, 'Please trade Gary Carter. See what you can get for him,' " Bronfman told Cook. "It was right away, as soon as I got there. Very little ever shocks me but I was surprised. It was such an untenable contract, the length of the contract and the amount. It was obstreperous. Seldom is when you trade a star player that would you get equal return, especially when there is money involved.

"Charles didn't like the way the game was going," Cook said. "My understanding is that he couldn't afford Gary Carter. Charles had very contentious negotiations with (agent) Dick Moss.

"I was the one who worked on it. I did the leg work. John McHale and Charles always had to approve. I kept them apprised of any trades. There were not a whole lot of clubs that would take on that kind of contract at the time. We talked with many teams. The Mets were the only true candidate. Everybody really had a decent catcher. The money wasn't worth pursuing for (most teams) for what they were going to give up."

So for several weeks, Cook had chats with Mets GM Frank Cashen and Mets assistant GM Joe McIlvaine. Then at the winter meetings in Nashville, the talks came to a head in a very unusual location. It was not in a hotel room or the phone.

"It was consummated on a stairwell," Cook recalled. "We made the

Fernand Lapierre photos
Charles Bronfman didn't like Gary Carter's contract

final decision but we didn't release it for several days."

Also there was another matter to be cleared up before the trade could actually be announced. Cook and McHale had to convince Carter to waive his no-trade clause and accept the trade. In the end, the Mets agreed to give up catcher Mike Fitzgerald, infielder Hubie Brooks, pitcher Floyd Youmans and outfielder Herm Winningham.

A Montreal Gazette report the next day suggested that Carter had requested a trade but Cook doesn't recall such an ask, adding that Carter was "pretty much controlled by his agent", who extracted more money out of Bronfman that he really wanted to give in the contract extension.

"The Mets offered Mookie Wilson but Winningham seemed like a better fit. He was a young player we thought had a solid future," Cook said. "He didn't quite achieve the heights we had hope for.

"Fitzgerald was established. We thought he was going to be a solid replacement (for Carter). Fitzgerald looked like the real deal until he broke his hand and it pretty much finished his career. He was never the same after that.

"Hubie Brooks was the key part of the deal. He was an established major-league player. He was a one-handed fielder. It was quite unique at the time. He never did have shortstop tools. Instead of using his two hands, the coach (Ron Hansen) taught him to be a one-handed fielder. He did most everything with one hand. It demanded less body control. He'd get 100 RBI and that would make up for his defensive deficiencies. Nobody thought he could play shortstop. It was fun to watch him."

Yeah, Brooks certainly turned out to be the best player the Expos got out of the deal. Fitzgerald was a tremendous leader, solid pitch-framer, game-caller and pitch-selector but didn't have Carter's offensive prowess. Actually, Fitzie was batting .282 when he broke his right index finger Aug. 1, 1986. Ironically, it was in the same game that Brooks tore ligaments and chipped a bone in his left thumb. What else could go wrong that night? To this day, Fitzie's finger looks awfully disjointed.

Juanita Moore photo
Gary Carter

Winningham amounted to no more than a solid backup player, a part-timer and defensive wizard. Cook and the Expos had anticipated that Winningham would become a full-time player but not so.

"As a rookie I was shocked because I found out later the Expos decided they wanted me in the trade for Carter," Winningham said. "They didn't want Mookie, they wanted me. I was glad to be part of the Gary Carter trade. I'm attached to him a little bit because of the trade. He got to the World Series in 1986."

The highlight for Winningham during his time with the Expos? It wasn't a game highlight. Something else. The Mets had "drafted me, taught me how to play and gave me a chance to play in the major leagues" but he had joined a new team.

"Just being there in the big leagues," Winningham said, in revealing the highlight of his time with Montreal. "I really appreciated the Expos for giving me the opportunity. I still have a place in my heart for the Expos and Montreal. I could run especially. That is how I got to the big leagues was with my legs. Over 60 yards, I had world-class speed.

"I was happy to be in the big leagues. I learned how to become a role player. I did the best I could. Oh man, I just learned how to play in the major leagues – those guys, Wallach, Raines, Dawson, Law, the pitching staff, Youmans, Dennis Martinez, Wallace Johnson, the guys on the bench."

One of those "guys on the bench" was Jim Wohlford, who kind of took Winningham under his wing. Wohlford was 32 in 1985, Winningham was 25.

"Herm was a young player. What I tried to tell him was that being a bench player was not easy, that you had to work that much harder," Wohlford said.

It was that kind of advice that Winningham appreciated.

Winningham enjoyed the season when the Expos almost pulled out the NL East title. He figures that if "we had five more games that year, we could have done some things" but the Expos fell short. He was glad the Expos "got that close."

By 1988 when the Expos faltered, Winningham had fallen out of favour with Expos management and the club wanted to option him to Indianapolis Triple-A. He balked.

"We were terrible. They wanted to send me to Indianapolis," Winningham said. "I told (Dave) Dombrowski that I wasn't going to Triple-A. I told him, 'If you send me down, I'm going to go home. I'm going to retire. Try to trade me. If not, I'm going home.' I left for home on a Sunday, they traded me on the Tuesday, the day of the all-star game. Ironic that the game was in Cincinnati. I was back in Montreal on Wednesday and on Thursday, I was in a Reds uniform. That was weird.

"I was there when Pete Rose was there and I saw the tail end of it when he had to step down. In 1990, the highlight of my career was winning the World Series. The ultimate goal is to win the World Series. We won the first three games and then if we win the fourth game, we sweep them. Billy Hatcher got hit on the hand, Eric Davis got hurt. Glenn Braggs and I weren't going to play but we ended up in the game. I ended up scoring the winning run. (Winningham was 2-for-3)."

As for him not becoming the star player the Expos expected of him, Winningham said, "It didn't turn out. It was too much expectations. They wanted me to produce. I became a role player."

Looking back, Cook felt the trade did have some benefit for the Expos, although the best player was Carter.

"I thought the return was really pretty good, considering the lack of teams we were able to generate interest in a trade," Cook said. "Seldom when you trade a star player do you get equal in return as a general rule, especially when you have money involved."

Was it the biggest trade Cook engineered in his days as a GM? Surprisingly, his answer was no.

"No, I wouldn't think so," Cook said. "It would be trading Dave Parker when I was with Cincinnati. Dave Parker certainly fits in. It was a pretty major trade. He was at the end of his career. The Carter trade had to be made."

To give this scenario some perspective, Parker was a Cincinnati native, who attended Courter Technical high school and grew up near old Crosley Field, playing pick-up baseball on the parking lots of the stadium. After more than 11 seasons with the Pirates, Parker signed a free-agent contract following the 1983 season to play for his hometown

Danny Gallagher photo

**Murray Cook with fan Paul Newsome of Cornwall, Ontario
at a recent Canadian Baseball Hall of Fame function**

team. It was big news at the time.

Parker enjoyed four solid seasons with the Reds with RBI totals of 94, 125, 116 and 97. In 1986, he played in all 162 games, the first time he had done so in his entire career. Then on Dec. 8, 1987, Cook dealt Parker, 36, to the Oakland As for pitchers Jose Rijo and Tim Birstas. Cook had history with Parker, going back to this days in Pittsburgh's front office.

"The genesis of it was that when Dave Parker first signed (1970), I helped sign him. Absolutely," Cook said. "I had worked for the Pirates for 20 years, including 15 in the front office. We developed him. He was one of those special players. He was a Cincinnati boy. We had a pre-draft workout in Cincinnati where we worked out about 100 players. He could run. He busted up his knee in high school. He had some off-the-field issues in high school that caused him to go down in the draft (14th round)."

"He was getting to the end of his career (in Cincinnati) and we needed pitching. It was a gut feeling. It was just time. I'd just gotten to Cincinnati (as GM). It put my mark on the club. Parker was more of a DH type. There was no DH in the National League. He had started to slow down in the field. He still had good numbers. He could hit.

"With Jose Rijo, the irony was that when I was with the Yankees, we were developing Jose Rijo so I had history with Rijo. It was a very positive history. We probably had a pitcher that was going to be good for a long time. Tim Birstas was a serviceable left-hander, another guy I had with the Yankees."

Cook chuckled as he related a "very funny anecdote" about an Oakland beat writer coming up to him at the winter meetings in 1987 after the trade to congratulate him. The writer told Cook that he "got two great arms for Parker' but as Cook told me in retrospect, "Unfortunately, both arms belonged to Rijo." Funny guy, that Cook.

So there – 17 years after Cook helped sign Parker for the Pirates, Cook traded him from the Reds to Oakland.

"When you think of any one trade that is bigger than the other, the Carter trade had to be made," Cook said. "The Parker trade was one that worked out for both clubs. The best trades are the ones that work out for both clubs."

When I got a hold of Parker to talk about the trade, he had no bad things to say about Cook and the Reds for trading him away from his hometown.

"I had four good years for Cincinnati," said, Parker, who is suffering from Parkinson's. "I was coming off a pretty good year. When the trade came about, it caught me off-guard. I was surprised."

Ironically, when I asked Parker in February, 2021 who his favourite Expos player was of all the ones he faced, he mentioned one name right off the top.

"Gary Carter. He played the game hard. He was a leader," Parker said. "It was obvious because it reflected in his play. We always seem to have a battle. He was a helluva player. I respected him. I enjoyed playing against him."

Photo submitted by Frank Albertson

Harvey Stone, centre, was the Expos equipment manager for about 12 years, beginning in 1969. He had previously worked for the Milwaukee/Atlanta Braves and New York Rangers. On this occasion in the photo, the Expos clubhouse employees feted Stone on his 80th birthday in 1979 with a plaque and a bottle of liquor. Left to right are Richard Beaudry, Dino Trubiano, Paul (Fitzie) Fitzsimmons and Frank Albertson. Stone was a lifelong bachelor, who was let go by the Expos following the 1981 season. He drove a "1955 Buick that was in perfect condition", said former head trainer Ron McClain. Stone died in a Florida nursing home at the age of 88. He had suffered from mild dementia and a "lot of health problems", McLain said. At one time, Stone boasted one of the largest collections of Expos memorabilia.

Career finished at 25

On Jan. 11, 2021, the volume on my cell phone was turned off while I was cooking so I never heard two calls that came through.

I looked at my phone shortly after and saw that two people had called me. One was from a 450 area code which I knew was from my friend Bill Young in Hudson, Québec.

The other call displayed a 615 area code. I was trying to figure out who that was. So I Googled 615 area code and found out it was Nashville before I checked my answering machine. I still couldn't figure out who it might be.

In picking up the recorded message from Nashville, the caller said, "How are you doing Mr. Gallagher? Good afternoon..It's Floyd Youmans. I'm just returning your call. Okay, have a nice afternoon."

I was shocked that Youmans would call me back. I had been trying to get a hold of him off and on for several years and most recently, I had obtained his number through Googling. I knew that he had been an Uber driver in the Nashville area after Pedro Moura, a sports reporter for California's Orange County Register newspaper, interviewed him while he was dropping people off at baseball's winter meetings at the Opryland Hotel in December, 2015.

All of a sudden, Youmans called me. His name has been put through the ringer so many times over his failed career and his involvement with drugs and alcohol but I still wanted to reach out to him for this book. After all, he was a promising Expo phenom when he was obtained in the Gary Carter trade.

"It's part of my life," Youmans said, when I told him I was surprised he called me because I thought he wanted to keep the Expos out of his mind. He didn't parry my request. He chose to talk with me and I commend him for it.

Youmans, for the record, told me he drove for Uber for about 18 months so it's been close to five years since he has dropped that gig. He says he's "retired" and enjoying life in Nashville where he lives with Dr. Regina Offodile, a breast-cancer surgeon at Nashville General Hospital at Megarry and a professor at Megarry Medical College. They met through one of his friends more than 10 years ago when he was a coach for Illinois' Joliet Jackhammers of the Northern league.

Denis Brodeur photo from Expos magazine
Floyd Youmans pitched
for the Expos from 1985-88

Youmans told me he first started dabbling in cocaine as a minor-leaguer in 1983 in the Mets organization in Columbia, South Carolina and continued it when he became part of the Expos system in late 1984. He made his MLB debut with the Expos in 1985 and started off his career that season with an ERA of 2.45 ERA. One of his stellar performances in '85 was late in the season in New York before 45,404 fans when he beat the Mets, the franchise that drafted him.

By the following season, he really showed the baseball world of his promise. Youmans was 13-12 with 202 strikeouts in 219 innings, although his ERA was a little beefy at 3.53 and he issued a concerning 118 bases on balls. If you needed a pitcher for one day in 1986, Youmans was the man.

Invariably, he was compared to his Tampa, Florida friend and high school teammate, Dwight Gooden. Youmans was the best man throughout his career, Gooden the groom. Youmans was the poor man's squirrel – compared to the more upscale striped chipmunk that was Gooden.

At times, Youmans was sensational in 1986, especially in July when he posted three shutouts and a 4-1 record, earning National League honours as pitcher of the month.

According to writer Chris Jaffe of The Hardball Times a few years ago, Youmans posted a glittering 2.40 ERA through one stretch of 21 consecutive starts. Here that follows are some examples of some masterpieces he rung up.

On June 13, Youmans and the Expos won 2-1. He gave up one run in eight innings and struck out 11.

On Sept. 7, 1986, Youmans allowed one run in eight innings and struck out 10 as the Expos lost 1-0 at home to the Giants. In five consecutive starts, his offence had only scored five runs.

"It's frustrating. I should have 15 or 16 wins by now," he said after the game against San Francisco.

"I won 13 games but I could easily have won 20 games but in the second half I was 3-7," Youmans said in our interview. "We just didn't score any runs."

Youmans threw a masterpiece on Sept. 2, 1986. He fired a two-hitter as the Expos beat the Dodgers 1-0 with the help of Vance Law's walk-off homer.

On Sept. 27, he won 1-0 with a 15-strike performance, the most Ks he ever posted in one game.

"I threw 98-99 on the old gun," Youmans said. "It would be over 100 under the gun they use now. The old gun was the one they used for cars."

Never revealed before was the fact that Youmans had been snorting cocaine in 1986 during the time he was with the Expos but he claimed to me that it never affected his performance.

Denis Brodeur photo from Expos magazine
**Floyd Youmans is married
to a surgeon in Nashville**

"It didn't affect me when I got to the park. I was never high on it. It never kept me from doing my job," Youmans said.

In 1987 when the Expos almost won the NL East, Youmans wasn't near as good as he was in 1986. At times, he pitched superbly but most of the time, he was somewhat mediocre. On July 9, 1987, he was dazzling, going head-to-head to beat a guy by the name of Nolan Ryan. He pitched seven hitless innings before Kevin Bass singled to lead off the eighth inning. That was vintage Youmans.

"My fastball had been blowing them away and then I threw a slider to Bass," Youmans recollected. "I just remember how so intense I was after the game, how so tired I was, really tired. I was so exhausted."

That season, Youmans went on the disabled list twice, once for elbow problems the other time for shoulder woes.

It was in the month of August, 1987 that the issue of cocaine use surfaced. The Montreal Gazette reported that two women said Youmans snorted in front of them. Youmans denied this claim and the Expos backed him.

Then on Sept. 15, he was involved in a car accident on the Trans Canada Highway north of the city of Montreal. He was driving a red Corvette he had borrowed from Tim Raines when he lost control and struck a concrete median. Québec Provincial Police said the accident occurred after two tow trucks collided and somehow, an anti-freeze solution spilled on the road, causing slippery conditions for Youmans.

"There was debris from another car that they didn't clean up," Youmans explained to me. "When I hit it, it was like ice. I couldn't control the car. I hit my head on the rear-view mirror. I went to a French hospital (Sacré Cœur). They couldn't speak English. Somebody had to come from the Expos office. I was in and out the same day."

In a strange twist of fate, his drinking problem was exposed right after the 1987 season ended. Expos vice-president of baseball operations Bill Stoneman, according to Youmans, advised him that he should report to a clinic in St. Louis for alcohol rehab, not cocaine rehab. There was speculation that commissioner Peter Ueberroth made a push to have Stoneman tell Youmans to go to St. Louis. All strange. Youmans told me he loved drinking Heineken but rarely any hard liquor.

"I was there for evaluation, to try to learn some things about yourself," Youmans said of the St. Louis sojourn. "And after I finished, I stayed in St. Louis four months. It gave me a little time to get away from everything."

The 1988 season was not so good. Youmans in the first half was 3-6 in 14 starts and then came the shocking news that the commissioner's office was suspending him in mid-June for "failing to comply with his drug-testing program". The test didn't show alcohol but rather traces of cocaine. He never pitched again that season and never pitched again for the Expos.

Youmans told me he spent about three weeks in rehab in Sarasota, Florida under the guidance of former MLB pitcher Dock Ellis and came back to Montreal to finish out his suspension for several weeks. Youmans was given clearance to take an on-field rehab assignment in Indianapolis. When I found out about him going to Indianapolis, I headed to Dorval Airport to interview him. I was the only reporter there. He was pissed at Expos management for not showing any interest in him following the suspension. My story for the Montreal Daily News sure hit the fan.

"Nobody from the Expos wanted to deal with me. I was upset," he told me in our phone interview earlier this year about the time he had spent in Montreal before he headed to Indianapolis. "I was one of the best prospects they had in a long time. It's like maybe they had given up on me. I was kind of forgotten."

I had not contacted Stoneman or his sidekick Dave Dombrowski to get the team's side of the story. Stoney and DD were pissed at me. In the press box the night the story appeared in the paper, Dombrowski asked me to come and talk to him.

"I may not be able to talk with you again," an angry Dombrowski told me. But he did.

That story fuelled the beginning of the end of Youmans' tenure with the Expos. The team had become very fed up with his antics. Oh yeah, big time.

From there on, testing of Youmans took place often. And Youmans knows why or at least he thinks he knows why he may have been sent to St. Louis and why the testing continued in the off-season and during the 1988 season. The reason: his buddy Gooden.

The commissioner's office linked Gooden with Youmans because they were friends from Tampa. Oh yeah, that is how baseball felt about Youmans. If Gooden has drug problems, why not test Youmans a lot? You get the drift.

"Gooden and I are best friends. That was the real reason why they were testing me because we were best friends," Youmans said. "Doc had been in trouble. Doc admitted to his problem. They were trying to clean up baseball.

"When you volunteer to go into rehab (in St. Louis) and come out, they can test you. They would call you on weekends (in the off-season) and during spring training, they'd come around and you'd get tested."

I asked Youmans if he would get Gooden to talk with me but it never happened. This was the same Gooden, who I approached with trepidation on the field near the batting cage prior to a 1989 playoff game in Los Angeles between the Mets and the Dodgers. I asked Gooden about Youmans and if there was anything new to report. Gooden said Youmans had a new girlfriend, Nadine Sunn. To this day, I remember her name and I even told Youmans I remembered her name without looking it up when we talked earlier this year.

Youmans and Sunn split up not long after Annette Williams, the mother of his son was murdered in Florida.

Getting back to Youmans' departure from the Expos: they dealt him and reliever Jeff Parrett to the Phillies at the winter meetings in Atlanta on Dec. 6, 1988 in exchange for pitcher Kevin Gross. Youmans never got on track in Philly either but he wants it made known that his career wasn't parried alone by drug use but that he also had shoulder problems.

"Everybody keeps forgetting," Youmans tried to explain. "They say that drugs destroyed me but I tore my right shoulder and had to have reconstructive surgery. That's what ended my career.

"When I was traded to Philly, I was hurting. My shoulder was not right. They said, okay, do this and do that. The Phillies didn't want to do surgery."

Youmans was 1-5 with a 5.70 ERA through part of the 1990 season before he shut the season down.

"My agent was Adam Katz and we decided to get a second examination with Dr. Jobe in California," Youmans said. "I had a torn labrum and I had loose (arthroscopic) surgery (Aug. 22)."

The following spring, the Pirates gave Youmans a tryout when he was still "throwing in the upper 90s" but they wanted to get him back on the field right away, as opposed to the normal recovery period from surgery of 1-2 years.

"In hindsight, I should have taken a bit longer and rested my arm longer," he said.

In any event, it was a shame that Youmans' MLB career ended at age 25. Oh my goodness, it was finished way too soon. He gave it a try later in independent leagues with New York's Sullivan Mountain Lions, New York's Newburgh Night Hawks and at age 39 with Canada's Saskatoon Legends.

It appeared that Youmans was non persona grata within MLB, that unofficially he was blackballed because of his drug problems and his attitude, just like Bill Lee was in 1982.

"I can't say I didn't have a drug problem," Youmans told me. "Don't get me wrong, it was my problem. A lot of people were doing the same thing back then in professional baseball. Remember in the 1980s, people would go out, party, have fun. That's how things were. You would hang out in clubs.

"I don't feel bad that things never turned out for me. Maybe life could have been better. I'm not bitter. I'm not mad. I had my problems. After baseball, I survived."

Youmans encountered some health problems about five years ago when he was forced to wear a portable pacemaker due to him gaining more weight than he wanted.

"What happened was that it (weight problems) caused my heart to overwork and I needed to wear the pacemaker for about 60 days," he said. "I was able to stop using it. Now I'm exercising and on medicine. I see my cardiologist once a year. I move around a lot. I'm not just sitting around."

There's the tendency to forget and forgive, pass over past transgressions instead of just throwing people to the curbside. Look at what happened to Ellis Valentine. Over the years, he has become glorified as if nothing happened. Same with badboys such as Bill Lee, Rodney Scott and Mike Lansing.

Youmans had worts, blemishes, moles, pimples and other stuff like the rest of us but that doesn't make him a bad person. He's what 30 years removed from his last time with the Expos. It was sad the way it all ended but we need to give Youmans his space and not throw him to the curbside.

Everyone has peaks and valleys in life, there are twists and turns, some positive, some negative. We've faced adversities that we didn't want to have. Youmans had his demons but we can't be negative for eternity. In the quiet there's not always peace in someone's life but we must show decency, mercy and respect at the same time.

Let's celebrate the great games he pitched for the Expos. Give him his due, instead of just criticizing or shunning him. Nobody is perfect.

Youmans, Floyd II, is happy in Nashville with his surgeon wife. He has a good life, a nice home. He has three grown children. One of his daughters, Meghan Youmans, is a lawyer. There is a Floyd Youmans III and there is a Floyd Youmans IV.

Youmans and Gooden talk regularly and try to meet every three months or so in spots such as Las Vegas. Youmans is also fairly close with former Met Wally Backman but ironically, he said he doesn't keep in touch with former Expos.

Youmans wants it known that he's a "very good cook". He says to check out his Facebook page. He loves making potato soup.

As former Expos GM Murray Cook, who made the Carter trade, looked back, he said, "Youmans never quite reached the heights we had hoped for. He certainly had the physical equipment, no question. He was probably as important a part of the trade as Hubie Brooks because of his ability but he didn't last very long.

"I saw him in high school and later on. How I gauged him was hits per inning. That was the criteria I used to judge pitchers. He was not a big kid, a medium-sized kid. He had a real, quick arm. His fastball was very deceptive – it looked better than it was."

Taking second chances

Pascual Perez, Dennis Martinez, two pretty darn-good acquisitions by Expos GM Murray Cook, all during a time frame of what six months.

Reclamation projects.

"Here's the situation," Cook was telling me in late 2020. "We know we give second chances for players. I knew Pascual from Pittsburgh. We knew the family. It's always been about second chances. Some people need to be straightened out. There is no guarantee of a major league job. Pascual became pretty good then. There was never any question about his ability."

Perez fashioned two wonderful seasons with the Braves: 15-8 and 14-8 but somewhere along the way, he was hit with a suspension for snorting cocaine.

Perez was dumped by the Braves in April 1986 because of his drug problems and sat out the remainder of that season. On Feb. 27 during spring training in 1987, Cook decided to sign Perez to a contract. Prancin' Pascual was getting a second chance. He joined the club that August.

Perez became a useful commodity. He was 7-0 with a 2.30 ERA in 1987, he was 12-8 with a 2.44 ERA in 1988 and he was 9-13 with a 3.31 ERA in 1989. And the Expos wanted to keep him as a free agent following the 1989 season but the allure of big money from the Yankees was too much for him to Perez to turn down. The Yankees gave him a three-year deal worth $5.7-million.

"Martinez? We got a call from Hank Peters, who is the GM in Baltimore. He instituted, started the discussions." Cook recollected. "He said, 'This guy is in rehab. We just can't bring him back to Baltimore from a PR standpoint. Would you be interested in taking him?' I said yes.

I didn't know he was available. We knew he had gone into rehab and was just coming out of rehab.

"Hank said they didn't want to bring him back. He didn't think it was wise. Hank felt that Dennis needed a change of scenery. Hank was very honest about it. Alcoholism, it's an illness, an insidious disease. It's like cancer. Remember Tommy Sandt? He drank himself to death (December, 2020).

Danny Gallagher photo
Dennis Martinez at 2016 Exposfest

"I never talked to Dennis. That was not the customary thing to do. We talked to Dennis' agent, Ron Shapiro. We made the trade. The rest is history. Dennis got his life straightened out. Back then, alcoholism, it was a pretty new thing.

"There wasn't much known about it. There weren't a lot of rehab centres. I knew of a guy when I was in Pittsburgh. He headed into rehab. It was much more private. Alcoholism weakens the character. Society back then considered it a weakness of character. It was different back then than it is now. That was a few generations ago.

"Mores have changed, times have changed, people are more understanding. People became a little more knowledgeable and showed more compassion," Cook said.

And then Cook pointed out to me that "Canadians were more accepting at the time", but more specifically that the Expos were more accepting of a troubled player back in the '80s. "Human frailty perhaps," as Cook put it.

"Martinez was grateful for the opportunity to come to Montreal. It was the only opportunity he had," Cook continued. "He had a (Canadian) hall of fame career from then on. He was dominant. It culminated in the hall of fame. It was kind of neat. We were inducted in the Canadian hall."

The revelation of Martinez's supposed stint in rehab in 1986 is a bit of a surprise because he has told me and others that he hasn't had a drink since 1983 when he was busted for DUI in December of that year. But it appears Martinez relapsed again close to three years later in 1986 and re-entered rehab, unbeknownst to many people.

If he did relapse, El Presidente wasn't about to get into details about it when I brought it up in late 2020. Yes, it happened a long time ago. Maybe that's why Shapiro never returned my email message. Do you

Tom Hagerty photo

Dennis Martinez poses at Wrigley Field in October, 1992

think there are many people out there who like to talk about admitting that they sought rehab treatment, that they wanted to dry out? It's all a private matter. It's embarrassing.

As Martinez recalled, he understood what the Orioles were trying to do. He said he never approached Peters about a trade because he was comfortable with the only MLB organization he knew. No way he wanted to be traded, even when manager Joe Altobelli left him off the roster for the 1983 AL championship series and the 1983 World Series which the Orioles won, the year Martinez quit drinking.

"Looking back, I know how this business work. I would do the same thing," Martinez told me in late 2020 about being traded. "They didn't want me anymore and wanted to get value before they cannot get anything. That's what most teams would do. I believe that they were not willing to sign me again.

"I was hurt because it was the only team I grew up with," Martinez said about the trade. "I was naive in some ways. It was the best thing that happened to me. The Expos were a low-market team that liked to get players from other teams and develop them."

Martinez went on to a stellar career with 100 wins with the Expos. All told, Martinez won 104 games in the National League and 141 in the American League, one of the very few to win at least 100 games in both leagues.

On July 28, 1991, El Presidente fired a perfect game. He finished his big-league career with a 245-193 record and 122 complete games. He is short on wins for Cooperstown and his ERA was 3.70 but those complete games, boy, they are impressive. In the olden days, he was golden, a workhorse. Nowadays, pitchers are held back by pitch counts and pitch very few complete games because of a team's desire to protect its greatest assets.

Talking of second chances, there was the case involving outfielder Mitch Webster, another solid transaction by Cook in 1985. Again, it was a phone call from an opposing GM, who initiated a trade discussion. This time, it was Blue Jays GM Pat Gillick.

And although the Expos and Jays made few trades over the years, Gillick just wanted big-league playing time for Webster, who unlike Perez and Martinez, was a clean-cut guy from America's midwest and had no dalliances with drugs or alcohol. He wasn't a reclamation project like Perez and Martinez but he needed a second chance with another organization.

"I always thought that was the most fun trade, the one for Mitch Webster," Cook said. "Toronto had a really strong club back then. Gillick called me up. He said, 'Hey, I've got an outfielder who should be playing. He can't get a chance to play here. His name is Mitch Webster. What do you think?' "

Webster was going nowhere in the big leagues at the time with Toronto because the Jays had a stellar outfield of Jesse Barfield, Lloyd Moseby and George Bell – 1985 was the first year the Blue Jays made the AL playoffs.

Without making any promises to Gillick, Cook said he flew to Portland, Maine, drove 25 minutes to nearby Ole Orchard, Maine where Webster was playing in the Triple-A ranks for the Syracuse Chiefs against the Maine Guides.

Cook saw Webster play both ends of a doubleheader and was impressed.

"I was enamoured with his speed," Cook told me. "I'd come from the Pirates. Speed was a big factor. We loved guys that could run."

A few days later, Cook called Gillick.

"We'd like to get Mitch Webster. What do you want?" Cook asked Gillick.

"Nothing. I just want to give him a chance to play in the big leagues," Gillick replied.

"I give all the credit to Pat for being caring for a player. Mitch became a good player for the Expos," Cook said.

Webster was called up from the minors immediately on the day of the June 22 trade and was a late-inning replacement. At one point during that 1985 season, Webster homered in four consecutive games, earning the nickname The Natural, a reference to the fictional character in the book and movie of the same name.

Webster had enjoyed cups of tea with the Blue Jays in 1983 and 1984 and finally got a chunk of playing time with the Expos for the remainder of the 1985 season.

Although Gillick said he didn't want anything in return, the official announcement was PTBNL. That came two months later on Sept. 10. The player to be named later going to the Jays was Cliff Young. Ever heard of him?

In 1986, Webster enjoyed an exceptional year. He batted .290, hit 13 triples to go with 36 stolen bases, eight homers and 49 RBI in his first full season but what really caught Cook's attention was something unusual, something very rarely seen today.

"The thing that was most interesting was that he had 11 bunt hits to shortstop. Kind of silly. That's my recollection," Cook said. "He could really run. Nobody does that, drag-bunt to the shortstop. Eleven bunt singles? It's a different world today. Mitch was a switch-hitter and he had power. He became a good player. He was a great guy."

In 1987, Webster was exceptional again in the Expos Cinderella run that almost netted them the NL East title. Webster hit .281 with 101 runs, 15 homers and 63 RBI.

Give Webster so much credit for his patience and resilience in the face of adversity. Here's a guy who spent what eight years in the minor leagues, including parts of two seasons in Lethbridge, Alberta. The guts and the courage Webster displayed was something to behold. Instead of throwing in the towel and going home to Kansas, he gutted it out and his patience paid off.

Webster's story is neat. He had spent some eight years in the minors with several cups of tea in the majors. And up until Gillick called Cook and engineered a trade, Webster would have continued to languish in the minors. Being buried in the minors is no fun for anyone. The good thing is that Webster was willing to ride it out for a while in the minors.

Webster was initially signed by the Dodgers but his first taste of the majors came with the Blue Jays. Ironically, Webster would finish his career with the organization that drafted him: the Dodgers.

"We had an infielder in Cincinnati when I was there as GM. Jeff Treadway," Cook said. "(Manager) Pete Rose didn't figure he would help. I called Bobby Cox with Atlanta and asked him if he had any interest in Jeff. We'll give him to you for nothing."

As a result of that trade, Treadway ended up playing a few years in the majors, not as long as Webster, but it was better than plying his time in the minors.

Webster, though, tailed off considerably in 1988 and was gone in a July trade to the Cubs for Dave Martinez in an exchange of outfielders. Just prior to that, Expos manager Buck Rodgers had talked vice-president of baseball operations Bill Stoneman out of a deal that would have

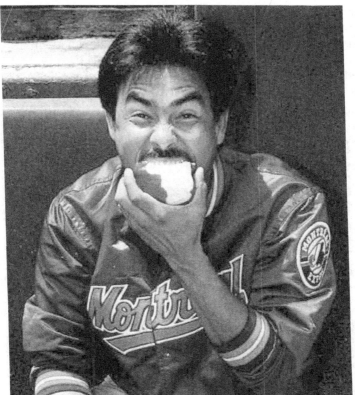

Courtesy Upper Deck
Dennis Martinez in this image from one of his cards

seen Yankees slugging prospect Jay Buhner traded to Montreal. Rodgers instead told Stoneman he wanted the light-hitting Martinez. Stoneman caved in but he told me years ago he regretted not trading for Buhner.

So on July 14, the Webster-for-Martinez trade was made. It had its own little side story. Martinez was traded because Cubs superstar Ryne Sandberg went to GM Jim Frey and issued an ultimatum: "Trade me or Martinez". Sandberg had found out Martinez had been fooling around with Sandberg's wife Cindy. Frey decided to trade Martinez.

The trade was announced by the Expos in the middle of a game in the press box and the way my Daily News sidekick James Baxter wrote it up, it wasn't a spur-of-the-moment transaction.

"I came to the park today knowing something was going to happen," Webster said following the trade. "It wasn't really a surprise. I am really looking forward to a fresh start. A change of scenery will really be good for me. I don't feel I'm a bench player at this stage of my career.

"I'm sad to be leaving. That's the sad part of being traded, leaving behind good friends.

Then a week later on July 21, the Yankees dealt Buhner to the Mariners and he would put up some pretty good numbers in playing the remainder of his career with Seattle until he packed it in, in 2001.

As for Webster, once he was traded to Montreal by Toronto, he never played again in the minors. Isn't that something – a great success story, thanks to Gillick and Cook.

Denis Brodeur photo from Expos magazine

Mitch Webster was acquired from the Blue Jays in June, 1985

"With the departure of Rudy May, the sale of Bill Atkinson's contract to the Chicago White Sox and the effects of the aging process on Woodie Fryman and Stan Bahnsen, the Expos bullpen could be a problem unless the team comes up with something in that area before spring training."
— my former newspaper colleague Ken Fidlin, writing in the Ottawa Journal Dec. 13, 1979.

James was a potential Goose Gossage

When Ken Fidlin called up Expos president John McHale and suggested this dilemma above, McHale replied, "That's true. We have to a take a long look at our relief corps. You know every year (manager Dick Williams) has a darkhorse pitcher ready to go.

"This year, he's counting on Bob James to develop into an outstanding rookie. He (Williams) says he's a potential Goose Gossage."

As in a fireballer, a flame-thrower. The blond-haired, dashing James was a first-round draft pick in 1976, a 6-foot-4, 215-pounder who had spent the 1979 season with Denver Triple-A before being tabbed as a September call-up during their unsuccessful pennant run.

Looking back, James told me about the Gossage reference, "It was a joke. They called me the Canadian Goose. The technology (radar) was around then with the Jugs gun, not as good as today. When I was drafted, I was consistently around 90-92 m.p.h.

"In '84, I was getting clocked at 94. With today's guns, which are meant to excite the crowd, I'd probably be around 97-100."

Before games when players would play catch on the field in front of the dugout, most of James' teammates didn't want to have to throw with James. The general rule of thumb with this tradition is that players would just engage in soft toss but not James.

"Bob James was not an easy guy to catch," Dan Schatzeder told me. "He threw hard and his ball moved. It hurt your hand."

James laughed at this story by Schatzeder and replied, "That's funny. It was no picnic trying to catch his knuckle curve either. My shins still hurt."

Canadian Baseball Hall of Fame
Bob James

James didn't pan out. He had a short MLB career but enjoyed his time with the Expos. Ironically, he had two back and forth stints with Montreal sandwiched around a trade with the Tigers.

"I played with lots of good guys. I came up through the minors with Rock, Gully, Charlie Lea, etc but the guy that sticks out is Jack Reardon," James said. "Great guy. Back then, we were bullpen rivals. I was up and coming and he was establishing himself as one of the greatest closers in history. He took it upon himself to befriend me and him, Dan Schatzeder and I would quite frequently go out for a few beers."

146

"I remember him driving down the street in Jamestown, N.Y. on a bicycle. He was a scarecrow on a bicycle with his size, his long arms and legs. He was a character. It took him a while to get his act together. In the first couple of years, he didn't show up but boy, the proof is in the pudding. That's what the minor leagues are for, for players to hone their skills. And he certainly did that. The rest is history."
— Murray Cook talking about Randy Johnson. Cook was the Expos GM when Johnson was drafted by the organization in June, 1985.

Johnson sure had a terrific career

Against his wishes, Randy Johnson started his pro ball career in Jamestown, N.Y. in 1985 and was having trouble finding the plate that year.

"I remember Randy some and also remember his first pitching outing when he walked four or five people in his first inning relieving," said his Jamestown teammate Mike Ahearne, who is a professor of marketing at the University of Houston. "Randy was a second-round draft choice who threw the ball over 100 mph. The team saw a lot of potential in him, given that he was a left-hander and threw the ball so hard. He just didn't get many outings his first year since his pitching was so wild. It really frustrated him."

But as Cook said, Johnson was able to "hone his skills" to turn it around.

On Sept. 13, 1988, Johnson stepped into the clubhouse at Olympic Stadium in Montreal for the first time. I was there. It was like history in the making, although we never thought of it that way at the time.

"I'm very excited. I couldn't sleep at all (Sept. 12). It's an unbelievable feeling. You get goose bumps," Johnson told us reporters shortly after arriving in the clubhouse Sept. 13.

"Everybody has had this type of feeling at one time. This is something I've been looking to all my life."

Darius Ramezani illustration
Randy Johnson

The Expos drafted Johnson in June of 1985 and just a little over three years later, he was up in the majors. Joining Johnson that day from the minors were infielder Johnny Paredes and minor-league manager Joe Sparks, who guided Indianapolis to the Triple-A title in 1988. In 1988 with Indy, Johnson was 8-7 with 72 strikeouts and a 3.26 ERA.

"I could've done better this year but I had some good quality starts," Johnson said. "It was a season of ups and downs. I started slow. That was a low point. Then I won five consecutive games and that gave me a lot of confidence. That was a high point.

"Then I broke my right hand June 14 and missed about 10 starts. That was a low point. I was out for six weeks but the important thing was that I ended up strong. The hand doesn't bother me.

"I think they know I can help this organization, that I'm capable of pitching."

He didn't make his first MLB appearance until Sept. 15 and he was a winner. He threw five innings as the starting pitcher, giving up six hits and two earned runs while fanning five batters to help the Expos beat the Pirates 9-4.

Those statistics you see of Johnson from 1988-2005 show he was worthy of Cooperstown. Of all the major homegrown, signed and developed talent the Expos brought forth, Johnson is my pick as the one who accomplished the most. The other top ones are Steve Rogers, Andre Dawson, Gary Carter, Tim Raines, Tim Wallach, Larry Walker and Vladimir Guerrero.

Big Unit struck out 4,875 batters, threw over 4,100 innings, compiled a 303-166 record and his ERA was 3.29. He was elected into

Cooperstown on the first ballot.

What made Johnson charming in other ways is that he had hobbies such as heavy-metal music and photography.

Montreal HMV retail clerk Steph Benoti was besotted with Johnson when he would walk into his store as a member of the Diamondbacks. Benoti found him "super cool" and discovered he was a heavy metal fan.

One day, Johnson said to Benoti, "Fill my basket with all the best metal bands from Québec".

Benoti and Johnson also talked some baseball.

"Cool guy and since I'm a pitcher, I asked him about his slider," Benoti said. "And he just showed me his hand and said, 'I just strangle the ball with these, man.' He had like nine-inch long fingers."

Benoti had another story about Johnson, one from the Big O. Johnson was warming up in the bullpen before a game. Some guy kept telling Johnson he was ugly, he couldn't pitch and blah, blah, taunting him non-stop.

"At some point, Randy stops pitching and says, 'Hey, buddy, fuck off,'" Benoti said.

Leading up to the big trade

On April 25, 1989, I quizzed Mariners GM Woody Woodward about the possible trade that would send Seattle pitcher Mark Langston to the Expos for Randy Johnson, Brian Holman and Gene Harris.

"We talked some names with the Expos but I'm not going to say who they are because it constitutes tampering," Woodward told me for a story for the Montreal Daily News. "First of all, the main objective is to get him (Langston) signed to a multi-year deal. We'd like him to be one of our pitchers for a long time to come. We signed him to a deal this year without going to arbitration but we couldn't get a multi-year deal."

On May 25, a month after that conversation with Woodward, the trade was made.

Prancin' Pascual

When I called up Expos GM Dave Dombrowski on Nov. 21, 1989, the day the deal was announced by the Yankees, he was emotional, shedding tears and hoping that the Yankees would look after Pascual Perez the way the Expos did.

Perez had earned $850,000 in 1989 with the Expos and from what I understood, the team offered not much more than $1.3-million in a new deal, about $4-million in total for three years.

"I just hope the Yankees have Pascual's best interests at heart," Dombrowski said. "I just hope they have the proper ways to help him. His problems are well documented. I hope they understand the care he needs. I like Pascual. I'm disappointed we lost him. We grew to have a great attachment to him. He had to do what was best for him but we were surprised he went elsewhere."

This was the breakdown of the Perez deal with the Yankees: $600,000 signing bonus, $100,000 relocation bonus, $1.2-million in 1990 and $1.9-million in both 1991 and 1992. Can you imagine. Even all these years later in 2021, this kind of money is ludicrous.

Days later on a late Saturday night in 1989, Nov. 25, I walked up the stairs to the newsroom at the Montreal Daily News on Ste. Antoine St. in downtown Montreal where I worked.

Outside the entrance to the newsroom was a security guard. I figured he might ask me what I was going there so late with no paper the next day, a Sunday. The paper was called the Daily News but we didn't publish seven days a week. I put my signature on the sign-in sheet and the security guard let me through without saying anything. I turned the key in the door and I went into find myself a desk and a phone.

It was eerie. It was barren and sparsely lit. I was the only one in the newsroom. I was there for one reason: to call this number I thought was one for Perez. Getting a hold of someone in the Dominican Republic or anywhere in Latin America wasn't/isn't easy. You never expect a number that will work.

To my surprise, Perez's wife Marisela answered the phone in Santo Domingo and soon, Pascual was on the line. I was elated. The phone number worked. More often than not, numbers in Latin America tend/tended to be "discontinued or no longer in service".

Dariush Ramezani illustration
Pascual Perez loved to entertain

I knew I had an exclusive, blockbuster story, beating all the newspapers and electronic media and the vaunted New York media, that drives on story-breaking adventures. This was akin to a cloak and dagger story out of a spy novel.

When I went into work the next day, I transferred the story from my Tandy to the copy editors.

"Can we hold this story?" editor Armand Thomas asked me, thinking there wasn't enough room in the paper to handle the story. Shocked, I told him, "No, it's a big story." Then I had to wait until Monday morning to find out for sure that no other media had talked with Perez. This was in the days when there were no cellphones to disperse the news immediately on social media.

In the story I wrote, Pascual tore a strip off the Expos for not trying hard enough to sign him.

"I love the people in Montreal, the fans, everybody. I'm disappointed about leaving but why did the Expos wait so late to sign me?" Perez asked me as we chatted. "Dombrowski said he was not going to sign anybody during the season but in the first half, they signed Dennis Martinez and in the second half, they signed Spike Owen. And they made that $9-million offer to Mark Langston for three years."

Hey, some people thought Perez maybe wasn't that smart but he knew what was going on. He was no dummy. Like I say about my wife, she doesn't have a degree in education but she has a degree in life. I could say that about Perez. What Perez was trying to say is that the Expos should have signed him long before the end of the season.

"After the all-star break, I asked Dombrowski: 'When are you going to sign me? What about me?' He said, 'We have to wait.' I was mad about that.

"Dombrowski always likes to be in the papers and on TV but never mind that. I said: 'Pay attention to me. Sign me.' On the last day of the season, Dombrowski said, 'We need you.' I said, 'Sign me right away.' One time, Bill Stoneman (VP of baseball operations) said, 'We want you for a long time.' But when I got back to the Dominican Republic, they didn't call me."

Perez told me that he and his agent Adam Katz told Dombrowski several weeks prior to the Yankees' signing that the Expos would have to fork out more than the $4-million they were offering for three years. Weeks earlier, majority owner Charles Bronfman had declared he was selling the team because of the heartbreak over the team's collapse in August and September.

"When we said that, Dombrowski said, 'You guys better deal with somebody else,' " Perez said.

There were many people who suggested that Perez should not have deserted the Expos after the way they bent over backward for him, considering his drug problems.

"I had problems in the past," Perez admitted. "And I appreciate the way the Expos treated me but all I'm concerned about is what is happening now. The Expos can be sorry for not signing me but it's too late. Why did they wait so late to sign me? I've been a big man with the Expos since I joined them in 1987. Look now, they made a mistake in not signing me.

"I'll miss it in Montreal but it's not my fault. It was the front office's fault. I had to look out for myself. I brought a lot of people to the stadium and they complain about paying me?"

Perez said the biggest compliment he ever received came from Bronfman.

"Bronfman told me, 'If every player with the Expos was like you, we'd win the World Series.' You know who showed a lot of everything with the Expos? Me."

Asked about getting into pinstripes, Perez replied, 'What's that?"

"You know the stripes on the pants the Yankees players wear?" I retorted.

"Ha, ha, ha, yeah," he said. "I like to be with the best. I want to win. When I play dominoes, cards, whatever, I don't want to lose. When the deal was done with the Yankees, I said, 'Thank you, God.' The Yankees have always been my favourite team. It's been a long time I've like them. I love them. They're a good ballclub with a good reputation. I love it. I waited so long for this to happen.

"I feel great for me. I came from a poor family. I cried a couple of times after the deal was made, I said, 'Now, God, look at me.' It's the best thing that ever happened in the world. When I go to the Yankees, I'm going to play hard and aggressive. I'll give my heart for the job. I'm never going to change."

As we wound down our conversation, I asked Perez if he had any advice for Expos management.

"Keep the players happy and keep the best ones," he said. "Management has to pay up. No pay, no play."

As some of us look back, the Expos should have re-signed Perez during the 1989 season when it would have been much cheaper. They probably could have signed him for $1.3-million per season, the amount they were offering months later in the off-season.

On Nov. 20, the day before the trade was announced, Dombrowski had told me he was not optimistic about signing Perez. The marketplace had turned upside down and the Yankees were part of it.

"We're aggressively trying to sign Pascual but the figures are so phenomenal," Dombrowski said. "It's like hitting a punching bag and the bag comes back to hit you all the time. You wince. It's beyond comprehension but you have to decide whether you want to play in the market.

"He got off to a 0-7 start so it was kind of tough to get into negotiations at that point. When I made him an offer a month ago, I thought it was a fair one but as it turns out, it was ridiculously low. I just never anticipated where the market would be. I've been caught off guard. So has Charles."

I had forgotten until I read online recently that Perez was in rehab for several months during his final season with the Expos. He escaped suspension when he agreed to a one-year suspension if he was caught again. Kevin Gross, one of Perez's teammates in 1989, told me at the time that he felt Perez owed the Expos some allegiance.

"I didn't think he'd leave the team after all the stuff the Expos have done for him, all the chances they gave him," Gross told me. "They helped him through drug rehab and all that. He should have given them every opportunity to sign him back. I'm very surprised."

Perez was a cartoon character, a colourful crowd pleaser with jericurls, fun to be around, a media darling who gave us endless copy. He put fannies in the seats. His games were quick, good for reporters' deadlines, good for fans to get on the road back home after a game. Expos management knew how important Perez was financially as far as attendance went.

He was the author of the eephus pitcher, a slow pitch thrown what maybe 40-50 m.p.h way up in the air and then it would land in the catcher's mitt, catching the batter off guard. French broadcaster Jacques Doucet would call it a "l'arc-en-ciel."

Perez would run back and forth from the dugout to the mound, dodging the chalk lines. He would also infuriate the opposition with some of his antics. He would pull his right arm back and forth or use a finger, emulating a strikeout like the umpire would. On occasion, he would peek through his legs to check the runner at first.

Perez only pitched three seasons for the Expos but his popularity made it look as if he had been there much longer. He was one of the more popular Expos of the late 1980s. In a tribute to Perez on YouTube, an anonymous, besotted fan hailed him this way: "Hats off to the most eccentric Expo ever."

As it turns out, Perez got into drug problems while with the Yankees and never played in the MLB ranks after 1991. He was suspended for one year prior to the 1992 season over drug use.

The baseball world lost a colourful figure when Perez was murdered in the Dominican Republic Nov. 1, 2012.

Expos lost out on Randolph

Did you know that Yankees second-base legend Willie Randolph was pursued aggressively by the Expos for the 1989 season?

Randolph opted for the Dodgers and real grass.

Randolph signed a two year deal with the Dodgers for $1.775-million. That meant he was going from the natural grass of Yankee Stadium to a similar surface at Dodger Stadium.

"One of Willie's concerns was playing on turf, rather than grass," Expos GM Dave Dombrowski told me after he struck out with Randolph. "Our doctors assured his doctors that there would be no problems (playing on turf).

"His agent (Ron Shapiro) was surprised that he decided on Los Angeles. Willie had said he wanted to play on a contender and we fit into that scenario. And his family lives on the east coast in New Jersey and he would've been only an hour's flight from home if he played with us."

At that time, Randolph had played close to 13 seasons with the Yankees and was 34 years old. A little long in the tooth but still useful.

Hubie was a great guy to deal with

Hubie Brooks was always accommodating in the two seasons I covered him with the Expos in 1988-89. Other reporters found him the same way.

Even when the 1989 season was over, he answered the phone at his home near Los Angeles.

When I called him to tell him in December of 1989 that Bryn Smith had signed with the Cardinals for three seasons and that Hubie was the only big-name Expos free agent remaining after Mark Langston and Pascual Perez had departed, he said, "I guess I'm the Lone Ranger."

The winter meetings in December came and went and Brooks had no deal and he had drawn no interest or offer from the Expos.

"There's nothing I can do about that," Brooks told me then. "I can't twist the Expos arms. You can't tell an owner how to spend his dollar. I guess they're not interested in me. They weren't interested in me in August either," he added, alluding to the fact that he was benched for six consecutive games.

"It forces your hand when they say they don't want to negotiate at $2-million a year. I'm a good player and I gave a lot of service to that team in every capacity."

He sure did. He was a clutch player through thick and thin and often played hurt, although his 1989 season wasn't so productive.

When I looked through some old clippings, I noticed that the Expos had wanted to extend his contract into 1990 and beyond following the 1988 season but Brooks told management he wasn't interested.

It was evident that relations between Brooks and the Expos had become strained. They didn't want to pay him a lot of money and they wanted to go with a youth movement that was considerably much

155

cheaper. Guys like Marquis Grissom and Larry Walker were coming into their own.

To Expos management working on a bare-bones budget, Brooks had become too expensive and a little bit old at 34. Before the winter meetings, Rodgers called Brooks to wish him the best of luck wherever he decided to play.

Heading into Christmas of 1989, Brooks finally got a deal with the Dodgers, for the same number of years and money – $6-million – as Bryn Smith got with St. Louis. The Expos offered something like $1.3-million per year after he had earned $850,000 in 1989. Brooks was elated to sign with a team located 20 minutes from where he lived.

Canadian Baseball Hall of Fame
Hubie Brooks

The deal was consummated Dec. 21 and all Brooks had to do was drive 20 minutes to Dodger Stadium for a news conference.

"I felt after last year that the Expos didn't have a lot of confidence in me," Brooks told reporters on the conference call. "I wanted to go to where a team would have confidence in me so that if I reached a low point (slump), people would know what I could do and wouldn't lose confidence in me.

"I don't have anything to prove to the Expos. I played five good years for them."

When Brooks was asked on the conference call if the Expos lacked leadership in 1989, he replied, "It depends on where you want to direct that question. Management, ownership and the dugout were probably parts of the reasons for the collapse in the second half."

When Expos vice president of baseball operations Bill Stoneman heard that Brooks had signed with the Dodgers, he wasn't taken for a loop. He had known for about a year that Brooks was reluctant to sign an extension with the Expos.

"After the 1988 season, Hubie appeared not to want to talk to us about a new contract," Stoneman told me back then. "His opinion all along has been consistent. He stuck to his pattern. He didn't sway from his objectives.

"He made it clear his top priority was to play in southern California so it didn't make sense to make a bid for someone who didn't want to play here."

Courtesy Hostess

Collage of photos produced in 1980s

And you know what Brooksie had agent Richie Bry install in his contract? He put it in writing that he couldn't be traded to Montreal. No kidding.

And wherever he was destined, he planned to be in even better shape than he was in 1989.

Sure enough, when we saw him in spring training in 1990, not only had he lost some weight – he sure looked good in Dodger Blue – blue lettering on a white uniform, boy, it looks stunning. But he confirmed the stuff about the no-trade-to-Montreal clause. Wasn't that a message that he didn't have much use for the organization?

"I don't think I'll ever have a chance to play there again because I'll be too old," Brooks said, laughing, as reporters like me stood around him. "But that clause was just something thrown in there. It really doesn't mean a lot. It wasn't something that was a knock on the Expos or a knock on the town. I always had fun up there.

"My contract was up and I got a decent offer (from the Dodgers). Not only that, all indications from Claude Brochu was that the club wasn't interested in giving me the kind of dollars I got in L.A. But if that's their policy, you can't knock that.

"I didn't go away mad at anyone. I thought it (L.A.) was the best deal for me. Closer to home meant something." Brooks had asked repeatedly during those trying moments when he was benched for six consecutive starts why was management blaming one person for a second-half slump.

"I don't think it was as much of a factor for me leaving as a lot of people thought," Brooks said. "I just think it was an indication that the club was most likely willing to go with younger players. Since I wasn't one of the younger guys, I think it was their idea that they were just going to go with younger players."

That same day in Vero Beach, Rodgers told reporters: "Of the four free agents we lost after last season, he's the one we'll miss the most. His offence will be the hardest to replace."

It was interesting that the Blue Jays had made a big push to try and convince Brooks to come to Toronto. On Dec. 19, just days before Brooks signed with L.A., Jays GM Pat Gillick personally called Brooks. And after the Dodgers began serious discussions on Dec. 20, the Blue Jays finally made their pitch, matching the Dodgers offer of three years and $6-million.

But sun and surf won out over cool weather and Canada.

In the last few years, Brooks has gone AWOL, except for events involving the Mets, his team from 1980-84 and in 1991.

We Googled him recently in California where he lives to try to get a phone number. We tried getting former teammates to help out. We tried Mets PR specialist Jay Horwitz but no dice. I guess Hubie just wants to be left alone. You have to respect him for that.

Too hard on Raines

Holy shoot. Looking closely at a lot of my newspaper clippings from the late 1980s and early 1990s, I see where I was really hard on Tim Raines. I picked on him because I felt he wasn't playing and hitting like he was capable of doing in 1988-90 with the Expos.

During those three seasons before he was traded to the Chicago White Sox, he was a figment of his former self and often, I criticized/critiqued him for what I felt was nonchalant play both for the Montreal Daily News and Ottawa Sun, but mostly for the latter paper.

So look below at what I said about him during the 1990 season for the Sun:

"Tim Raines says the Expos shouldn't consider trading him. But it has come that time when they should trade the outfielder and get a quality body in return while he has some market value. He hasn't been useful the last three years, he's loafing and he's getting injured more frequently. Most of all, his enthusiasm for the game has waned. Where he shows most of his enthusiasm is around the batting cage when he clowns with teammates and opposing players. No longer is Raines considered one of the top players in the game. Raines claims he's happy in Montreal but it's doubtful he would veto a trade. He would welcome a change in scenery in an attempt to revitalize his career. Raines has been a solid franchise player for the most part since he came into the league but loyalty is no longer guaranteed in this game."

Yeah, I was hard on Raines. My father would often say to me, "Don't be too hard on them." Meaning athletes.

On the last day of the 1990 season, some of us reporters went up to Raines in the clubhouse and he told us he didn't expect to be traded in

Danny Gallagher photo
Tim Raines listening to questions from reporters at the Big O in 2018

the off-season but added he wouldn't be surprised if he was.

"I wouldn't be stunned," Raines told us. "There's been a lot of talk about it the last two years."

Raines said he preferred that he stay in the National League and go to a team that plays on natural grass.

"And it doesn't necessarily have to be in California," he said. "I don't want to play in San Francisco because of the cold, fog and earthquakes."

Two months later, I attended the 1990 winter meetings in the Chicago suburb of Rosemont. It was there that the Cubs, were looking to trade for Raines.

When I called Raines up at his Florida residence during those meetings, he said he had heard he might be sent to the Cubs in exchange for outfielder Dwight Smith, closer Mitch Williams and catcher Damon Berryhill.

"That would be a good move for both teams if it's more than a rumour," Raines told me that day. "The Expos would be getting another outfielder, a switch-hitting catcher and a guy who can be a stopper."

Wielding the power of 10-and-5 status, meaning 10 years in the majors and the last five with the same team, the Expos, Raines turned down trades to the Kansas City Royals and Boston Red Sox. Raines didn't want to play on Royals' turf and he wasn't too fussy about going to Boston because of the racial tensions there.

From what I had reported many times, Raines had been rumoured a number of times about being going to Boston in a 1-for-1 trade for Mike Greenwell. There was even speculation that Raines turned down a 1-for-1 transaction that would have sent him to Atlanta straight up for Tom Glavine. Now, wow, if that trade had taken place, what a boon that would have been for the Expos.

Juanita Moore photo
Tim Raines in 1981

Know what? Not long after those winter meetings, Raines was swapped to Chicago, not to the Cubs, but to the White Sox on Christmas Eve for Ivan Calderon and Barry Jones.

From 1981-87, a span of seven seasons, Raines was one of the most impactful players in all of Major League Baseball.

At spring training in 1991 with the arrival of Calderon, veterans like Dennis Martinez commended the move, sensing that a new atmosphere was starting to take shape.

"The attitude and work habits are there," Martinez told reporters during one scrum. "We're more serious. That kind of attitude is always positive. I think we need that sometimes if we're in the business to win things."

And what caused the change? Martinez was asked.

"You know why but don't ask me," El Presidente said.

Although Martinez wouldn't mention the departed Raines by name, reporters knew Martinez meant Rock, who had a reputation as a joker.

"Calderon is one of the guys I see already talking to some guys about a situation, what they have to do to light a firecracker under everyone else. We've added somebody who wants to play. We need leadership like that. We don't get it from the Cat (Andres Galarraga) and we don't get it from Tim Wallach.

"So maybe Calderon's the type of explosive guy we need. We need some fire. He's new here but like us Latin guys, he has killer instinct, the attitude of being fearless, that you want to win."

Raines resurrected his career with the White Sox and later helped the Yankees win two World Series titles. He even had the great privilege of returning to play for the Expos in 2000.

Danny Gallagher photo
Tim Raines looks dapper in a suit, posing in a Toronto Maple Leafs baseball cap at a Leafs fan forum in May, 2019. The Leafs play in Ontario's Intercounty league.

Buck gets canned

On June 3, 1991, I was in West Palm Beach on a mini holiday to check out a possible condo purchase which never materialized.

While there, I found out that Expos manager Buck Rodgers had been fired by GM Dave Dombrowski.

So sitting at the Crazy Horse Tavern while sipping on a few beers across the street from the now defunct Expos spring-training home, Municipal Stadium, I banged out two stories, the main story, and a sidebar, on my trusty Tandy computer for my employer, the Ottawa Sun, even though I was technically on holidays.

Instead of me being at Grumpy's bar on Bishop St. in Montreal where Rodgers convened his going-away news conference, I called Buck at his Montreal residence. We put a place line of Montreal on the story, pretending I was in Montreal.

Rodgers got the call from Dombrowski at 6:30 on the morning of June 3. The Expos had lost five straight and 10 of their last 11 so the end was nigh.

"No thank-you handshake. No person to person discussion. Just a phone call," I wrote in the Sun.

Thus was the exit of who some believe was the most popular manager in Expos history. The debate would be whether he was more popular than Felipe Alou.

"It was very short and sweet," Rodgers told me on the phone about his brief chat with Dombrowski. "He said 'We've decided to make a change and we have to let you go.' I said, 'Okay, that's fine' and I hung up and went back to sleep. Ninety-nine percent of the time, a manager gets fired in person but I was expecting it this way anyway.

"I'm leaving Montreal with my head held high, with a real gusto. I think the firing was inevitable. I'm not happy about it but I'm not sad. I don't have any plans but I want to manage again."

There was friction and a rift between Dombrowski and Rodgers. The GM inherited Rodgers, who had been hired by Murray Cook in the fall of 1984. There were times during or following both the 1989 and 1990 seasons that Dombrowski wanted to fire Rodgers but majority owner Charles Bronfman intervened and put the kibosh to those plans.

Later that month when Bronfman's 60th birthday party was held in Montreal, an occasion that saw comedian Bill Cosby as the surprise guest speaker, Rodgers was invited but Dombrowski wasn't.

"If we'd won the championship this year, I wasn't going to be back anyway," Rodgers said on the day of his firing. "When I didn't get my contract extension late last season, I figured that was going to be it. I was not part of the GM's plans.

"I was not his man. I was forced on him. He wanted me to change my personality. One time, he wanted me to be Tommy Lasorda. Another time, he wanted me to be Tony La Russa. Another time, it was somebody else.

"I told him three times going back to 1989 that if he didn't like me that he should fire me. I told him I wasn't going to change."

Rodgers was leaving the Expos tickled most about the 1987 club that wound up 91-71 when it wasn't expecting to do much.

"And last year (1990) we had 85 wins and we saved the franchise," Rodgers said. "I was real proud. If we'd finished last and 900,000 people had showed up, not many people would have invested in the club. Probably, there would be no baseball in Montreal."

Yet, on the last day of the 1990 season when Rodgers won his 500th game as Expos manager, he didn't get a contract extension. He figured he was doomed. He was right.

Rodgers was replaced by rookie Tom Runnells, who was the Expos third-base coach. Jerry Manuel, the third-base coach at Triple-A, took over similar duties with Montreal.

Up until that point, Rodgers was the winningest manager in Expos history with a record of 520 wins and 499 losses. He lasted six and half seasons, a pretty darn-good stint. He was being paid $450,000 to manage in 1991.

When I got a hold of veteran third baseman Tim Wallach, he took the blame for the manager's demise.

"In the name of the Expos, I accept responsibility as team captain," Wallach told me. "We didn't play for Buck and he paid the price. I hate to see a guy lose his job like that but the issue was out there. There are too many players playing for themselves and not to win."

On Sept. 26, 1989, it was announced that Rodgers would return for the 1990 season when there appeared to be some doubt after the Expos folded like a tent and lost the NL East they had held for a good portion of the season. It was a disaster the way the '89 season ended.

On that day in late September, Rodgers and Dombrowski had met for two and a half hours at Dombrowski's Mountain St. condo. On Sept. 25, Dombrowski told the Expos board of directors that he favored retaining Rodgers if the manager would meet certain conditions.

Those conditions included Rodgers spending less time in his office and more time on the field prior to games, overseeing workouts. Rodgers was Prince Charming, a media darling, who would spend considerable time with reporters, spilling out eloquence and a genuine personality to go along with his good looks.

Dombrowski had also asked Rodgers to reduce the country club atmosphere in the clubhouse that was considered much too free-swinging and carefree. I could see that players would be in the clubhouse and some not on the dugout steps during the national anthems.

Ironically, just what about a month later, Dombrowski left the Expos to become the GM of the expansionist Florida Marlins, who were to begin play in 1993. Runnells turned out to be a disaster and a beam fell off the stadium, forcing the Expos to play all of their remaining games on the road. The one good thing that happened that season was Dennis Martinez's perfect game July 28.

When Cook was hired as GM in the fall of 1984, his first task was to hire a new manager, the second task was to trade catcher Gary Carter.

"We thought Buck would be a pretty good manager," Cook said of hiring Rodgers, who had managed the Milwaukee Brewers in 1980-82. "I didn't know Buck at all. I was instrumental in his hiring. He was our Triple-A manager.

"We didn't interview a whole lot of people. We did interview Earl Weaver. He'd been out of baseball a year or two."

That's true. Weaver had spent 15 and a half seasons as Orioles manager before retiring at age 52 following the 1982 season. Wouldn't you know it, the Orioles won the World Series in 1983 with Weaver gone. That's why he was available for the taking by another team. He agreed to be interviewed by the Expos.

"John McHale and I flew to Miami and met Weaver in one of the airport lounges," Cook said in late 2020. "All he could do was talk about the Orioles. He was great to talk with. He could tell a story, oh boy. He was the only one we did consider. I just felt that he didn't seem to me a fit for a young team in Montreal.

"We did consider Felipe Alou, who was a minor-league manager for us. I just felt we needed to go with more experience. Felipe was a managerial prospect but Buck was more than ready. I always felt that Felipe was better served by having more time in the minor leagues. He had never managed anywhere (in the majors). I felt that experience was important."

Wallach's exit was unpleasant

It was a shame. The departure of Expos third-base stalwart Tim Wallach was not pleasant. Rather unfortunate.

He was in his declining years with the team and had three years remaining on his contract worth about $10-million when general manager Dan Duquette, with nudging from vice-president of baseball operations Bill Stoneman and managing general partner Claude Brochu, began the process of doing everything he could do to move Wallach and his salary.

Eli had produced two consecutive seasons of similar hitting – not good. In 1991, he batted .225. In 1992, he hit .223. For a front-line player, who was in the lineup pretty much every day, this kind of production was not acceptable. He had only nine homers and 59 RBI in 1992 so it was easy for Duquette and Co. to try and get rid of his contract.

First, before making an attempt at trading his contract, the Expos tried to convince him to waive his 10-and-5 rights as a player so that they could expose him in the Nov. 17, 1992 expansion draft that would supply players for the two new teams, the Rockies and the Marlins.

On one condition, Wallach was willing to consider this waiving of his special status of longevity – at least 10 years in the majors, the last five with the same club. By that time, Wallach had accumulated 12+ seasons of service time with the Expos. He needed a concession from the Expos: financial compensation.

"If I'm going to waive my rights, there has to a financial offer," Wallach told me in an interview for Toronto's Globe and Mail as the clock ticked toward D-Day. "If there's no offer, I'm not going to do it. They know I'm not going to do it for nothing. I have a dollar amount in mind but I'm not going to say what it is."

As it turned out, he got no financial offer to tease him into waiving his rights. So what happened is that Wallach had to be protected by the Expos on the 15-man list submitted to Major League Baseball in advance of the draft.

At that time, I had written that Duquette was telling his aides to guard against releasing scouting information to other teams or the media, especially after the protected lists were submitted.

"Any leaks within our organization that undermine the collective interest of our baseball operation will not be tolerated," Duquette said in a memo to staff members. "Please report any transgressions you see or hear to me."

When Wallach declined to make himself available to be exposed in the draft, the Expos continued to try to deal him away. And finally, the Expos did trade him on Dec. 24, 1992 to his homestate Dodgers for little in return: minor-leaguer Tim Barker. A Christmas gift of sorts. I was in the touristy town of Stowe, Vermont on a Christmas holiday when I found out about the trade and I joined a conference call with Eli that day.

Even then, it wasn't an easy transaction. It was complicated. Wallach told the Expos he would accept a trade if the team would sell his Montreal-area condo. That was one other condition. Wallach also had to adhere to a Dodgers' request that he take a pay cut on the remainder of his contract. Hrmmph.

So on Christmas Eve in 1992, Wallach was gone. He was 35 years old.

In the spring of 1991, he became the first captain in the history of the Expos. Wallach's last few seasons with the Expos were marred by some unhappiness on his part in terms of his contract. I don't know how many times I wrote stories about Wallach and his contract negotiations. When Andres Galarraga received a three-year deal worth $6.85-million in late 1989, he was making more money than Wallach.

When reliever Tim Burke was given a three-year deal worth $6-million in late 1989, it ruffled Wallach's feathers at least to the point where his agent Rod Wright would personally complain to Expos management. And the sad part is that when Wallach still had three years remaining on his contract with the Expos and was traded, the Dodgers wanted him to take less money in a trade.

To this day, Wallach remains one of the most popular Expos of all time.

167

Anatomy of Walker's route to the Expos

It's a page out of a movie script.

Not one, but two residents of Portland, Oregon were on the hustings as scouts looking to sign Larry Walker in the fall of 1984. Can you imagine, two U.S.-based scouts from the same city in the Pacific Northwest wanting to put this Canadian prospect from British Columbia on the dotted line?

Not only that, two other Portland-based scouts, Larry D'Amato of the Pirates and Clint (Rocky) Granato of the Twins looked at Walker but passed on trying to sign him.

As for those two guys wanting to sign Walker, one was the better sleuth: on the one hand was Bob (Whitey) Rogers for the Expos. On the other hand was Andy Pienovi for the Cubs.

Although the exact date is unclear, it is believed that on Nov. 12, 1984, out of pure luck and coincidence, Rogers got on the phone at his home in Portland and called the Walker household in Maple Ridge, B.C.

Rogers called out of the blue to see how Larry Walker Jr. was doing since they last communicated. Larry Walker Sr. picked up the phone and started talking with Rogers, who worked full-time as a walking boss foreman/longshoreman on the waterfront in Portland and was a part-time scout covering the Pacific Northwest, including Idaho, and the Canadian Prairie Provinces for the Expos.

Nicknamed Whitey because of his white-blondish hair, Rogers had watched Walker Jr. play a number of times in tournaments and was merely following up by doing what an inquisitive scout would do. Rogers, as he told me one time, had been stalking Walker at tournaments for years. The first time Rogers saw Walker play, the kid was 14. Rogers saw the potential in Walker and kept travelling to see him play.

I love underdogs and characters behind the scenes and Rogers is one of them. Rogers had been a Little League coach in Southwest Portland and later became a scout under Granato with the Twins before taking on a stint of close to 10 years with the Expos.

The story goes that B-C.-based scout Wayne Norton had given Rogers the heads-up that Walker wanted to quit school, meaning he would be available to sign soon.

"The long story, he (Rogers) called the house," Walker Sr. was telling me. "It was just to see how Larry was doing when we informed him that Larry had decided to drop out of school. He just happened to call just to see how things were and it was by coincidence a couple of days after Larry quit.

"He (Rogers) got pretty excited and wanted to meet with us. I took a look at my schedule. With three brothers and myself playing or reffing hockey, I informed him that I had a day off in two days and the next one was in two weeks."

So you know what Rogers wanted to do – he took up Walker Sr.'s offer of meeting in two days. He sure wasn't waiting two weeks. He knew that it was important to beat out other teams who might be interested in the prodigy. And there was no way he was telling Pienovi of his plans!

"Bob made arrangements to fly to Vancouver and asked if we could meet about signing Larry," Walker Sr. said. "The Vancouver airport is in Richmond. We met two days later at the Airport Inn in Richmond. Richmond is across the bridge from Vancouver about 17 miles from Maple Ridge. We were at the hotel for probably less than an hour as I recall."

Larry Sr., his first wife Mary, Junior and Rogers were in the room. The official date for Walker's signing is listed as Nov. 14, 1984, which may be the date it was registered with MLB and the MLBPA.

Rogers and the Walker clan knew that as long as Junior was in school that he couldn't be signed. Prior to Rogers making that fateful phone call, Walker Jr. had no plans to do anything after he quit school, according to his father.

Twice in consecutive years, Walker Jr. had undergone goaltending tryouts with the Saskatchewan-based Regina Pats junior hockey team. In September of 1984 after being cut the second time by Pats GM Bob Strumm, Walker was asked if he wanted to go to a Tier Two team in Western Canada. So Walker and friend Rick Herbert stopped in the town, Swift Current, Sask., looked around, didn't like what they saw and Walker declined Strumm's offer.

"As long as he was attending school, they could not (sign him)," papa Walker said. "As soon as they found out he dropped out, then they were right on it. In the U.S., you had to be finished your Grade 12. In Canada, if you were not attending school, then they could talk before the Grade 12 year was completed. I believe he was in the 11th year, maybe the 12th at Maple Ridge high school."

As Mr. Walker recollected, Rogers came to the meeting only to talk contract.

"We didn't really talk about anything except that they had limited funds but wanted to sign him," Mr. Walker said. "He offered Larry $1,500 if he would sign. I looked at Larry and said, 'Do you think you want to play baseball for a living?' He said, 'Yes' so we signed the contract that day.

"I think they had first seen Larry play at a major tournament in Grand Forks, B.C. and then at the junior worlds in Kindersley, Sask. in 1984. By the way, Larry never received any messages from the Blue Jays. The Cubs called a few days after he signed with the Expos," Walker Sr. said.

Canada at world juniors in Kindersley in 1984	
USA 8	Canada 2
Canada 11	Dominican Republic 3
Canada 31	Belgium 2
Cuba 9	Canada 2
Nicaragua 8	Canada 0
Canada 7	Panama 3
Korea 6	Canada 2
Australia 6	Canada 4
Chinese Taipei 11	Canada 2
Canada didn't qualify for the playoff round.	

That's right, Pienovi was too late but you had to hand it to him for at least calling the Walker house. Pienovi had obtained a master's degree in education from the University of Portland and was a teacher and baseball coach while adding scouting roles as time passed on. He also scouted for the Twins, Royals, Padres, Dodgers and finally the Blue Jays, according to his obituary.

"Andy was pissed at me," said Don Archer, a coach for Walker in 1984. "He said, 'Why didn't you call me and tell me that Larry was going to sign?' I told him I didn't know."

Larry Walker Sr. remembers when the Cubs scout called the house.

"He asked, 'How is Larry?' We said he signed with the Expos and that was it. If I recall, it was a week or two after the signing. I don't think it was much of a serious pursuit (by the Cubs). They were just checking."

As for the Blue Jays, their lack of interest in Walker was puzzling to say the least. Here he was a Canadian in the Jays' backyard with some potential and the Blue Jays had no interest? I was told in late 2020 that the Blue Jays backed off on Walker, not because of any lack of talent but because they were concerned about off-the-field intangibles such as partying too much. But teenagers love to drink and have a good time, don't they?

"His reputation hurt him," said a former Blue Jays scout. "I think his reputation kind of hurt. You know, with that life, having a few beers. It's one of those things. I did it. You know when you are with men."

In the next breath, the scout said, "He was a great athlete."

The Pirates were among the teams that also took a pass on Walker, not because of any party-animal tendencies but because they thought he was slow afoot.

"My impression was that he was a below-average runner. For Pittsburgh, he had to be able to run," D'Amato said. "To be honest, Walker wasn't very impressive. His athletic ability was borderline.

"The Pirates philosophy was based upon the Branch Rickey theory. (1) If you cannot run, you cannot score runs. (2) If you cannot throw, you could not throw runners out. (3) If you buy the bat, you shall die by the bat. Simple as that.

"Pitchers were simple. Look for hard-throwing pitchers with good arm extension and balance. Fastball, curve and change. I used this theory all throughout my scouting career.

"Walker was a raw, very green type player. He only played baseball in the summer. He was an athlete. He looked like a football player, very strong. I give him credit, when he came to the Rockies, he made himself into a player."

The Grand Forks International is some fancy-dan tournament. Founded by Larry Seminoff, it has attracted teams from all over North America, Cuba and other countries. It's a "senior" tournament, meaning adult-aged players. For all intents and purposes, it's a men's event. The tournament is an "open" age group, said tournament organizer Steve Boutang.

"The teams that attend are made up of college players and senior men's calibre, ex-pros, pros between contracts, and guys who are hanging on or trying to play their way into a pro contract," Boutang said. "Lots and lots of high-level players. It's the best amateur tournament in Canada as far as I'm concerned.

"In those days, the GFI was held over Labour Day weekend. Larry Seminoff was left scrambling for a team to fill in. He contacted Wayne Norton of Baseball B.C. Wayne said he would try to cobble together some players. Two hours after he spoke to Larry Seminoff, Wayne called back to say he had enough players to come up with. They were called the B.C. All Stars."

Seminoff recalls that there was no vacancy and no team had dropped out but another team was wanted.

"Baseball B.C. initially said they weren't sure they could send a team," Seminoff said. "By luck, they did. At the 11th hour, they said they would come. We needed another team and we were counting on Team B.C. to be that team.

"What I remember is that Larry Walker – we knew he was a hot potato. When it came to scouts in the major leagues, the Expos were at the top of the list. The Expos were all over it. We knew Walker was coming, we knew the Expos would have their people there. The Giants were here, the Blue Jays were here, the Cubs, too.

"That was the first year that I recall that major-league scouts showed interest and the main reason was that Walker was playing in the tournament. He became one of the best players in Major League Baseball."

No doubt about it, Walker was indeed the player scouts were watching.

Walker was 17 at the time in Grand Forks and playing against players older than him. Teams such as the Alaska Goldpanners, Seattle Studs and Lewiston-Clarkson Truckers, a highly rated college team from Idaho, have come and played in the tournament. Besides Walker, such future major leaguers as John Olerud, Tim Lincecum and Josh Beckett played in the tournament. The event is an economic boon for the little town, bringing in about $1-million for the week, except for the 2020 pandemic year.

"I told Larry that year that he was going to be a good player," said Archer, who was his coach with the Coquitlam Reds during the 1984 regular season and in Grand Forks as a co-coach along with Norm Caig and Sandy Robertson. "Larry said, 'I don't know about that.' I said, 'Wait and see. You're going to be good.' Oh yeah, everybody did (thought he would be good).

"We were playing a team in Bellingham, Washington in an exhibition game and the Cubs scout Andy Pienovi was there. Larry buried one in the centre-field scoreboard.

"Larry was a competitive guy. He could really hit. I mean, he could hit. He was a natural hitter, he could run, he had a strong arm. He was what you'd call a five-tool player. You know, I mean he was unbelievable. He had the work ethic which I tried to instill in our guys. He started to show at the end of the year, he started to gel.

"At the Grand Forks tournament, he started to really stand out. Against the Washington State University summer team, Larry hit a long home run and Bobo Brayton their coach, said, 'Who the heck is that guy?' We played Lewiston & Clark, a small college team, a really good team, with mostly dropouts from Division 1 schools. We beat them 6-4 and Larry hit two home runs. Their coach (Ed Cheff) went off on his team, saying, 'That fuckin' high school team beat you guys.' Little did he know that Larry would go on to win a few batting titles in the majors."

Not to mention, get elected into the Canadian Baseball Hall of Fame in St. Marys, Ontario and the National Baseball Hall of Fame in Cooperstown, N.Y.

The story goes that Walker and Rogers met secretly underneath a grandstand in Grand Forks to lay the ground work for a contract. Rogers was determined that he wanted to sign Walker for the Expos.

"They were pretty darn serious in Grand Forks," Seminoff said of an impending contract signing between Walker and Rogers. "Something did happen here. Both parties left Grand Forks that something was going to happen. I remember saying hello to Rogers in passing, only in welcoming him and that it was nice to see a major-league scout at the tournament."

This is how Archer assessed Walker in the Grand Forks event: "He was average in the first two games, did not struggle, played strong defence, went off in the third and fourth game and the rest is history. Larry never really struggled at any time."

Walker has been heard on television over the years, talking about the time he drove back home to Maple Ridge from Grand Forks and that he told himself he needed to decide on a future in either hockey or baseball. He dumped hockey and opted for baseball.

Walker had arrived in the Coquitlam Reds camp in early 1984, a reluctant visitor. Archer used the power of persuasion and the proverbial twisting of the arm in February of '84 to convince Walker to come out and play for his team. In 1983, Walker was talented enough to play for B.C.'s entry at the 1983 Canadian bantam championship in Ontario so Archer knew of his potential.

Archer placed five phone calls to the Walker residence, two to Larry Jr. and three to his parents.

"Finally, he showed up, the rest is history. He came out to one of our early March outdoor workouts at Mundy Park. It's not a BS story. If it wasn't for those five phone calls, he probably doesn't have a baseball career," Archer said. "In his own mind, he thought his athletic career was over. He was going to play softball. He was our best player. He played short and he pitched, mostly in relief. The best athlete on the team is usually the shortstop.

"In the B.C. championship that August, he threw a no-hitter against Richmond Auto Body. One time we played North Shore, a rival team, and we won 4-3. We brought Larry in to pitch in the bottom of the sixth. He struck out six in a row to finish the game."

Of course, he got the save.

Interesting, too, that two months earlier in Kindersley at the World Youth Baseball Classic tournament, Walker didn't have a banner event. But Expos scout Jim Fanning saw him there and was impressed with how he handled himself defensively and at the plate.

In Kindersley, Walker started off 0-for-8 at the plate and finished 7-for-33, which comes in at an average of .212. Not that impressive. The good thing is that Walker got a wee bit better and better as the tournament went on. In a 31-2 romp over Belgium, Walker hit a home run over the right-centre field fence. He finished the tournament with four RBI.

"The home run brought Walker out of a slump he's been in since the tournament began," Don Thomson wrote in the Kindersley Clarion newspaper.

"I wish I would have only hit .212 at the world championship and have the career Larry had," said Martin Robitaille, a teammate of Walker's who hit a dazzling .388 at the worlds.

"I do remember that Larry actually did play some shortstop at the time of the event," said Baseball Canada executive director Jim Baba, who was a guest coach for Team Canada in those days along with his job as director of parks and recreation for the town of Kindersley. "I know he played more positions than that during the event. I also remember him drawing big-time interest from scouts at the time as that event was well attended by scouts and fans alike."

2009 Inductee
Canadian Baseball Hall of Fame and Museum

Larry Walker

Kindersley tournament chairman Earl Berard remembers Walker and Fanning in particular.

"Fanning was instrumental in picking up Larry (for the Expos). I remember being in the office and we received a lot of calls from the Expos. They wanted Jim Fanning back in Montreal," Berard said.

Why did the Expos want Fanning to return to Montreal? Berard had "no idea." I do know that about a month later, Fanning was hired to replace the fired Bill Virdon as Expos manager to finish out the '84 season.

Berard said that it was a coup that the small village of Kindersley could even pull off a tournament of that stature. Berard told his wife that he was going to make a presentation to Baseball Canada and she said, "You must be nuts."

Berard and a committee made a presentation in October of 1981 at a Baseball Canada meeting in Saint John, New Brunswick, where officials from the Expos and Blue Jays were also present. So the Kindersley group had earned the right to be the Canadian host for the tournament if the International Amateur Baseball Federation was to choose Canada.

The next hurdle was to impress IABA executives that this small town in Saskatchewan could successfully put on a great show. So Berard, fellow Kindersley committee executive Jerry Flanagan and another 15 or so people, including wives, travelled to Holland to an IABA meeting, while making it a holiday at the same time. It sure helped that IABA vice-president Cas Pielak of Regina was pushing all the right buttons to convince his committee members that Kindersley would be a good choice.

"First thing that caught their eyes was when all of us and our wives walked into the meeting. We walked in with red jackets (Canadian colours) or top coats. We were all dressed the same," Flanagan said.

"There wasn't a word said for five minutes. Then after about 15 minutes, they said, 'You got it.' That's all there was to it."

Meaning tiny Kindersley was awarded the 1984 world youth tournament. That was in January, 1982, meaning Berard, Flanagan, marketing specialist John Boquist, transportation manager Bill Sullivan and their group had two and a half years to lay the foundation for a successful event by getting diamonds up to snuff, erecting new and bigger grandstands, rounding up several thousand volunteers and arranging for communities in and around Kindersley to billet the incoming teams from Panama, the Dominican Republic, Korea, Belgium, Canada, Chinese Taipei, Nicaragua, Australia, the U.S. and Cuba.

For close to 10 days prior to the tournament, Walker and 29 other prospects from across Canada were invited to a tryout camp in Kindersley. These prospects played against local senior teams like the Eston Elks and Kindersley Royals in exhibition games to be assessed by general manager Harvey Bailie, head coach Jim Ridley and assistant coaches Tom Erasmus, Rand Rasmussen and Marc Gélinas, a Pittsburgh Pirates minor-league prospect.

In the end, Walker was one of 18 who survived the final cuts. The other 17 were Robitaille, Barry Petrachenko, Dan Demchuk, Steve Hodges, Cam Lane, Christian Cantin, Carlo Boniferro, Winston Brown, Loris Mazzocca, Galen Sonntag, Mike Dorrington, Yvon Coriveau, Bill Vanderwel, Darryl Rowley, Michael Cariel, Daniel Desgagne and Peter Ballance.

Walker and the other 29 had to live through some gnashing of teeth as the Team Canada brass made its cuts. Some 12 players had to be told they would not make the team for the tournament, causing a little bit of drama.

"I know that all the cuts were done in the arena stands – very Canadian," Petrachenko recalled.

Corriveau was one of a number of hockey prospects invited to the baseball camp. He went on to a career in the NHL and other leagues after a two-season stint in junior hockey with the Toronto Marlboros. Petrachenko thought it was pretty cool that three guys from Welland, Ont. made the team: himself, Corriveau and Lane.

"Which is pretty amazing when you think about it," Petrachenko said. "That summer has stuck with me over the years. Kindersley was a very small town but they were terrific hosts. It was very much like Groundhog Day – wake up, walk to breakfast at a local restaurant, walk to the park, practise till noon, shower and hop on the bus for a three+ hour ride to play a team in the Saskatchewan senior league."

So each day, as Petrachenko jokingly said, it was "rinse and repeat"– the same ritual. Walker, Petrachenko and Co. were in Kindersley for about a month, including the tryout camp. The parks they played in were terrific. Some had skinned infields and fans were parked around the perimeter of the outfield fence in a sort of a tailgate party watching games. Other venues had modern facilities and medium-sized stadiums.

Of course, the calibre of ball was excellent with a strong mix of teenagers and college players. Among those who found their way to the majors from that Kindersley tournament along with Walker were Jack McDowell, fellow Americans Albert Belle and Gregg Olson, Juan Guzman of the Dominican Republic and Australians Graeme Lloyd and Mark Ettles. Lloyd, like Walker, played for the Expos.

For a kid like Petrachenko getting his taste of some serious competition, "it was an unbelievable way to spend a summer."

Walker, Petrachenko and their teammates saw the charm in their surroundings. The Canadian clubhouse was the dressing room of the local Kindersley senior hockey team and it was located, get this, at the top of the stands in the arena.

"Every day, I wondered what it must be like for that team to walk up through the crowd to get to their room between periods," Petrachenko said, smiling. "The cool of the arena was welcomed after practice but the room itself was hot and cramped. Showering only provided short-lived relief as you were sweating again within seconds.

"Being in a national environment for the extended camp was also pretty eye-opening. It was the first time I had seen my peers chewing or dipping tobacco."

Petrachenko would see many of the guys on the team or at the tryout camp when they would cross paths at the Canada Games, at national team camps, at school and in the Cape Cod league, even at hockey meetings years later.

When the tournament commenced, "a blur of games" faced Team Canada and their competitors. By this time, Walker and his teammates had moved in with their billet families.

"It was on those bus rides (back and forth from Kindersley) that I got to know Larry a little bit better – two kids away from home trying to figure it all out.

"Black Jack McDowell shut us down with his slider on opening night in front of a packed house," Petrachenko said. "We were mediocre as a team at the event, with lots of guys in new positions and lots of pressure on us all for really the first time in baseball."

Said Boquist: "The part that played a huge role was that each country had its own team billeted in communities. That was a real decision maker, it was absolutely a great concept, it was absolutely great. That community was cheering for its team. There were times when we really questioned ourselves if we had the ability to pull it off but the weather was on our side. Every day was absolutely gorgeous for 10 days. We didn't have a hiccup."

Okay, there was the problem with the picky, demanding Cubans,

Photo supplied by Martin Robitaille

This is Canada's entry at the world youth tournament in Kindersley, Saskatchewan in 1984. Front row, left to right, are Carlo Boniferro, Peter Ballance, Mike Dorrington, Darryl Rowley, Winston Brown, Martin Robitaille, Steve Hodges and coach Randy Rasmussen. Centre row: head coach Jim Ridley, Christian Cantin, Daniel Desgagne, Cam Lane, Loris Mazzocca, Dan Demchuk, Barry Petrachenko and coach Tom Erasmus. Back row: pitching coach Marc Gelinas, Larry Walker, Galen Sonntag, Bill Vanderwel, Michel Carle and Yvon Corriveau.

who, when they arrived, told the organizers that they didn't want to stay in their designated billet communities of Smiley/Flaxcombe. They demanded that they be put up somewhere in Kindersley. Boquist told me that "we could have sent them home. We had every right to do that."

Flanagan, when he heard of the Cubans' discontent, was discontent himself, showing up where the Cubans were temporarily staying and rapping on the door to tell them in no uncertain terms, "I can invite you to stay in Saskatoon."

The Cubans weren't enthralled on staying two hours away in Saskatoon. Then Flanagan and Co. suggested to the Cubans that they could stay in beds put up at the town hall in Blackstone. The Cubans said no. Then the Cubans agreed to stay in trailers that had been set up in Kindersley.

Then the Cubans didn't like the trailers and wanted to be billeted, after all, in a community nearby. By that point, the community that was supposed to billet them in the first place, said no to the Cubans so the Cubans ended up staying in trailers the whole tournament, using washrooms at a nearby curling rink. Go figure.

As far as the Canadians were concerned, Kerrobert was fine.

"The town was all in, and they made us feel like real superstars," Robitaille said. "We stayed with host families and we were very well taken care of. It was hot and windy.

"But Kindersley was a small town on the Prairies with very little excitement. There might have been a disappointment with the fact that the tournament was not in a more exotic place.

"The hopes were high for the Canadian team and the training camp was very competitive. Jim Ridley was a great leader."

In the end, the Cubans, led by shortstop sensation Omar Linares, won the championship, despite their dissatisfaction with accommodations.

"I have fond memories of the tournament and being chairman. It was unbelievable that we did it," Berard said. "We had about 1,400 volunteers. I'm the only person living on earth to chair a world youth championship and win the gold medal for Team Canada (as business manager) and that was in 1991. It was never done before or after."

Following the worlds, Walker returned to his home province to play junior ball for Archer and the Coquitlam Reds, located some 20 minutes from Maple Ridge. Then about a month later, the Grand Forks tournament came along.

I made many attempts to get a hold of Rogers' family in Oregon to try and find out more about this scout but all trails were closed. Rogers died in the late 1990s from what I was told. I had talked with him about Walker in 1992 but somehow, I never kept his phone number. From what I was told, the Expos fired him following the 1985 season.

D'Amato told me that Rogers "disappeared" and people heard "hide nor tale of him" and that he had moved to Washington and later Hawaii.

Rogers would tell me that he first started scouting Walker when he was only 14, meaning he would have seen him play when Walker was playing under the late coach Lorne Upsdell.

"When my dad brought Larry up in bronco ball, he was 10 years old. He was just an average player but two years later, he got better and better. You could see the power in his hitting, his ability to field and his pitching was outstanding," said Danny Upsdell, son of Lorne Upsdell, who played with and against Walker. "There was one tournament, the Don Brue tournament, and Larry hit nine home runs over the fence at Pitt Meadows field."

No word of a lie. This is not hearsay or one of those rumours about Walker's nine home runs. It's true and the stuff of legends. It's a tournament record that has never been broken. The headline in the Maple Ridge News went this way:

Larry Walker Jr. still holds Victoria Day home-run record

The newspaper revealed that the left-handed hitting Walker hit his nine dingers in a mere 13 at-bats. Long before major-league teams were obsessed with The Shift against mostly left-handed batters, Walker's power resulted in the Walker Switch, meaning the opposing infield shifted to the left. The first time Walker saw the switch, he called a time-out and scooted down to the third-base coach's box and asked Lorne Upsdell if he could bunt to the unguarded bag at third.

"Nobody's there. I'll get a double," Walker told Upsdell in his plea to bunt.

"Larry, go back and hit the ball," Upsdell replied.

"The way he hit the ball, his swing was so even. He hit the ball so hard," Danny Upsdell said in general about Walker. "He would crank the ball and the outfielders didn't know where the ball would go. When he came up to bat, the outfielders would back up and move back.

"When Larry was pitching, when he was on, he was on. When he was playing mosquito, my dad always told me the story that when Larry was nine years old, he'd always go up to my dad and say, 'I wanna pitch, I wanna pitch.' He was a fair teammate. He was never conceited. Nobody guessed that he would make the majors. I don't think people saw any indications he would make the majors."

A few weeks after Walker signed a contract for Rogers, the Expos sent Walker a plane ticket and off he flew to West Palm Beach, Florida for spring training in 1985. Just a few weeks before he flew out, some of his real-close friends gathered at a hall in Maple Ridge to send him off.

"We were there to wish him luck in pro baseball. Larry's girlfriend at the time was there," Danny Upsdell said.

Walker was homesick for awhile at spring training but he got over it. To make up for missing home, Walker made daily collect calls which the Walker clan "gladly accepted" when the operator interceded.

"That's why the phone rang every day. We just sat at home, answering the phone on a daily basis," Mr. Walker said. "There was a big telephone bill that month but he withstood the homesickness."

Walker would spend the 1985 season at Class A Utica in the New York-Penn league where he hit a paltry .223. He sure improved after that. In 1986, Walker hit 33 homers and drove in 90 runs in a combined season with West Palm Beach and Burlington, Iowa. According to writer Carl Gusten, Walker, Cubs legend Billy Williams and Paul Molitor are the only players, who played out of Burlington to get inducted into Cooperstown.

Walker was almost as good in 1987 with Jacksonville Double-A with 26 homers and 83 ribbies.

Walker was forced to sit out the entire 1988 season due to a knee injury sustained in Hermosillo in the Mexican winter league.

"He was running to home on a play," his father told me of this injury. "He had shoes with plastic cleats on because his metal cleats broke and that is all they could get on a last-minute call. He slid across the plate and when he hit the dirt behind the plate, he went over forward and hyper-extended his knee, causing the anterior ligament to break."

Submitted photo
Larry Walker
in Burlington, Iowa
Class A

Just think, Walker's rise to the top and a Cooperstown nod began when he made his first appearance with the Expos on Aug. 16, 1989 after he spent part of the season at Indianapolis Triple-A.

Walker went on to play until the 2005 season when he packed it in. Because of what? Knee injuries. The hockey injuries, playing on the turf in Montreal and the knee injury in the Mexican league caught up to him.

Today, he lives a quiet, elusive life, going back and forth from his homes in West Palm Beach and the idyllic resort community of Los Cabos, a municipality located at the southern tip of Mexico's Baja California Peninsula, in the state of Baja California Sur. It encompasses the two towns of Cabo San Lucas and San José del Cabo linked by a 20-mile resort corridor of beach-front properties.

I wrote Walker a typed-up letter to his house in West Palm Beach, requesting an interview in 2020 but I never heard back from him.

"He's private and we certainly respect that," said marathoner Brent Underdahl, Walker's growing-up friend from Maple Ridge. "We were buddies when young. We spend time with him in Cabos – as neighbours."

In either location, Walker has been working on his induction speech for Cooperstown whenever that might be. Hopefully, he will make note of saying thanks to Bob Rogers in that speech. You can bet he will also mention Lorne Upsdell.

Back in 1999 while he was employed by the Rockies, Walker paid tribute to Upsdell by having someone build a specially made Louisville Slugger bat ensemble.

On the bat are these chiseled words from Walker: "To Lorne, congratulations on all you have done for baseball in Ridge Meadows."

And behind-the-scenes people like Archer could be worthy mentions in the speech. During one of Walker's appearances in Seattle as a member of the Rockies, Archer arranged for Walker to participate in a commercial, promoting the Coquitlam Reds. When Walker got word that he was selected into Cooperstown, Archer sent him a congratulatory note and Walker replied with an email, thanking Archer and the team.

Walker's billet

Sandy Campbell and her family in Kindersley billeted Larry Walker for the 1984 world youth tournament and they have fond memories.

"Larry was pretty young. My husband Jimmy and I enjoyed having him," Mrs. Campbell said. "We thought he was a fantastic guy. He was a nice young man. Very polite. He was just like a son of our own. He was pretty young to be away from home. He was on his own. We made him feel comfortable. We kind of spoiled him. There's a baseball he signed for me and I still have it."

"I was concerned once we got it. Oh man, I'll tell you, I wondered if we could really do it. I don't know how many trips I made to Kindersley for meetings. They put on a helluva show, one of best there was. I had already talked to the IABA executive before they went to Baseball Canada. Japan wanted it but they dropped out of it."

– Cas Pielak of Regina, Sask., who worked behind the scenes in 1982-84 to help make the 1984 world youth tournament a reality and a success in Kindersley. Pielak was a VP with IABA and had a lot of clout with fellow board members in getting the 1984 event approved.

MacKenzie had a hand in landing Walker

Would Larry Walker have been signed by the Expos had Bill MacKenzie not intervened on a sun-splashed day in July of 1984 in the small town of Kindersley, Saskatchewan?

If he had not intervened, Expos scout Bob Rogers of Portland, Oregon would still have signed him late that fall but how MacKenzie got involved sure makes for interesting fodder.

MacKenzie was the technical director for Baseball Canada when Walker played for Team Canada at the World Youth Baseball Classic in Kindersley. MacKenzie had never seen Walker play before. When MacKenzie saw the skill set that Walker produced, he went to the phone almost immediately to call Expos scouting director Jim Fanning in Montreal.

That's true.

"Hey, Jim, there's a kid here playing in Kindersley you should have a look at. He's a diamond in the rough. His name is Larry Walker. He's a horse, athletically," MacKenzie told Fanning.

"OK, I'll come out and see him," Fanning replied. Fanning had never seen Walker play before either.

So MacKenzie got into his rental car and drove close to four hours to Calgary to pick Fanning up at the airport to deliver him to Kindersley and vice-versa when Fanning returned to Montreal after watching a few games. Can you imagine – MacKenzie saw a future for Walker and drove close to four hours to get Fanning so that the Expos would get a closer look.

"I didn't mind doing it," MacKenzie said of picking up Fanning, "because of the respect I had for him and the Expos. Jim was only at the tournament maybe three or four days. When we drove back to Calgary,

Jim was very excited by what he saw about Walker. Jim called up Bob Rogers and told Rogers to sit on Walker and not to let him out of his sights."

MacKenzie was a little biased toward the Expos because he had been a scout, front-office assistant and jack of all trades for the Expos through much of the 1970s and 1980s until he switched to Baseball Canada in 1987 before returning to the Expos in 1989 until 1993.

What MacKenzie did in favour of the Expos was made at the expense of the late Jim Ridley, a Blue Jays scout, who was also Walker's coach in Kindersley. Imagine. You can't make this stuff up. Ridley was this-close to Walker all through the tryout camp and the ensuing tournament and for some reason, didn't think he was a prospect. Hrrmph.

Baseball Canada photo
Bill MacKenzie

"The funny part is that Ridley was right on top of Walker, sitting on him. As far as I know, he never wrote a (scouting) report on him. He didn't even write him up," MacKenzie said. "Rids is dead now but I would have liked to have found out from him what he thought when he first saw Walker.

"I don't know how these teams messed up on Walker. Rids saw him every day in Kindersley. How could you not see the potential? As big as he was, Walker could run like hell.

"Larry showed up at the tryout camp as a shortstop. That lasted about one day. He didn't have the quick actions to play in the infield. He was an athlete but not at that position. He had a really good arm but he just didn't have the body to play shortstop.

"It was like Gary Carter out of high school. You knew he wasn't going to be a shortstop. He was very athletic but he didn't have much range at shortstop."

In consultation with Ridley, MacKenzie suggested that Walker be worked out in the outfield in Kindersley.

When I told MacKenzie that Walker started the world tournament 0-for-8 and finished up a little bit better at 7-for-33 (.212), MacKenzie replied, "A lot of those were strikeouts. He swung through a lot of balls. He swung and missed a lot in batting practice. He was a hockey player.

"No question Walker had the potential. We knew he had some upside. He had the size and the great arm and great running speed. He could run. He had the bat speed. Thing is he had this really nice swing. He had the quick hands. He just persevered."

183

MacKenzie was also instrumental in getting the Expos to look at a "skinny, young fart" who also became a Hall of Famer – Tim Raines in 1977. An anonymous woman called MacKenzie up at the Expos spring training facility in Daytona Beach, Fla. to suggest that someone go and see Raines at a high school game nearby.

MacKenzie took in the game and saw, as he saw in Walker and Carter, that Raines wasn't suitable for playing shortstop but he sure saw a lot of potential. On MacKenzie's recommendation, Raines was signed out of the Expos front office against the wishes of Florida area scout Bill Adair, who for some reason, didn't see much value in Raines. Hrrmph.

MacKenzie was also the scout who saw potential in Matt Stairs of Fredericton, New Brunswick. MacKenzie signed Stairs for $15,000 in 1989 in Marysville, N.B. and Stairs climbed the ladder to a pretty solid MLB career, including a short stint with the Expos. MacKenzie tried Stairs out at what position? You're right: shortstop, although he never played there in the majors.

This baseball-wise man of MacKenzie lives in Brockville, Ont. with his wife Donna and looks back fondly at a life that took him all over North America and the world as a player, executive, scout or as a Team Canada coach.

I first ran across MacKenzie in late 1978 when I lobbied him and fellow Baseball Canada executive Paul Lavigne to have the South Korean national team play an exhibition game in 1979 in Sudbury, Ont. where I worked and played baseball - against the Nickel Region Senior Baseball League all-stars as part of a cross-Canada tour.

By late 1978, I had left Sudbury for the Ottawa Journal but while I was in Ottawa in early 1979, MacKenzie and Lavigne informed me that Sudbury was placed on the South Korean tour. I was elated. I even went back and played in the game played before several thousand fans and won easily by the South Koreans 17-4.

Because I didn't play in Sudbury that year, I was a late-inning replacement in the game against South Korea, turning a double play with future NHL defenceman Neil Belland.

Another story: in 1984, the same year MacKenzie saw Walker in Kindersley, I invited MacKenzie, a Team Canada coach at that time, to come to Sudbury, where I was based again, to conduct a tryout camp for prospects. He came up and the plan was to recommend one prospect for a camp held later that year. We put a number of teenagers through drills and MacKenzie picked a lanky pitcher by the name of Rick Kilganon, who never went anywhere in the game, but it was all a memorable experience.

Another story: in the fall of 1989, I invited MacKenzie to be part of a two-pronged event on the same day in the Upper Ottawa Valley involving the 20th anniversary of the Douglas Expos winning the South Renfrew Senior Baseball League championship.

I was a member of that team and I organized a reunion that involved both a pick-up game in the afternoon at the diamond in Douglas and then a party at night at the Best Western Inn in Renfrew with MacKenzie as the guest speaker.

So I arranged to meet MacKenzie in Renfrew and as we drove north out of that town, he suggested we had to drop into the bar at Butson's Valley Motor Hotel on the outskirts of town on Highway 17 for a pint or two of Blue. I agreed, although it meant we would be late for the game. All in fun in the name of friendship. MacKenzie was the pitcher for one side in the game, I was the pitcher for the other side.

MacKenzie spent a total of 14 years in the Expos' organization in multi-faceted roles, seven years in the employ of Baseball Canada as a national senior team coach and technical director and eight years as a scout for the Colorado Rockies. Not to be forgotten, MacKenzie was a former Expos' minor-league player and a former Expos' minor-league coach.

"I was with the Expos two different times for seven years each. I was with Baseball Canada for seven years. I don't know if that was lucky or unlucky," MacKenzie said. "Then I was with the Rockies for more than seven years, eight to be exact."

MacKenzie was born in Pictou, N.S. but made his way at a young age to Sarnia, Ont. where he started playing baseball. The Detroit Tigers, especially bird-dog scout Harry Moore, gave the catching prospect a lot of looks when he played at St. Clair County Community College in Port Huron, Mich. near Sarnia. Those looks were enough to prompt the Tigers, after much persistence by Moore, to sign MacKenzie to a contract in 1966.

"Harry kept recommending me to the Tigers," MacKenzie said.

The Tigers put MacKenzie on a bus in Port Huron and sent him to Lakeland, Fla. for seasoning. The trip was 22 hours long to Tiger Town. He would go on to play in such exotic locales as Statesville, N.C, Lakeland, Erie, Pa. and Dubuque, Iowa. One of his roommates he recalls with some amusement was John D'Auria, who had returned from a stint in Vietnam and was never the same mentally.

"I drank a few pitchers of beer and ate some pizza with John," MacKenzie said. "He was funny."

During spring training in 1969, the first for the Expos, the Montreal organization was looking for bodies so the Tigers sent MacKenzie's contract to the Expos.

Even though the Expos had killer Bs behind the plate in John Bateman, John Boccabella and Ron Brand, MacKenzie was happy to be with Montreal.

"You being a Canadian, you have a good opportunity," somebody with the Expos told him.

MacKenzie is part of a piece of interesting Expos' trivia that I didn't know about until I sat down with him in Brockville and stuck a tape recorder in front of him.

"Ernie McAnally and I formed the first battery in a regular-season game for the Expos' organization in their first season of operation in 1969," MacKenzie revealed with a lot of satisfaction. "Ernie was the pitcher, I was the catcher. I even got a hit. Joe Mook hit the foul pole in that game for us and the place went nuts.

"That year, the Expos only had one minor-league affiliate and that was the one in West Palm Beach, Fla.," MacKenzie said. "Then the next day, the major-league club played its first game in New York. How's that for trivia?"

West Palm Beach Expos owner Freddy Whitacre, who respects MacKenzie like he is a son all these years later, brought up an interesting tale when I talked to him.

"Bill had a shoebox full of baseball cards, including Pete Rose cards, and he gave them to my son Michael," Whitacre said.

MacKenzie's tenure with the Expos' organization as a player was literally shattered when he was bowled over at the plate by a Lakeland runner halfway through the 1969 season. One of the runner's shoulders rammed into MacKenzie's right shoulder.

MacKenzie spent part of a day in a hospital recovering and tried to return weeks later but found he had no juice on the balls throwing to second base.

"I could throw batting practice for an hour but I had nothing on the ball to second," MacKenzie said.

So what did Mackenzie do? He returned to the Tigers' system and spent three seasons as a minor-league coach, including time with the likes of Jim Leyland, Bill Lajoie, Lance Nichols, Max Lanier and Stubby Overmire. Following the 1972 season, MacKenzie was let go but it wasn't long afterward that he called Expos scouting director Mel Didier, seeking employment.

"Bill was multi-gifted," Didier told me a few years ago. "We used him in multiple situations, in various places, in the office, as a technical instructor, as a manager, as a coach, as a scout. He had a good way about him with young players. He was a true, solid coach, especially in catching.

"People respected him. He had a knack for pointing out things that other people didn't see. He called a spade a spade. He was a reliable person who I feel was a big part of the Expos the first few years of their existence."

As part of his multi-tasking duties, MacKenzie worked often with Paul Shubin out of the Expos' office on the mezzanine level at the Dominion Square building in downtown Montreal and later at Olympic Stadium. In unison, the two would produce three organizational programs on franchise news once a month.

Other catchers MacKenzie taught along with Carter were Barry Foote and Bobby Ramos. Some of the other prospects he found or recommended besides Raines, Walker and Stairs were David Palmer and he also coached future Expos in Dawson, Larry Parrish, Warren Cromartie, Dale Murray, Rick Down, Jerry White and Tony Scott.

"When Gary Carter was elected into Cooperstown, he mentioned me in his speech. I went online and pulled up his speech to see what he said," MacKenzie said. "When I was teaching him how to catch in Cocoa Beach, Fla., his work ethic was second to none. He kept me in the rain and dark, working him out.

"Gary had very quick hands from behind the game. He'd squat. Dennis Blair threw fastballs right by Gary until he got used to squatting back there. It was very unique – with Carter's body size, he kept his arms inside his knees, instead of holding them out. He locked himself up. He was such a quick learner to get the hands out in front."

As for Parrish, MacKenzie said, "He was signed as an outfielder but we converted him to third base. We thought his arm and feet were better for third base. He had that mental toughness you don't see in many people. He played hurt a lot."

MacKenzie recalls with some glee being in the Expos war room at the 1973 winter meetings in New York when the club was talking trade with the Dodgers.

"We had a chance to get Willie Davis. They wanted Mike Marshall. Willie Davis was a nutcase," MacKenzie said. "We looked at manager Gene Mauch and said, 'Can you control Willie Davis'? And Mauch said, 'I can handle him.' "

As the 1970s came to a close, the people running Baseball Canada began bugging MacKenzie off and on to join its organization out of Ottawa on River Road in Vanier. He called his father for advice and the elder MacKenzie said, "Do what is best for you."

So Mackenzie moved from Montreal to Ottawa and became technical director and head coach of Canada's national senior team. MacKenzie jumped head-first into the job, implemented coaching-certification courses and developed coaching manuals when he wasn't coaching the national team.

"I didn't know any of the players so I didn't know what I was getting into but I realized it was a golden opportunity to develop the program," Mackenzie said. "When I took over, Canada was ranked 11th in the world in men's baseball and when I left, we were fourth."

MacKenzie was barely into his tenure in 1978 with the national team when the contingent headed to Italy for the amateur World Series tournament. Mackenzie also guided Canada at the 1979 Pan American Games in San Juan, Puerto Rico and the 1984 Summer Olympics in Los Angeles, where baseball was a demonstration sport. Canada went 1-2 in L.A., upsetting hotshot Japan in the process. The Olympic club

187

roster included Stairs, who signed with the Expos five years later.

As time went on with Baseball Canada, MacKenzie was getting frustrated with his superiors. One day, Fanning just so happened to call MacKenzie out of the blue. This was years after the world tournament in Kindersley.

"Bill, just calling to see how things are going in Ottawa," Fanning said.

"Oh, Jim, not very good," MacKenzie replied.

MacKenzie let it be known he'd like to work for the Expos again so Fanning arranged for GM Murray Cook to call MacKenzie. Cook promptly said, "Bill, get your ass to Montreal and we'll have lunch."

It wasn't long before MacKenzie was back with the Expos and to facilitate the move, Cook said he could stay in Ottawa and work out of there. He was in charge of Canada, upstate New York, Vermont, Maine and New Hampshire, mostly during the reign of scouting director Gary Hughes. He remained with the Expos until near the end of the 1993 season when he was fired by Hughes' successor Kevin Malone.

MacKenzie hooked on shortly thereafter with Colorado and his coverage included all of Canada and upstate New York. He was responsible for pro coverage of the New York Mets' organization and six International League teams under Pat Daugherty, a former Expos' alumnus, going back to the 1970s. The most notable signing for MacKenzie for the Rockies came in 1994 when he inked left-handed pitcher Mike Kusiewicz, a Montreal native, who pitched for the Ottawa-Nepean Canadians under manager Don Campbell.

One of Kusiewicz's best seasons in the minors came in 1995 when at age 18, he led the Class-A South Atlantic League with a 2.94 ERA, going 8-4 in 21 starts. Three years later, he was 14-7 with the Rockies' Double-A team in New Haven, Conn. He was never able to duplicate that season and injuries throttled his possible ascent to the majors.

When Rockies GM Bob Gebhard was fired in 2003, MacKenzie was gone, too, as part of a wholesale shake-up. Seven years later, MacKenzie managed the Ottawa Fat Cats, a senior team in Ontario's Intercounty league, for one season.

Along the way, MacKenzie was also a consultant to two manufacturers of baseball bats, including the Original Sam Bat Company founded by Sam Holman. In fact, it was MacKenzie, who recommended to Holman one day over beers at the Mayflower Pub in Ottawa that he produce a bat that would not break easily.

Today, Sam Bat produces bats for 120 big-league players out of a manufacturing facility in Carleton Place, Ont., although Holman is just a consultant.

Upstairs in a room at MacKenzie's Brockville home are a number of Expos' and Rockies' jerseys hung on the wall with MacKenzie 23 on the backs. Downstairs in another display room are framed jerseys of two of his favourite Dodgers' icons with no names: No. 42, the other 24.

"Okay, 42 is Jackie Robinson and 24 is Johnny Roseboro?" I asked MacKenzie.

"No, Walter Alston."

On an opposite wall is a cherished autographed photo of Roy Campanella, the Dodgers' catching great, MacKenzie's hero. Safe to say you know what team was MacKenzie's favourite growing up and still is, especially the Brooklyn version. He never did get to work for the Dodgers along the way but what he did with other teams and Team Canada is what counts.

"Bill was a very good baseball man. He was one of the finest scouts and minor-league instructors that the Expos had when we were assembling the team that became the 1994 club," Hughes said.

"Bill richly deserves induction into the Canadian Baseball Hall of Fame," Didier said. Many other people agree. I nominated MacKenzie a few years ago but so far, he hasn't been elected.

MacKenzie knew his way around a diamond, he had the eloquence and communication skills to deal with the personnel surrounding him, he knew a prospect when he saw one and he still knows how to peel a potato better than I do.

August 10, 1977

Dear Jim,

Upon completion of our 1977 try-out camps, we have selected what we feel are the better players who attended.

It is always difficult to observe and judge a player's ability one a one day look and we must judge the tools a player demonstrates during the day to determine if, in our minds, he shows ability enough to merit another look and, possibly, upon further evaluation, become a signable ball player.

You have been selected as one of these players and are invited to a special, closed, camp here in Montreal on Saturday, September 3rd beginning at 10:00 a.m.

The camp will be held at Robillard Center, a beautiful new complex built for the 1976 Olympic games. Enclosed please find directions to that center.

We hope you can attend and we look forward to a good workout. Following the work out, everyone attending will receive a complimentary ticket to attend the Expos - Houston game at the Olympic Stadium that night.

If you are unable to attend, please reply as soon as possible. We look forward to seeing you on September 3rd.

Sincerely,

Bill MacKenzie
Assist.Director of Scouting

BM/pldeW

Club de baseball Montreal Ltée, Montreal Baseball Club Ltd.,
C.P. 500, Station "M"/P.O. Box 500, Station "M", Montreal, Quebec H1V 3P2. Telephone : 253-3434 (514)

This is a letter Canadian-born Expos prospect Jim Kaludis received from Bill MacKenzie

Santovenia was a can't miss prospect

Nelson Santovenia was one of the good guys in baseball when I knew him from my days as an Expos' beat writer.

Kind, unassuming, polite were just a few words to describe him. He hasn't changed.

Santovenia was one of those prospect-type players the Expos discovered out of two post-high school institutions. He's a trivia item of sorts: he was one of those few players drafted twice by the Expos. We don't exactly know if this is true but it isn't often a player is drafted twice by the same team.

Santovenia had first caught the eye of the Expos when he was a catcher at Miami-Dade College. So what did they do? They selected him in the third round of the 1981 draft but he didn't sign.

"I guess I wanted to play another year of college. I had a scholarship to the University of Miami," Santovenia was saying about not signing with the Expos the first time.

So a year later after he had switched to the U of M, he was selected a second time by the Expos in the first round of the draft's secondary phase. This time, Santovenia signed with the Expos and received a $30,000 signing bonus, not bad considering that Larry Walker received a mere $1,500 when he signed in 1984.

Santovenia was born in Cuba and was fortunate to move at age 5 in 1966 to the U.S. following the Fidel Castro invasion to be with an uncle who was in the U.S. army based in Fullerton, Calif. Santovenia moved off the Caribbean island with his mother Caridad, father Antonio, sisters Mirta and Alyeda and brother Luis. Later, the family would spend time in the Boston area before moving to Miami.

That was all one nice stroke of luck to escape the communist regime.

So was getting drafted by the Expos. So was the opportunity to be called up to the majors by the Expos.

It took a few years before Santovenia really opened up the eyes of the Expos' brass. From 1982-86, Santovenia even admits that his pro career had become sluggish with middling results and he noticed that other catching prospects were bypassing him. Then the winter of 1986-1987 rolled around.

"Actually, I went into that off season thinking that was going to be the year where I pretty much said to myself that if I keep struggling and not having success, that I was really planning to give it up," Santovenia said. "It was my sixth year with the organization and a couple of players had kinda passed me. I was not an everyday catcher and I had to wait my turn. I had to prove myself at a higher level or that was going to be it. It paid off. They gave me a chance."

That chance was with the Jacksonville club, a talent-stacked team of future Expos in Double-A. They were nicknamed the Jaxspos. Walker played on that team. So did Randy Johnson, Rangers' castoff George Wright, John Dopson, Rex Hudler, Brian Holman and the list goes on.

Santovenia's contribution was pretty heady: .279 BA, 19 homers, 63 RBI in only 117 games. To cap that wonderful season off, Santovenia got The Call in September.

"I have goosebumps on my body telling the story," Santovenia said. "Manager Tommy Thompson called me in and gave me the news. The Expos had purchased my contract and I was being called up to the big leagues. It was one of the most exciting moments of my career.".

Santovenia could never live up to those Jacksonville days in his short tenure with the Expos, although he did hit eight homers in 1988. He spent time with the Expos from 1988-1991 with sporadic success. On July 28, 1989, Vince Coleman of the St. Louis Cardinals was caught stealing by Santovenia, ending Coleman's MLB streak of 50 consecutive stolen bases

Santovenia was released by the Expos at the winter meetings in 1991 on Dec. 9 and that very day, they traded to get Darrin Fletcher from the Phillies for Barry Jones. Subsequently, Santovenia had cups of tea with the White Sox and Kansas City before packing it in at age 32 in 1993. Knee problems didn't help.

"Nelson was a great catcher," remembered pitcher Rich Thompson, who spent time with him in the minors and with the Expos. "Nelson, Gilberto Reyes, Larry Owen, Dan Bilardello, and Doug Simunic were my five best catchers over 15 years."

While with the Jacksonville club, Thompson had told Santovenia, Johnson and Walker in the bullpen that they were going to the hall of fame in Cooperstown. Only Santovenia didn't pan out. Pretty head praise for a guy, who fell hard from the Expos' depth chart.

"I'm not sure. It could have been anything," Thompson said. "I recall Buck Rodgers seemed to prefer Mike Fitzgerald at catcher and he got the majority of playing time over Nelson. Both players were great teammates. Mike always played hard and was a gamer, but I preferred Nelson defensively."

Santovenia, while with the Expos, received some recognition by public-address announcer Richard Morency, who would bring him up in to the plate from the on-deck circle with this rendition: "Now batting, the catcher, le receveur, Nel-son San-to-ve-nia."

Subsequently in order to help his wife Nancy pay bills and raise their two sons Nelson Jr. and Anthony, Santovenia elected to go and work for his brother-in-law in the not-so glamorous underground construction business, something he did for 13 years from 1996-2009. In 2008, he was hurt by the economic crisis that affected the world but he was fortunate enough to keep the house he has had since 1990 by refinancing it with a loan modification.

"I'm one of those guys hanging in there. It's an OK life. I still own a nice house and building equity," he said.

For several years, Santovenia worked with former major-league pitcher Alex Fernandez at a baseball school in Miami and he helped out coaching a high school team.

For a point in time, Santovenia was the hitting coach for the Detroit Tigers' Class-A team in Lakeland, Fla.

A one-time prospect, Nellie never panned out but he was a class guy.

Fletcher had solid career

It was a culmination of events that took place Dec. 9, 1991 at the winter meetings at the Fontainebleu Hotel in Miami.

I was there when it was announced that long-time organizational catching prospect Nelson Santovenia was released. The Expos under GM Dan Duquette made a trade the same day to bring in another player to add to their behind-the-plate portfolio."

His name was Darrin Fletcher. It was the beginning of a remarkable odyssey that saw Fletcher play 10.5 seasons for Canadian teams, six for the Expos, the next and final four and a half of his career for the Blue Jays.

Fletcher doesn't recall anyone from the Phillies or the Expos calling him about the trade. He thought it was more him watching on television that he was changing teams. But there was no mistaking his happiness at leaving the Phillies, the same happiness he experienced when the Dodgers traded him to the Phillies in mid-season in 1990. Fletcher had been drafted and signed in 1987 by the Dodgers but his tenure was short. He appeared in only 16 games in 1989-90.

"I knew my time in Philly was shortlived," Fletcher told me in 2020. "They had Darren Daulton. He wasn't going anywhere. I'm not sure why the Phillies held on to me. I was very happy to get a chance in Montreal. No, I wasn't surprised at the trade.

"The Dodgers, at the time, had won the World Series in 1988 and were at the top organization-wise. I had no ability to be an everyday catcher with the Dodgers because they had Mike Scioscia and Mike Piazza. So I had a couple of organizations where I had no chance ever at playing every day.

"Both the everyday catchers with the Dodgers and Phillies were left-handed catchers. My skill-set was that I was a left-handed catcher. Scioscia and Daulton were veteran style players so I was destined to be moved."

The way Fletcher observed things in his eloquent way, he felt Expos organizational employee Kevin Kennedy was the ruse who put it in Duquette's ear that Fletcher would be worth a gamble. Kennedy had worked for the Dodgers during Fletcher's time with L.A. so he knew what Fletcher could do.

"What helped the story was this guy, who wasn't there very long, Kevin Kennedy," Fletcher said. "He was advising Dan Duquette and he really was the guy that was probably Dan's ear on myself and John Wetteland (acquired later in a trade at those same winter meetings)."

Fletcher's status with the Expos in 1992 was a platoon role with former Expos franchise great Gary Carter, who had been claimed off waivers the previous November from the Dodgers. The Expos also gave some playing time behind the plate to aging Rick Cerone and youngsters Tim Laker and Rob Natal.

Fletcher admits his 1992 season was less than impressive. He hit .243 with two homers and 26 RBI but he was delighted to be around Carter, not so much for gaining expertise at catching but to learn more about off-the-field stuff, raising a family and combining professional life with a family life.

"That was the most memorable thing about 1992 was Gary. He came back to Canada. It was his swan song," Fletcher said. "He was a really nice man, a good leader. His approach was that you should have fun. He really enjoyed the game of baseball. It was not a job. He really enjoyed playing and that he was putting on a show."

Ironically, when Carter doubled for what would be his final at-bat in Montreal on Sept. 27, 1992, a subtle scenario presented itself at second base in the ensuing euphoria: Carter was replaced as a pinch runner by Laker. They hugged each other in what some perceived to be the passing of the torch: the franchise legend being replaced by the prospect.

And what that meant was a semi-message that perhaps Laker was being groomed more than Fletcher.

"I interpreted that the same way. I was playing okay but not great," Fletcher said in analysing the Laker-for-Carter switch at second base and the message. "Laker obviously ran better than I did. I think the Expos were not sure about me. Laker was the up and coming prospect and had the potential to be the next guy."

So that was it. What it boiled down to was a battle the following spring and during the early part of the 1993 season between Fletcher, Laker and also Tim Spehr for playing time to see who would emerge as No. 1. During most of the first month of April, as I learned through research at retrosheet.org, Spehr got most of the playing time and Fletcher was still trying to make his situation work for the better.

Eventually, Fletcher got hot and he got most of the playing time the remainder of the season. A little animated discussion between Fletcher and Alou was the spark that got Fletcher going.

"I had missed a sign from Felipe at the bench and he wanted me to get my eyes checked," Fletcher was telling me. "So he got the head trainer, Ronnie Mac (McClain) to come to me and say that Felipe wanted me to get my eyes checked, that I had missed a couple of signs and that my bat was not coming around as it should.

"I was upset and angry. I was pissed off. I think Felipe did it on purpose to get me riled up, that he didn't see a lot of emotion from me. So I went in to see Felipe and I said, 'I don't need my eyes checked.' I need to get better. He put me in the lineup and I got hot."

The turnaround started April 21 and 22 when he went 2-for-4 with a ribbie in each of the last two games of a series against the Dodgers in Montreal. He called the Dodgers performance a "good series" that was a "confidence booster for him." He went on a streak where he went something like "12-for-18."

Fletcher finished the season with a .255 average with nine homers and 60 RBI in 396 at-bats. Both Laker and Spehr had almost identical opportunities to impress. In 86 AB, Laker batted .222 with no homers and seven RBI and in 87 AB, Spehr batted .230 with two homers and 10 RBI.

Canadian Joe Siddall of Windsor, Ont. collected 20 AB in a catcher's role, including the Sept. 6 game when he caught in an historic game for fellow Canuck Denis Boucher with Larry Walker of Maple Ridge, B.C. in right field.

Laker faded into oblivion and never panned out with the Expos or any other team. For most of his life, Laker, currently the hitting coach for the Mariners, has had to deal with a stomach ailment that requires medication.

"It was a competitive year. We battled it out and I emerged," Fletcher said of the battle for No. 1 catcher. "It was my little breakout year. I had a good big-league season as a catcher and I swung the bat well, at least as a platoon player or the extra guy in Montreal. I was catching well and hitting well."

And to boot, Fletcher and the Expos almost pulled off a playoff berth by winning 94 games and losing only 68. Following the season, the Expos approached Fletcher about a multi-year extension of his contract even though he was still under club control with no arbitration rights.

Fletcher went for security and signed a team friendly deal of three years plus an option that began with $615,000. There were some who criticized him because he surrendered a fair amount of arbitration money but at the same time, the deal meant security for him.

"I thought it was a good fit. I was young and I wanted some security," Fletcher said.

Back on the field in 1994, Fletcher and his mates were primed to win in 1994. Fletcher "started off real good" in 1994 with 10 homers before the end of May and 50 RBI prior to the all-star break.

"I felt really good," Fletcher was saying. "I knew I was good at the receiving end but I needed to hit. I had to produce. I felt I could be a threat. As a left-handed hitter, I was always an offensive-minded catcher."

So what should happen? Fletcher impressed voters enough to be voted to the all-star game along with shortstop Wil Cordero, outfielders Moises Alou and Marquis Grissom and pitcher Ken Hill.

Fletcher was the underdog player of the five, a thick-set guy, who couldn't run much, an unheralded catcher, the champion of the underdog. With Fletcher catching more often than not, his efforts steered the team pitching staff to lead the National League in winning percentage, ERA and tied for the lead in shutouts with eight.

For the native of smalltown Illinois who played independent ball in the Cape Cod league, this nod for the all-star game was met with much gratitude. He was undeterred in the wake of the stack of odds against him because he was marginally talented but he made up for any slights by being committed to his art and having success doing it.

He possessed that indomitable spirit that inspired those who he played with and against and those fans who watched him. He was an inspiration to people of all walks of life that enthusiasm overcomes any adversities in life.

It sure must have been a frisson moment, sending tingles of joy through his body, the moment of being told the news about his selection, the joy of walking into the NL clubhouse to be with the other stars, and putting his uniform on for the game itself. Fletcher was a late-game insert behind the plate and the memories will last a lifetime.

"Personally, that was a career highlight for me, making the all-star team. That was a pinnacle moment for the Expos with the five of us at the all-star game," Fletcher said. "The all-star game was a high point for the Expos organization. It was a neat time to be an Expo. We were enjoying ourselves. All of baseball was talking about this young Expos team. Our talent level was off the charts."

Fletcher continued to play for the Expos through the 1997 season before becoming a free agent and signing with the Blue Jays.

"That was an enjoyable year in 1997," Fletcher said. "We played the Blue Jays in Toronto on July 1 in the interleague game. The place was packed, a beautiful day. A lot of Expos fans were there. It was a highlight moment for me. Clemens vs. Juden. I liked the feel of that game and the city. It was a cool series, really cool series."

By the end of the 2001 season, Fletcher said it was getting "harder for me to stay in the game" because his production was going down so he decided to pack it in following that season.

"It was a tough decision but it was the right decision. I never looked back," he said. "I was banging on 36 years old and I had a lack of passion for the game."

The combination of six years with the Expos and five with the Jays makes him a bonafide candidate for selection into the Canadian Baseball Hall of Fame.

"I think I'm the only player in MLB history to play more than 500 games with both franchises, Toronto and Montreal," Fletcher said.

A trailblazer on Expos telecasts

Claudine Langan was a trailblazer, even if she was not a household name to many in Canada.

She was behind the camera, not in front of it but the Expos family, TSN and RDS will remember her from the late 1990s through to the strike year of 1994. She was an associate director and then director of Expos games on those Canadian TV cable stations.

"It was a fun — for the most part — and challenging career and I made some terrific friends along the way but I honestly don't think I have anything to recount that would be of any real interest," Langan said in an email exchange. "Of course, when I stepped into the director's chair for the first time, I became the first woman in the world to direct a Major League Baseball game. But that is more of a personal accomplishment that would not be of interest to most and is only really tangentially connected to the Expos."

During her time in TV sports, she covered Super Bowls, World Series, NHL, the Winter Olympics and many MLB games. Following the strike year, Langan moved on to other projects. Her resumé is rich with accomplishments.

She joined AOL as director of consumer marketing, working at their headquarters in Dulles, Virginia. Following a long stint with AOL, Langan decided to move back to Canada where she joined a subsidiary of the largest telecom company in the country as vice-president of consumer marketing, overseeing a large team responsible for generating just under $1-billion in annual revenue.

Her broad experience as a sales, marketing and communications executive provided an excellent foundation for her thriving career as a real estate agent in San Miguel de Allende, Mexico.

Langan retired Dec. 31 of 2020 and her and her husband got their visas and decided to move to Portugal in February, 2021.

"We've been in San Miguel de Allende for almost 12 years and it has been really great but we feel it is time for a new adventure and Europe now beckons," Langan said.

Langan obtained her bachelor's degree in mass communication from the University of Ottawa where she graduated Cum Laude and a master's degree in mass communication and marketing from the Cronkite School of Journalism at Arizona State University in Tempe where she was named graduate student of the year with a 4.0 Grade Pointe Average.

Furthermore, she obtained a post-graduate fellowship in Media Management from the Poynter Institute for Media Studies in St. Petersburg, Florida.

"Good luck with the book," Langan told me. "And if you happen to be talking with Rich Griffin, Dave Van Horne or Ken Singleton along the way, please say hi to them from me. I've lost touch with them but they were such wonderful guys to travel and work with. They watched over me while on the road and I will always be grateful to them for that. It wasn't always easy being the only woman around."

Cabrera's IQ was what made him tick

Orlando Cabrera had vision, the ability to read the game. He had ESP. He possessed a sixth tool.

When he was young and growing up in Colombia, he played in a semi- pro league with men a few years older than him. He said he was the "youngest guy" on those teams of older men and he was getting a "lot of recognition" from scouts, He could pick up stuff right away that he could use to his advantage. He was always looking a play ahead. While playing with these veteran-type players, he began to accumulate his ESP know-how and display his ideology.

It helped, too, that his father Jolbert Sr. was a scout for the Marlins and his brother Jolbert had played in the Expos minor league system to help to understand what it took to reach the majors.

Cabrera was discovered while playing at a tournament in Santa Marta, Colombia. He was 16 years old. The Colombia national team was playing against a team from Mexico. The Mexican team had a couple of players who were sick so Orlando got clearance to play shortstop for the Mexican team. No word of a lie.

"Orlando was the most valuable player in that tournament between the two countries. He was the best player," Jolbert told me. "An Expos scout was doing a report on the tournament and he said to me, 'Who is that guy?' I said, 'That's my brother.' "

Oddly, Cabrera was signed not in person per se – but on the phone.

"I didn't do any tryouts like they do in international markets," Cabrera told me. "My dad had me signed on the phone. $7,000. They sent me a contract."

The official signing date was June 1, 1993, exactly three months after Expos director of international scouting Fred Ferreira had signed a guy by the name of Vladimir Guerrero. Ever heard of him? Oddly enough, Ferreira told me he couldn't recall doing the Cabrera contract on the phone, although he said it was "entirely possible."

When it was arranged by Ferreira that Cabrera would report to Santo Domingo to work out at the Expos Dominican Republic academy, Ferreira had a scout/coach, Titico Pascal, go to the airport to pick up Cabrera, who had flown in from Colombia.

For close to two hours at the airport, Pascal couldn't find Cabrera, who was 5-foot-10. The scout wandered in circles around the airport but Cabrera was there all along, standing in the middle of the airport – it was a somewhat hilarious scene that played out fine in the end.

"The guy thought Orlando was tall. He was looking for a taller guy for one to two hours," Jolbert said. "They thought he was as tall as me. I'm three inches taller than him. I'm 6-foot-1. Finally the guy found him. 'I've been looking at you for two hours.'" the scout told Orlando.

As Ferreira recalls, "Orlando had been turned down by other MLB teams because they considered him too small. They thought he was very small but I saw him. I liked his actions, his arm strength, his running speed. It's how it looks in your eyes. They all count in my book.

"I had to make a decision (to sign him) because someone else might come around. If you like something, you buy it. I saw his leadership. His size was no matter. People may have told me he was too small but he played like he was 6-foot-3. He persevered."

One of the scouts who looked down despairingly at Cabrera was Marlins scout Javier Vasquez, not the same Javier Vasquez, who pitched for the Expos. Jolbert tells the story that when his brother reached the big leagues with the Expos in 1997, Vazquez was fired by the Marlins as somewhat of a punishment.

"That scout didn't want to sign him. He said he was too small and that he wasn't going to be a good player," Jolbert said. "He thought Orlando might get better but he didn't want to sign him. He said Orlando wasn't going anywhere but Orlando had determination and drive. He was a very smart person. He learned the major leagues. He adapted and continued to adapt to what the league (especially the pitchers) were doing. He was a winner. He had all those instincts playing with older guys."

Once Pascal found Cabrera at the airport, Cabrera spent part of that summer in the Dominican Summer League and the following year, he played for the Gulf Coast Expos in Florida. By 1995, he really began to show what he could do in a full slate of Class A games – combined with the Vermont Expos and West Palm Beach Expos. He had three homers and 33 RBI while batting .281.

Then in 1996, he was assigned to another Class A outpost in the Delmarva Peninsula, an unique portmanteau occupied by the vast majority of the state of Delaware and parts of the Eastern Shore regions of Maryland and Virginia. This was the very first season of operation for the team after a group called Maryland Baseball purchased Georgia's Albany Polecats, an Expos affiliate for many years, and relocated them much further north.

Home games were played at Arthur W. Perdue Stadium in Salisbury, Maryland. The team entered into a two-year affiliation agreement with the Expos. The team was called the Shorebirds as a tribute to the marine waterfowl of the Delmarva Peninsula. The team was managed by Doug Sisson and finished with an impressive 83-59 record.

Cabrera enjoyed a solid season with 14 homers, 65 RBI, 51 stolen bases, 86 runs and a .252 batting average. What a season.

The 1997 season was also memorable for Cabrera because he played with four teams. He did a lot of packing of suitcases. He played Class A for West Palm Beach, Fla., Double-A in Harrisburg, Pa., Triple-A in Ottawa and also Montreal.

It was in Ottawa that Orlando and Jolbert got to play together, a thrill for both of them. Jolbert said it was "a time we cherished" and he had hoped to be called up by the Expos along with Orlando but it didn't happen. Jolbert, though, did get to enjoy time in the majors with other teams.

Cabrera made his MLB debut on Sept. 3, 1997 as the first player from Colombia to play for the franchise. The debut was in Boston as a fourth-inning replacement at short for Mark Grudzelienek, who had been ejected by home-plate umpire Bob Davidson for arguing balls and strikes. Cabrera went 0-for-2 in his debut.

Cabrera split time with Ottawa and Montreal in 1998 and became the everyday shortstop when Grudz was traded to the Dodgers on the trade deadline day of July 31.

O-Cab had fielding woes in the early part of his tenure with the Expos but turned the corner in 1999 with a streak of 42 consecutive games when he didn't make an error. He also had a streak of bad luck when he severely sprained his left ankle when he stepped on first base on Aug. 1, forcing him to miss the remainder of the season.

Not long before the injury, he popped up for the last out in the perfect game notched by David Cone by the Mets on July 18 in New York.

By 2000, Cabrera was getting to play more often. That season, he accumulated the most number of at-bats to that point with 422. He recorded 13 homers, 55 RBI while batting .237. 2001 was an exclamation mark season when he played in all 162 games with 176 hits, 14 homers and a career-high 96 RBI.

"The highlight of my career," Cabrera said of 2001. "I had the most number of RBI I ever had with 96 and I won my first Gold Glove."

2002 saw him play in 153 games and admits he missed some time with a bulging disc. There was a reunion of him and Jolbert in a series in Montreal in June. Jolbert was playing for the Indians.

2003 was another exclamation mark season. He played in all 162 games again. Only two Expos have played in every game in one season in their 36-season history. Ken Singleton did it in 1973, Warren Cromartie did it in 1980.

"Not many managers let you do that," Cabrera said of playing every game. "Playing every game, you can provide some type of way to win games, that I need to be in the lineup, every game, no matter. Managers understand that. You're not going to be getting 2-3 hits a game but defensively, you can be managing the team in the field."

Which brings up a point – during his tenure with the Expos, at least during the Felipe Alou era, Cabrera was frustrated with Alou over the shortstop's inability to create his own management of opposing batters when it came to possible shifting. Cabrera, on occasion, would want to shift certain batters such a way but Alou opposed it.

"Felipe was old school," Cabrera said. "He was very controlling. I couldn't use my biggest tool which was my IQ. Other players can hit 30 home runs and hit .300 but I can use my IQ every day, anticipate what was going to happen. It was my frame of reference. That is a frame of reference. My baseball IQ was so advanced. Like wow, the freedom you get. You try to take advantage and win games."

Except that Felipe didn't want the confident, perhaps cocky Cabrera to express his freedom and his IQ.

"I was put almost into this bubble," Cabrera said. "I couldn't expand (his freedom). I wanted to do shifts for guys like Barry Bonds, Ken Griffey and Ken Caminiti. I couldn't express myself. I couldn't play my game. It was a tragedy for my game. I couldn't use my biggest tool which was my IQ. We were the first team to do the shift but I never got the credit."

Cabrera said he and infield coach Perry Hill would take in "all this data" and draw up plays that they wanted to use but some of them never came to pass.

"Orlando had a very good baseball mind," Hill told me in late 2020. "He was a very heads-up player. He anticipated situations. He knew exactly what he wanted to do. Felipe was one of the best baseball minds I've ever been around. He was good at overseeing things. He ran a very good game. Not many things got by him. He was an outstanding manager."

Hill knew what he was doing, too. He has coached 10 Gold Glove winners during his time in the majors as an infield coach, including Cabrera and former Expos second baseman Jose Vidro.

"With Orlando, it was just a matter of time for him to be a force. He was a force defensively and offensively in his own right," Jolbert said.

By 2004, when it was determined that it indeed would be the last season for the Expos in Montreal, Cabrera wondered about his future with the organization. He wasn't unhappy when he was dealt to the Red Sox on deadline day on July 31. What he won't forget is that he was part of a four-team trade.

"What happened in those days, there was a lot of controversy about where the team was going to go," Cabrera said. "Was I going to be offered a contract by (GM) Omar Minaya? Where were we going? Are we going to Puerto Rico? Are we going to Washington? There were a lot of questions that couldn't be answered.

"It was sweet, an awesome experience to be traded to the Red Sox. It was truly, truly amazing. It put my name on the map. We won the World Series. It's not only about the money but the recognition to be one of the best, to dream to be the best that year. I learned how powerful my mind was that year."

And then O-Cab started laughing.

"A lot of people don't know that I was traded so many times. It was always a challenge," he said.

Yes, that trade to Boston led to a string of swaps to other teams and signings by other teams. After half a season with the Red Sox, Cabrera was with the Angels as a free agent. It was in 2006 with the Angels that he amassed a streak of 63 consecutive games whereby he reached base. At the time, it was the sixth longest streak in MLB history. Ted Williams still holds the record with 84.

Danny Gallagher photo
Orlando Cabrera
a few years ago

"With all the greatest players to have played the game, to even be on that list is crazy," Cabrera told reporters at the time. "I'm a free swinging hitter. Reaching base every day? It was hard to believe I was doing it."

Cabrera ended up playing with nine teams before packing it in. For the most part, he has been living in South Carolina, running his foundation, operating a podcast and helping other prospects get to the majors through his baseball academy.

When I complimented him on his eloquence, he laughed and said, "Thanks", and began to explain how he would often hang around media scrums so that he could get more and more experience speaking English. He relished interviews.

"When you practise something, you get better," he said. "I would always answer questions. I wasn't afraid of making mistakes (in talking). I was always available for the media. When you are learning the language, you need to communicate. You need to connect by talking and talking. I wanted to learn."

Looking back and forward

Even though he was the majority owner of an American League team, George Steinbrenner wasn't averse to criticizing something going on in the National League.

I got him to talk twice about the Expos more than 25 years ago as he scolded Montreal fans for not supporting the city.

"Principally, they love their hockey in Montreal but I speak out hoping that that great city will support baseball because if you don't, you're showing everybody that you don't want the sport," Steinbrenner told me in an exclusive for Toronto's Globe and Mail newspaper. "You'll regret losing it very much after it's gone. That's history.

"A lot of us are concerned about the situation in Montreal. I'm concerned for the fellows who own the club. The fans should appreciate it and support it. If you don't want the team and don't support it, then don't blame the people who own it. I know Claude Brochu works very hard.

"They're doing everything humanely possible. They've given the fans a very good, entertaining team. Now it's up to the city to support them and if that means a new stadium to play in, they've got to do it or face the prospect of losing the team. They've got to consider giving them the same as Cleveland, Texas and Baltimore have done for their teams.

"If Montreal comes to the owners and said, 'We have to move, we just can't do it,' I would be very sympathetic. I wouldn't necessarily vote for it but I know how badly Claude wants to keep the team in Montreal. He really does. He has convinced all of us of that. The Bronfmans were a tremendous group of people. God, how we hated to lose them out of baseball but Claude and his people are going the extra mile. You just can't expect them to sit there and pour money down a rathole."

It was around that time of the 1994 season that Brochu talked about the "behavioural problem" as it related to the ticket-buying patterns of the francophone-dominated population in Greater Montreal. In my interview with him, Brochu told me 1993 season-ticket sales topped out at 8,300 and 1994 sales were more-or-less stuck at 8,000.

"It's a little disappointing coming off our great season but the economic situation in Montreal is pretty serious," Brochu said at the time. "It's tough to get people to commit to half-season and full-season packages."

Brochu described the apparent apathy of Montreal ticket buyers as a "monstrous problem." It was a problem that befuddled various Expos ownership groups for years, including Bronfman.

"Some people think our problems are marketing related but most of our problems are from a revenue perspective, either related to structural problems (The Big O's location in the east end) or as they are related to consumer-behavioural issues.

"This is a very particular case here. The behaviour of francophone consumers, especially, is different from anglophones. Very different — how they buy tickets, these are cultural and social issues. The francophone is more of an impulsive buyer. The decision to buy, the decision to go to a game is made the day of a game, whereas the anglophones will plan — he will know six months ahead of time that he's going to a game on a certain date and he'll buy a ticket.

"It's a complex situation. It's not a matter of incompetence of the marketing department."

Brochu said in that interview that 85% of Expos season-ticket holders were corporations. He was not aware of the breakdown of those buyers in terms of francophones and anglophones but he realized there was an "untapped market" in the French population.

"Definitely, definitely," Brochu told me. "A lot of people don't come to the park. They follow the game on television or radio and read about it but getting them to the park is another issue.

"We felt that if we could maintain the nucleus of this club, we would get the support that would pay us back in terms of attendance and ticket sales."

On the eve of the 1994 season, Brochu was very open with me in a revealing story for the Globe and Mail that ran April 4. The headline read:

Poor season could put Montreal Expos on life-support

or better still, it should have read:

"It's simply a miracle that we operate" – Brochu

The Expos were coming off a solid 1993 season when they won 94 games and were destined to go all the way in 1994 but a players' strike loomed. I asked Brochu if the 1994 season was a "watershed" season for the franchise.

Brochu was quick to say he "wouldn't classify it that way" but it was clear it was a make-or-break year because 1995 would prove significantly more expensive to keep the team's core of talented players.

"I'm not one for using terminology or handles or artificial deadlines," Brochu told me. "I haven't really thought about '95. It's all hypothetical. I'm going through this year first. Our margin of error is so small that we can't afford to make one mistake. We're real careful and frugal but not stupid. It's simply a miracle that we operate. It's a testimony to our system that we're able to hang in."

Pretty sobering thoughts from Brochu, huh? Gall-darn right. He told me that the Expos were already "behind the eight-ball" financially in 1994 with a payroll hovering around $19-million. Expenses were being cut to the bone, although Brochu disputed reports that vitamins wouldn't be supplied to players and that players wouldn't be given taxi fare if they ventured to the park early for batting practice on the road.

Curiously, Montreal has always been considered a small-market baseball city but is labelled a large-market hockey metropolis. Ronald Corey, the president at the time of hockey's fabled Canadiens, who also scrutinized the Expos from his season-ticket seat along the first-base line, passed along some interesting thoughts for that story for the Globe and Mail.

"Definitely for sure, no question, we constitute a big-market hockey team," Corey said. "But population is not necessarily relative. It's not only city population but the meaning of the club to Montrealers.

"We've had good teams and we've won 24 Stanley Cups. I'm not going to talk about the Expos too much but in Montreal, hockey is the sport. It's the first love for Montreal. It's part of your blood."

Corey was talking less than a year after the Canadiens had won the 1993 Stanley Cup. And here we are all this time later and this storied franchise hasn't won another NHL championship since. Who would have thought the Canadiens would go through this drought of close to 40 years?

When I called up then Blue Jays chairman of the board Peter Widdrington about the dicey situation with the Expos, he was reluctant to offer a critique.

"It's a tough situation in Montreal," Widdrington said. "Claude Brochu is working 24 hours a day, trying to make it work. It's a big city. I've never thought of Montreal as a small-market city but fact of the matter is that it has a difficult stadium. It's not an ideal stadium."

In other similar stories I wrote in the 1990s about the Expos attendance problems, then mayor Jean Doré admonished Montreal's business community for not supporting the Expos, saying that the Expos did not have enough tickets sold through the "corporate citizens" of the city.

Doré felt the business community had taken the franchise for granted.

"The club has to be supported more by the smaller, medium-sized businesses," Doré told me. "With a metropolitan population here of about 3.1-million people, we should have 15,000 to 17.000 season tickets, double the norm."

Sure enough, the future of the Expos was really clouded in the winter of 1994-95 during the players' strike which had started Aug. 12, 1994. It took in fact 10 years for the Expos to leave town but some say the beginning of the end took place with the players' strike, the cancellation of the season by commissioner Bud Selig and the subsequent firesale of players Ken Hill, John Wetteland and Marquis Grissom and the inability to sign free agent Larry Walker.

A few years earlier, Brochu was a hero in Montreal for saving the club from going to the U.S.

Charles Bronfman dropped the Expos following the team's disappointing 1989 season when they led the NL East for a good portion of the season before finishing 81-81.

"It was very tough on all of us," Bronfman said about 1989. "It maybe was the toughest experience I've had as an owner. I knew we were going to win. No question about. When we didn't win, it was tough to take."

Bronfman appointed Brochu to find a new owner or owners. As it turns out, it was a very difficult procedure in the midst of a recession when no billionaire was willing to take over the ownership reins.

"I want freedom," Bronfman told me in early 1990 about the desire to drop his ownership of the franchise. "I've had enough. I've been held captive by baseball from February through September for 21 years. I'm going to be 60 soon and I want to spend more time with my wife and family.

"Being an owner is a very taxing thing. You give an awful lot of yourself. After awhile, you get burned out. It's a question of whether you want to continue to give it your all year after year. I've enjoyed being an owner. I've given the game a lot but now is the time for someone to take the team to the next plateau. For 21 years, we pioneered it. We've had some great years and some exciting teams. Now, I just want to be a fan and not an owner anymore."

Bronfman said he had no wish to be a minority shareholder in the new ownership group headed by Brochu.

"I think that would be bad for the new owners," Bronfman explained. "It's very tough for somebody whose rear end has been in the saddle for a long time to suddenly sit on the arm of the chair."

I remember close to nine months following Brochu's campaign to find new owners that it wasn't going very good. Brochu was fit to be tied when little or no support was forthcoming.

"Sad as it seems, a billionaire owner will likely have a government buying him out. Bronfman doesn't want the team anymore so if it takes the Bourrasa government to keep the boys of summer in town, so be it," I said in an opinion piece in the Ottawa Sun Aug. 17, 1990. "There are many individuals who do have the money to buy him out but as Bronfman has said, they don't have the enthusiasm for sports."

A week later in another story I wrote, no sale had been concluded to take the Expos off Bronfman's hands. So people put a lot of blame on Brochu for what happened late in the 1990s and before the team was taken over by this clown Jeffrey Loria but these same people don't remember how hard Brochu worked to try to get a consortium together in the midst of a recession.

Covering the possible sale of the Expos had become an almost daily duty of reporters such as myself but annoying to say the least, trying to compete with the other media outlets to see who could break stories and release names of companies coming on board as minority shareholders. The soap opera had dragged on far too long for my liking.

In the midst of all this struggle to find investors, White Sox owner Jerry Reinsdorf, who was then the chairman of the MLB's ownership committee told me, "I hope Charles never sells the team."

There was even a report by Marty York of the Globe and Mail that beer magnate Molson's was interested in getting involved in Expos ownership. York said the source of this information was fabled legend Reggie Jackson.

With Brochu struggling to find investors to come on board, there was much speculation that non-Canadians such as Martin Stone of Lake Placid, N.Y. wanted to buy the team and even keep it in Montreal. And a headline in the Ottawa Sun above a story I wrote went this way:

Expos sound good to Nashville

Yes, you saw that in 2020 Nashville put together a major committee of owners and managerial executives. But 30 years earlier, Nashville wanted more than just country music to entertain the folks there. Larry Schmittou, general manager of a group pursuing a MLB franchise for Nashville, called Expos vice-president of baseball operations Bill Stoneman in August of 1990 to enquire about the Montreal club's possible availability.

Schmittou made no offer for the Expos but Schmittou, GM of the Nashville Sounds Triple-A team, told Stoneman where he could be reached if Québec buyers couldn't be found.

"We would make an offer under the right circumstances, if we were invited by the Expos," Schmittou told me.

Miami even was being touted as a possible landing point for the Expos at Joe Robbie Stadium. Then there was Buffalo throwing its hat into the ring. Remember back in 1968 when the Montreal franchise was having trouble getting money from investors to keep the team in Montreal before Bronfman saved the day. Buffalo was rumoured to be a spot where the fledging Montreal franchise would be moved had Bronfman not moved to the forefront with major money.

Buffalo had also filed application to be granted an expansion team but was rejected.

Then some 22 years later, Buffalo was showing interest in the Expos again. In his book The Right Angle: Tales from a Sporting Life, Buffalo Bisons Triple-A owner Bob Rich talked of his communication with Bronfman about taking over the Expos.

"Along the way, Charles seemed to have become disenchanted with the economics of the game and the collective mentality of the other owners," Rich said in his book. "We had heard of his unsuccessful attempts to sell the Expos to Canadian buyers, who would keep the team in Montreal.

"His vote was very important to Buffalo's chances, but I also felt we needed a backup plan. After pitching our city, I asked him if he would consider an offer to sell us the Expos. He didn't say no, so a week later, I sent him a registered letter, offering to buy the Expos for $90-million (U.S.) in cash.

"A few weeks later, he called me and said, 'Bob, I want to thank you for your offer but I love this team and I love this town and I won't be known as the person who sold them to another city.'"

Rich countered that comment by saying this: "Charles, if it's a matter of dollars, that was just our opening offer." Bronfman's reply: "Bob, I appreciate that. I have a lot of respect for you and your family. Your offer was more than fair and generous. I just cannot sell you this team."

Rich was disappointed that he struck out but said, "I will always respect Charles Bronfman as a true gentleman. Charles was a quiet, understated gentleman with a passion for his family, baseball and Israel. He almost seemed out of place with the other owners and took an independent course of action, developing players from within and not paying outrageous amounts of money to superstar free agents."

I tried hard to land an interview with Rich but he declined my overtures. As a compromise, he had a secretary send me a copy of his book.

So yes, there was much worry that outside interests would buy the Expos because Brochu was having much difficulty in bringing investors on board. In the end, a number of companies came on board paying $5-million to $7-million, more-or-less as a community responsibility. They really didn't want to be there but they pitched in to help out of civic or national pride. They were not sports enthusiasts.

For years, there has been a resurgence of enthusiasm to get a team back to Montreal but it may take years.

"Brochu ran the team like a corner grocer, minding every nickel rather than investing in the team on the theory that a winning squad just might make some money," said Jack Todd in a Montreal Gazette column in August of 2020.

"Did the baseball strike kill the Expos? Or was it the Big O? Blue Monday? Brochu's ineptitude? Jeffrey Loria's naked greed? Bud Selig's behind-the-scenes machinations? The indifference of the fans? Truth is, the Expos were swept away by a perfect storm of bad luck and bad management.

"The strike played a huge part but to survive long-term, the club was going to need an owner with deep pockets and real vision. Brochu had neither. They were also going to need a new, well-planned and well-built downtown ballpark — and Brochu's niggling ways would have led to an inadequate stadium and the eventual death of the team. If Stephen Bronfman can pull off his attempt to revive the Expos in a real ballpark, the strike and the eventual loss of the club could turn out to be a well-disguised blessing," Todd added.

As he sat on the deck at the Jube Pub and Patio in Oshawa, Ontario in August of 2020, former Montreal resident and Expos fan Vic Cupidio shook his head when he was asked if baseball would ever return to Montreal.

"No way," he said. Cupidio agrees that a big problem is lack of support from the French people for the team. He said the majority of people who supported the Expos were English and many were Jewish.

Joel Kirstein, a transplanted Montrealer living in Dallas, believes that if Montreal does attract a new MLB team in the next few years that it will need to do a better job of attracting francophone followers. But as Bronfman, Brochu and others tried, it's easier said than done.

"I believe that the Expos didn't do enough to attract more francophone players to the team and what little they did was ineffectual," Kirstein said in an interview. "Just having Québécois players wasn't enough because they were few, far between and fleeting.

"An exceptional ballpark experience in a vibrant entertainment destination with lots of options including within walking distance from the ballpark is a good start. The team should leverage Québécois celebrities as brand ambassadors for the team to create excitement."

Kirstein feels that a new Montreal team should get players to do public relations in French all season long, a move that would appeal to a francophone audience.

"They would need to create very family-friendly ticket plans that are affordable," Kirstein added. "They would need to create multi-partner promos with brands that francophones are loyal to, including product discounts and add shuttle buses from francophone neighbourhoods to make going to the games seamless and easy. I would suggest that they bring more Québécois culture to the ballpark. I could go on all day."

A good guy to talk to about this theme was Mike Cohen, a man about town in Montreal, a renaissance man, who calls himself a "multi-tasker." He's been a councillor for District 2 in the City of Cote Ste. Luc since

2005, he has been writing a weekly column for The Suburban newspaper for many years and he's the full-time communications and marketing specialist for the English Montreal School Board.

Cohen believes that "if and when" a team does return to Montreal, that what is in the franchise's favour is "local ownership." Cohen pointed out that prospective owners Stephen Bronfman and Mitch Garber provide the kind of financial support that is equivalent to Geoff Molson's stake in the Canadiens hockey team.

"I find it hard to think it will ever happen again," Cohen said of Montreal's chances of getting a team. "Montreal has a bonafide ownership group. They will do whatever is necessary to bring the fans in. The pandemic might actually make this happen. Tampa Bay may move to Montreal quicker. People would fall in love with a new stadium because of location. Stable ownership would make it work."

Like Kirstein, Cohen believes any new Montreal team would need to try and attract players from Montreal and Québec but of course, that is all easier said than done.

"I do believe that the Expos did not try hard enough to get local talent. I remember being at Olympic Stadium in 1993 when Denis Boucher pitched. The atmosphere in the crowd was something else. He never got a decision," Cohen said.

"The scouting staff needs to go out of their way to find a number of French Canadians. Claude Brochu was very positive, He did a lot of things in the French community. He tried very hard. He warned everyone about Jeffrey Loria. Claude managed to keep a team on a shoestring and it was still competitive. The biggest failure if the team comes back is if they don't go out of their way to find French Canadian players."

Cohen said any new franchise would need to do a better job of community relations, something what Warren Cromartie and Perry Giannias have been fostering for years. Cromartie got the ball rolling with reunions of the 1981 and 1994 Expos and was the catalyst for Exposmania. Giannias has pitched in with fund-raising autograph festivals involving former Expos players.

"If the Expos had a guy like Perry in the early 2000s, they might never have left," Cohen said. "The Expos memories are still alive."

Cohen said former French language broadcasters Jacques Doucet and Rodger Brulotte keep the Expos fever alive with commentary in Le Journal de Montréal and they also continue their work by doing Blue Jays games in French. Legendary talk-show host Mitch Melnick, Cohen said, is "constantly doing Expos stuff on his show."

Loria "worst memory" from brain injury

Jim McCoubrey can't remember the exact date but it was in the early 2000s when he was involved in a bad car accident during an ice storm in Canada's capital of Ottawa, a mishap that left him with a "serious brain injury."

He was told by some medical personnel that he would never recover, that he would spend the rest of his life in a wheelchair in a long-term care facility.

His good friend and critical-care specialist Dr. Arnold Aberman of Toronto helped to nurse him back to a more manageable way of life and miraculously, has made an excellent recovery after he was transferred quickly by ambulance from Ottawa to Toronto where he would receive superior medical care. He was nicknamed The Miracle.

"This brain injury erases your memory. I don't have my photographic memory anymore but the only name I remember, the very worst memory I have, and Loria is one of them," McCoubrey said in an interview.

Loria, meaning Jeffrey Loria, who was a majority shareholder of the Expos at the time and McCoubrey was a representative of Télémédia, a broadcasting and magazine conglomerate, which was one of many shareholders in the franchise going back to the days when Claude Brochu headed up a group that purchased the equity shares of Charles Bronfman, the original majority owner of the team.

"Loria was a con man, a bad businessman," said McCoubrey, who was an Expos board representative for more than 10 years and attended all of the limited partnership meetings held by either Brochu or Loria. "Loria came in as the good guy. He went from a good guy to a bad guy.

"What I remember vividly is that Loria was losing money every year and the shareholders would put in more money to make up for the losses. All of the guys didn't want to do that and he ended up owning 51% of the team.

"At one meeting, Loria said, 'You're idiots. You're losers. I want a winning team. I'm going to spend money. The rest of you can go to hell.' He signed up players in free agency with enormous amounts of money. The team went bankrupt. Maybe not bankrupt (but close to it)."

Yeah, remember that folks, when Loria, on his own without so much as consulting GM Jim Beattie, signed Graeme Lloyd to a three-year deal worth a crazy amount of money: $9-million and he was just a set-up guy in the bullpen. Because of tendonitis and shoulder pain, Lloyd pitched very little that season and although he was 9-5 in 84 games in 2001 the jury had voted against him and Loria.

Lloyd was signed by Loria because he won two World Series rings with the Yankees. Around the same time, Loria acquired pitcher Hideki Irabu, another bust, from the Yankees. Loria was a Yankees fan because he grew up in Manhattan and has operated his art empire out of there for decades.

That same year, 2000, according to McCoubrey, Loria had told the minority shareholders at a meeting that "you don't know how to negotiate" broadcast rights with English-speaking radio and television stations. So Loria attempted to negotiate new deals with media companies to carry the team's games – only to find out his demands were too high.

McCoubrey said Loria "thought he was a genius" and added that Loria pushed "all of the broadcast companies out". That season, fabled broadcaster Dave Van Horne had to do his play-by-play of Expos games on the internet. Very embarrassing.

When Loria kept losing money, he asked the limited partners to fork out money to make up for the losses. Some gave money, others didn't. When some companies didn't want to contribute more money, Loria became a 51% owner of the franchise and later the percentage climbed to 93%.

"Obviously, Loria's spending increased the losses and as he was unable to get broadcasters interested in buying at his price," McCoubrey said. "The team went downhill fast and nobody was interested in buying pieces of a losing minority team and we would not/could not pour money into this losing business. So what followed was to be expected and as you know he had his son-in-law (David Samson) running the team and he was not a businessman or leader anybody believed in.

"I believe that we all wanted out but Loria did not want to buy or pay for our shares. We tried to sue him but to no avail."

What infuriated McCoubrey and his fellow limited partners from the other companies was the deal Loria struck with commissioner Bud Selig and the team owners to sell the Expos to Major League Baseball in exchange for Loria acquiring the Marlins while Marlins owner John Henry was allowed to come in and scoop up his dream team, the Red Sox.

That shyster of a Loria bamboozled the Expos out of Montreal and then coerced politicians in Florida to pony up to build the Marlins a new stadium in Miami. Hrmmph.

Loria got MLB to pay him $112-million for the Expos and then he purchased the Miami franchise for ….Then when he sold out to a group headed by Bruce Sherman and Derek Jeter a few years ago, he pocketed $1.2-billion. Ah shoot, outrageous. When MLB took the Expos and gave the Marlins to Loria, McCoubrey was "amazed, completely amazed. They let that guy buy the Marlins."

Compared to Brochu, who was forced out by partners, Loria was bad news.

"Loria put two teams into bankruptcy," McCoubrey told me, mentioning that the Marlins were the second team along with the Expos. "I thought Brochu was the best guy for the job. He was pretty fair. All he wanted to do was keep the team alive. He was a hard working, very honest guy. He had no personal money. The team was losing money. We had no money. It got worse under Loria. The other partners were very good businessmen in their own right but they were not into baseball."

Danny Gallagher photo
Jeffrey Loria

As for the possibility of baseball returning to Montreal, McCoubrey had no hesitation in saying that it would never happen, even with a new ballpark downtown.

"There is zero chance a team is going there. It wouldn't be supported," McCoubrey insisted. "Montreal is no longer a baseball town. Montreal is good for amateur baseball, not a professional team.

"Olympic Stadium is in the east end, very, very far from where the majority of the fans live – downtown and in the west end. In the east end, there are no baseball fans. They are all immigrants from Nigeria or France, French Caribbean. There are no real Canadians in that area.

"The francophone population has changed. It's not a baseball group of people. They're not baseball fans. Many of the francophones have died or moved to Ontario replaced by Caribbean francophones, North African francophones. I lived in Shawinigan Falls, Québec for a while. It was totally francophone as it is now. There are no baseball fans. Hockey? Yes."

Montreal part of futuristic age in baseball?

Raymond Burns, a productivity specialist for iNet6 in New Hampshire, in what some may interpret as outlandish, says baseball and other sports are changing so much to the point that technology will play a bigger part in how we view the game and how the players will perform.

"Players definitely will be digitally enhanced so that they don't have to play as much," Burns predicted in an interview. "Merging live play with online gaming will become more of a reality. With Microsoft, live fans is a huge step toward a new age.

"Montreal will be on that new wave along with London, Sydney, Tokyo, Berlin, Paris and so on. Things are becoming global."

Burns' theories, guesses or predictions, he feels, will take place in about five years. Futuristic technology will be chic and owners, even the old school ones like Bill DeWitt Jr. of the Cardinals, Bob Castellini of the Reds and John Henry of the Red Sox, will have to adapt to the changes and they will have to start to realize it will bring in more revenue on a global scale.

"Baseball will be the new future past time for millennials and Gen Z because it will be interactive and it can serve as a tool financially for equality & equity," Burns told me. "If baseball has a purpose, I believe it will bring people together like it did when baseball first started out.

"With the new Microsoft technology seen at NBA (bubble) games in Orlando, team owners will see new revenue from this. Let's say an arena has a 24,000-30,000 seat capacity – that capacity could grow to 500,000-1 million with digital seating. Certain features online include close-up camera game play. With the use of VR (Virtual Reality) you'll have a courtside seat view."

And consider this view by Burns as far as gaming, players and drafting. It boggles the mind but it might happen. As far as gaming, players and drafting go, Burns predicts that with virtual reality, we will see gaming added to baseball where holograms will be in place of the players in a 162-game season.

This type of play will give players a chance to stay home and be with family and work on their careers outside of the sport. Imagine, if that ever came true. Players staying at home for part of the season to work on a second career outside baseball?

"Players will play 50-75 physical games," Burns predicted. "Gamers can actually enhance how the player plays by creating new moves and make moves that the player could possibly work on in a physical game. Gaming can also bring early drafting for kids when they're in T-Ball and Little League.

Submitted photo
Raymond Burns

"Gamers can make the kids adults in the virtual game which can create a salary for those kids to bring more money into the family. This will boost economies around the world. Physical players can earn a percentage of earnings, kind of like a royalty check in music from fantasy sports and betting through FanDuel and DraftKings."

Burns also sees global expansion of MLB made easier by his prediction of technology. He feels that Montreal's prospective ownership group would benefit greatly by this technology, making it easier to bring in additional revenue on top of the traditional mores of ticket sales, corporate boxes, merchandise sales, etc.

"With players playing less with VR gaming, we will have a larger league globally," Burns said. "It opens up the expansion to places like Montreal, Tokyo, Seoul, Paris, Berlin, London, etc. Other smart cities can be included like Bill Gates' new planned city in Arizona, Southport in Boston, Mountain View (Google, Facebook area), a new smart city proposal by singer/songwriter Akon in Senegal etc."

Sounds wild but that's how Burns looks at it. He believes his off-the-wall theories might help Montreal when it comes to expansion or relocation "because unemployment is high and people will be eager to have a team following the pandemic."

Burns also was handing out advice as far as improving transportation to and from a new stadium within Montreal and attract more people for attendance.

"They did it to the Celtics arena in Boston near where I live and it's real profitable," Burns said. "The Golden State Warriors' new arena in Frisco provides free transportation to the arena. It's included in the ticket price.

"Market the neighborhood where the stadium is. This will include apartment buildings, new business offices, and fun spots for teenagers. You need the right investors, real estate agents and lobbyists who can get the zoning and approval to build. Montreal is a beautiful, cozy city and if it's marketed right, it could become bigger than Toronto.

"Cafes and shops provide a great experience for those who come on business or millennials, who want to find a place to relax and have fun with amenities. People nowadays love amenities included in their experience."

Tout fini for the Expos

The end of the Expos came Oct. 3, 2004 at Shea Stadium in New York but for many Expos fans, it was Sept. 29, 2004 in Montreal.

It was the last home game of the Expos but as part of that scenario, a 2 p.m. news conference in Salon A in the cold, sombre catacombs of Olympic Stadium spelled the finality of the Expos after 36 seasons following several mis-fires earlier that decade. This was the e-n-d end.

Salon A is where the Expos staged only major news conferences. One big one I can recall years earlier was when Felipe Alou was introduced as the manager on May 22, 1992. The Expos would also use that room for annual January news conferences to get the manager, management, players, office workers and fans hyped up for another season.

But many reporters recall the really-big gathering Sept. 12, 1994 in Salon A, following acting commissioner Bud Selig's directive that the season would be cancelled, thus upending the talent-packed Expos chances of going to the post-season.

The event on Sept. 29, 2004 was even more surreal and disappointing than the one 10 years earlier. Expos president Tony Tavares was the major spokesman for the event, speaking only in English. Some francophone reporters felt someone like French-speaking vice-president Claude Delorme should have been on hand to handle questions in French.

The end of the Expos on Oct. 3 meant many Expos employees were losing their jobs and many reporters were covering the team for the last time. Veteran beat writers such as Serge Touchette of Le Journal de Montréal, Stephanie Myles of the Montreal Gazette and the La Presse Canadienne duo of Richard Milo and Michel Lajeunesse, who covered the team home and away for years, would have to find other beats.

Submitted photos

Expos president Tony Tavares, inset, speaks to reporters on Sept. 29, 2004 prior to the Expos last home game. Left to right are Stephanie Myles of the Montreal Gazette, Cathy Newton of CIQC/TSN Radio and Sylvain Bouchard of the Sports-Labs website.

The same could be said for broadcasters Jacques Doucet, Rodger Brulotte and many other radio and TV play-by-play folks like Elliott Price. Then there were other reporters, who covered the Expos at home. That group included the likes of Cathy Newton of CIQC/TSN Radio and Sylvain Bouchard of SportsLabs.com.

"My fellow reporters and I were just numb, thinking we're just having a nightmare," Bouchard recalled of that Sept. 29 presser. "I can still hear Tony Tavares, very stoic, borderline insensitive, declaring: "Today, the sun is setting in one city, but rising in another." Or something like that.

"Not a single expression of sympathy that I can recall about all the employees that would then be losing their jobs within the Expos organization, not to mention stadium staff.

"It was a first for me having front-row seats to witness a team announcing its relocation to another city, so I had no reference for comparison. One can't objectively say that Tavares was dishonest or whatever.

"He was the MLB-appointed executioner of the transfer of that lameduck Expo team into a city (Washington) that, ironically, had previously lost a MLB franchise not once, but twice. But still, the news struck us all like a stroke of a two-by-four upside the head, which prompted a colleague to ask Tavares: 'Aren't you concerned about security at the game, tonight?' ".

Bouchard said Tavares' reply was that it was a business matter, not at all related to the game on the field.

"Try selling that to the dozens of broken-hearted fans who had come prepared to express their fury with golf balls, batteries, and various other items to throw onto the field of play," Bouchard told me in late 2020.

As for the game itself and the post-game, Bouchard said, "The Expos, I guess, were as numb as everybody else in the stadium, that night. The players may not have all expressed it in words, but life between the lines was just gutted out.

"That game just may as well have been cancelled. To be totally honest here, the only lasting image of the game that I have is the very last out: A Terrmel Sledge pop-up to third base, ironically caught by former Expo Mike Mordecai. And, of course, when former Expo player and team employee Claude Raymond, in full uniform, tearfully addressed the crowd, flanked by an equally emotional Brad Wilkerson, who said 'Au revoir, Montréal!'"

Montreal Expos photo
Livan Hernandez

So that was the end of the Expos and Bouchard said he left the journalism industry all-together in 2005 following a season of NBA coverage for RDS. Newton, who had covered the Expos for almost 10 years for broadcaster Mitch Melnick, was saddened by the turn of events.

"When the Expos left, it was pretty heart breaking," Newton said. "It actually formed part of my decision to head home to Kelowna (British Columbia) where my family is. My sister was having a baby and I wanted to be part of that. Plus my hubby was up for a change so we decided to head out here in 2005.

"With no more baseball, I saw long, dull summers ahead as a sports reporter in Montreal. Then hockey in the winter just wasn't going to make up for it."

As Myles recalls of the last home game, she remarked to me in late 2020, "I was just impressed that I put on a suit for the occasion."

It was the end of an era. Who can forget lovable, portly pitcher Livan Hernandez in the Expos final season? After going 15-10 with the Expos in 2003, he came back and logged 255 innings with an 11-15 record in 2004 with a respectable ERA of 3.60. And at the plate, the defector from Villa Clara, Cuba hit an impressive .247 with seven doubles, a homer and 10 RBI.

I made brief contact on the phone with Hernandez in Miami on Feb. 23, 2021 but we were unable to get together for an interview. He said he "was busy at something" when we first connected and we never connected after that when I called again.

It's somewhat understandable because he filed for bankruptcy in 2017 despite career earnings of $53-million U.S. so he probably doesn't want any publicity. Online reports say he gambled away millions at south Florida casinos. A shame.

Two brothers and their love for the Expos

Andrew and Nathan Clopman grew up in Massena, New York, population 13,000, about an hour south of Montreal so it's not surprising that they attained an immense love for the Expos.

Andrew was a newspaper writer in Northern New York after he finished college and loved receiving Expos guides in the mail. From there, he started collecting Expos magazines, books, postcards, media guides, and "ephemera", as he calls it.

He has collected every Expos media guide except for the one for 1969. He has collected 10,000 different Expos baseball cards, postcards and other similar type pieces of memorabilia. Over the years, he has slowly but surely been scanning copies of Expos related articles in his Baseball Digest collection (mostly from the 1980s), baseball books, and other magazines.

Eventually, he plans to scan pages from old Expos team magazines and media guides. Since the pandemic hit, he has also been going through old Montreal Gazette files on the Google news archives page and saving PDF images of Expos articles. He is saving it all in OneDrive. He had started the project by printing articles off Montreal-area library microfilms in the late 1990s/early 2000s, but discontinued it when he moved away from Montreal in 2006.

"I haven't watched more than a couple of live baseball games since the end of the 2004 season, and it has left a large void in my daily routine," Andrew said in an interview. "I figure I spent three hours by the radio or television 160+ times a year, plus I spent countless hours checking the box scores and transactions from various publications and listening in to radio coverage of the Expos.

"I filled my new-found free time with law school, at first, and then long work hours once I started my legal career," Andrew said. "When my kids were born and I'd stay up with them at nights when they were babies, I watched every Expos game I could find on YouTube. I also had old VHS tapes with games, and my brother converted them to digital copies.

"I've now seen all of the available games a couple of times, so I decided to start reading old Gazette articles when recovering from a broken knee in 2018-19. I dabbled with adopting the Jays, Red Sox, and Mets as a new favorite team, but I decided instead to just remain an Expos fan by digging into books like the ones you write, reading old Bill James books, watching old videos, and now reading old newspapers."

Nathan is cut from the same cloth.

"I have a crazy Expos collection," Nathan said from Florida where has worked for years as a funeral director. "My man cave – I have a whole room dedicated to the 'spos. When I was in Massena, we went to a few games a year in Montreal with my father.

"As soon as I could drive, I went to 20+ games a season. It helped that the drinking age was 18. My family had an apartment in Montreal so I spent a lot of time there. I was there for the last home game Sept. 29 in 2004."

Nathan's first true recollection of the Expos was when his father would sit outside with a black and white five-inch television and a radio listening to Dave Van Horne. For no good reason, he enjoyed watching Mitch Webster before he was traded to the Cubs for Dave Martinez. And watching Otis Nixon, Pascual Perez made his Sunday afternoons a little brighter.

Andrew and Nathan would often see their parents take them to Montreal to watch the Expos, including many Father's Day events at Olympic Stadium. Nathan can remember Felipe Alou's kids, "barely out of diapers" hitting baseballs in the outfield. Often, the Clopmans would go to Expos games to see the Houston Astros play because one of their starting pitchers, Jim Deshaies, came from Massena.

On Sept. 27, 1992, Nathan was at Olympic Stadium to see Gary Carter hit that famous double over the head of former teammate Andre Dawson as the Expos beat the Cubs.

Having grandparents living in Lake Worth, Florida had advantages, too, because the clan from the north could take in a few spring training games. In 2005, after 23 years in Massena, Nathan moved to Florida.

"I always dreamed of moving to Florida, being by the beaches, having warm and sunny winter days," Nathan said. "They do not call Florida God's waiting room for nothing. Growing up in the frozen tundra that is Northern New York, there was not much to get excited about.

"Early April was different, as the snow began to melt and temperatures broke out of the negatives. Early April meant my birthday was arriving on April 6 and it meant the beginning of the MLB season. Sometimes, the two events would coincide. We were only a couple of miles from the Canadian border and Ottawa and Montreal seemed like a hop, skip or jump away."

Nathan first moved to Melbourne but for a number of years now, he has been in Port St. Lucie as a worker in the funeral industry. He had studied mortuary science back home in college.

"I will remember sitting in Albany, New York when I saw on the news that Gary Carter had a malignant, fatal brain tumor, praying that he would have a miraculous recovery, as I am sure many people did," Nathan said. "I also remember the local news on February 16, 2012. I was running on the treadmill at the gym when the local news made a breaking announcement that Gary had passed away. This shows how much Gary meant to the South Florida community, that this was breaking news."

Working in the funeral business, Nathan was blessed that Dignity Memorial, where he worked, was honoured to serve Carter and his family. Nathan recalled that among the former Expos at Carter's funeral were Rusty Staub, Tim Raines, Andres Galarraga, Warren Cromartie and Tommy Hutton, who delivered one of the eulogies.

"Gary's family opted to have him cremated and he is resting peacefully at Riverside Memorial Park in Tequesta, Florida, which is the closest and nicest cemetery within a 20-minute drive, of where Gary lived in Palm Beach Gardens," Nathan said. "The cemetery sits at the end of a street and is beautifully maintained. The musician Perry Como is also laid to rest there. The population of Tequesta was 5,629 during the last census. With Gary, it makes it 5,630. Gary was an icon who is still missed by many.

"The Expos will always be a part of me," Nathan said. "I still have my 25-year-old Youppi keychain that I carry daily. Also living in Florida, the first thing that I did was sell my four-wheel drive sport utility and purchase a new Mustang convertible. Also living in Florida, you have a longer boating season than Northern New York and Montreal had.

"After purchasing a boat, I needed something that could tow it. I purchased a new Jeep Wrangler Sahara. I wanted to be different and decided to put an Expos tire cover over the back spare. Finding a place to do such as task proved difficult but I eventually found a place in Tampa three hours away that would honor my request.

"It has served as a conversation starter. I was at Buffalo Wild Wings in 2017 and the McHale family happened to be there and they stopped me. So did Charles Bronfman and Andres Galarraga."

Having the opportunity to watch Vladimir Guerrero's raw and natural talent had to be one of the highlights of Nathan's childhood. The home opener in 2000 was memorable for him. With traffic, he didn't get home to Massena until 1 in the morning.

Despite little sleep, he made it to school and his first-period teacher, Burt Peck, a huge Expos fan, allowed him to sleep on his desk.

"Another great memory occurred in 2001," Nathan said. "I was watching the Expos warm up and (reliever) Anthony Telford came over to me. I had the same Expos hat that I received as a gift in 1992 when Montreal changed jerseys and caps. I grew as did my head, but that didn't stop me from wearing the cap. This cap went to school and everywhere with me. It was more than likely covered in beer and sweat.

"Anthony took one look at that cap and told me to get a new one and donate this one to the Expos hall of fame. Anthony did indeed grab the cap and sign it for me. This cap sits in my Montreal Expos collection, in which my brother, Andrew and I have been collecting for over 25 years."

Photo by Nathan Clopman

**Nathan Clopman is proud of his Jeep
with the Expos logo on the spare tire**

They played for both Expos & Jays				
Luis Aquino	Rob Ducey	Maicer Izturis	Sandy Martinez	Jon Rauch
Michael Barrett	Scott Downs	Anthony Johnson	Jim Mason	Bill Risley
Miguel Batista	Ron Fairly	Randy Knorr	Orlando Merced	Juan Rivera
Tony Batista	Darrin Fletcher	Tom Lawless	Bailor Moore	Randy St. Claire
Denis Boucher	Willie Fraser	Ted Lilly	Dale Murray	David Segui
Sal Butera	Brad Fullmer	Graeme Lloyd	Steve Nicosia	Scott Service
John Candeleria	Damaso Garcia	Luis Lopez	Otis Nixon	Tony Solaita
Rick Cerone	Rene Gonzales	Ken Macha	Charlie O'Brien	Matt Stairs
Raul Chavez	Alex Gonzalez	Mickey Mahler	Tomo Ohka	Hector Torres
Darwin Cubillan	Shawn Hill	Fred Manrique	Al Oliver	Mitch Webster
Omal Daal	Tommy Hutton	Dave Martinez	Robert Perez	Brad Wilkerson
Source: Clay Marston, Canadian Baseball News				Kenny Williams

Dawson's sacrifice led to Curt Flood award

When Andre Dawson stood by his principles and decided to leave the Expos following the 1986 season, he was without a contract heading into the 1987 season.

It was an off-season of collusion when team owners ganged up and decided they would not get into a free-agent frenzy by signing players. It was collusion at his finest. Crazy nonsense.

Dawson had to wait until March 9, 1987 long after spring training had started to sign a contract elsewhere. Can you imagine waiting that long? He signed for far less money than the last offer made by the Expos: $1-million.

That offer by the Expos was a cut in his salary by $200,000 from 1986. Dawson was insulted. He had been chatting initially that winter with GM Murray Cook and vice-president Bill Stoneman but when Dawson made his decision to leave, he was dealing with president John McHale. He thanked McHale and told the Expos he was moving on.

In an interview Dawson did with me Feb. 16, 2021, he said the Expos offer was a "slap in the face" and there was no way that he was going to return to the team for the 1987 season. He did say owner "Mr. Bronfman made the money available to sign me" but his executives in the baseball department didn't do anything about it.

"I've been in baseball long enough that it's part o the game. Sometimes decisions have to be made," Cook said in an interview with me in 2020, in studying Dawson's departure. "Jeff Reardon (traded that winter to the Twins), Dawson, it's just part of baseball. Clubs were starting to move players because of contracts and a lot of different reasons. In this day, players hardly seldom stay with clubs their whole career."

After a decade of service with the Expos, Hawk was looking for an-

Submitted photo

Andre Dawson poses with the late Juanita Moore on Camera Day in 1981

other employer.

"I was putting that chapter of my career behind me," Dawson told me. "They offered me a cut in pay. At that point, there was a lot of bitterness, especially when I was dangled in trade rumours. It had left a bad taste in my mouth. That (trade talk) never manifested itself but I knew the writing was on the wall.

"I just kind of took it to heart about what objectives they had of trying to do with me and what their plans were for me. As a free agent, I wanted to get fair market value. I'd been there for 10 years, having a career like I had, it was time to move on and test the free-agent market. In my last year, I had gone on the disabled list for the first time. I injured my hamstring and then re-injured it the day before I was supposed to come off the disabled list so I ended up spending a month on the disabled list."

226

Although it would have made some sense in the form of wishful thinking, there was the story going around in the winter of 1986-87 that Dawson and his good friend Tim Raines had discussed the idea of both of them signing with the same team as free agents. But nothing ever came of it.

"It would have been nice to have both of us on the same ballclub and continue our careers together," Dawson said. "That was going to be a tough go for the most part. No team would be looking for two outfielders, maybe one but two at the same time, not likely."

Dawson even told me that he considered "going to Japan and make more money" but it's something he didn't consider "that seriously".

As Dawson and his agent Dick Moss studied their options upon leaving the Expos, they decided on a rather brazen move because as Dawson said, "We got no offers at all." They decided to travel unannounced, without any advance notice to the Cubs and showed up at spring training in Mesa, Ariz., looking to see if Chicago would be interested in his services. The story about him going to Chicago without the Cubs' prior knowledge is something I'd never heard before until now.

"We went to Arizona. They were caught off-guard. They weren't expecting us to show up in the middle of spring training," Dawson said. "We wanted to get something into Mr. Green. We were feeling our way in. We didn't know his agenda or itinerary for that day."

I was curious as to why Dawson picked the Cubs and he made some interesting comments.

"My preference was to stay in the National League and play on grass and I felt I performed better in day games," he said, alluding to the fact that in those days, the Cubs never played night games until the lights went on Aug. 8, 1988.

So Dawson and Moss got chatting with the Cubs and this is what Hawk did: he handed the Cubs a blank contract and asked GM Dallas Green to fill out a salary that the team deemed appropriate for his wealth of talent. Everyone knows that story.

Green came back with a less than glamorous figure of $500,000 but Dawson bit his lip and accepted it.

"I just said to myself, 'Hopefully, it won't be overly embarrassing,'" Dawson said of the Cubs' offer. "I put my neck on the fence. Looking in the mirror, I got the offer and realized it was an offer for me to refuse. Their offer was for me to turn down."

So what Dawson said without admitting it, was that the offer was more or less lower than what him and Moss were looking at but they accepted it. But then that's when the scenario got interesting.

"They weren't supposed to be negotiating with free agents," Dawson said of the Cubs. "I accepted it right away. I went in there, not knowing how they would react. I said, 'Thank you, Mr. Green.' And he got quiet for a few seconds. I thought I lost him."

Yeah, Green was stunned that Dawson accepted the offer. Green offered him that amount, not figuring he would accept it.

"Can I get back to you in an hour?" Green politely asked Dawson and Moss.

"Sure," they replied.

"We knew what that was all about," Dawson told me. "They had to clear it with the commissioner's office. They weren't supposed to do it (negotiate a contract)."

But commissioner Peter Ueberroth advised the Cubs they had the OK to accept the offer.

"We'd love to have you," Green told Dawson.

Dawson told me that if there had been no deal with the Cubs that he had no intention of returning to the Expos. He said "Montreal was not going to be an option" but he did say that he had been planning to talk with Atlanta, if the Cubs deal fell through.

What did Dawson do in 1987? It's the stuff of legends. He produced a banner season of 49 homers and 137 RBI to show that he still had a lot of pop in the bat. It was some kind of sweet revenge on the part of Dawson against the Expos.

"I'd heard later that they (Expos) were saying my best years were behind me, that I was limited to a degree because of the Astroturf," Dawson said.

Fast forward to 2020 when the Major League Baseball Players Association selected Dawson as the winner of the inaugural Curt Flood Award, given to a former player who "demonstrated a selfless, longtime devotion to the Players Association and advancement of players' rights."

Yes, the players association group looked at Dawson's "selfless", unselfish decision in 1987 and deemed him 33 years later to be a worthwhile winner of the award which recognizes the legacy of Flood, who pursued judicial help in an attempt to end baseball's reserve system.

Flood was unsuccessful in his own personal case but his efforts sure laid the pipeline for free agency to be much better in the long run.

"Myself, my agent, we did some creative thinking and we devised a plan," Dawson said in a video released by the players association when the award was announced. "I didn't know what the outcome was going to be as a result. I guess I made the right decision. It's not about the monetary issues. It's about pride and principle moving forward."

Dawson's sacrifice paid off in the long run for him and other free agents like Raines, who were bypassed that off-season season by the collusion-beset owners. Raines waited until May, 1987 to re-sign with the Expos.

What Dawson's sacrifice helped to manifest was a lawsuit against the owners, accusing them of collusion. It resulted in Dawson and other players being awarded vast amounts of money to offset what they had to endure in the face of next-to-no offers from most teams. His decision to accept an inferior offer is seen in many circles as a landmark time for the rights of players and the end result was the production of a $280-million collusion settlement between players and team owners.

"The Expos were telling Andre he was washed up and no good," Russ Hansen, Dawson's close friend of close to 45 years, told me in an interview. "He used to share that with me. Because of Andre taking the stand for half a million, that opened up the catching of all these guys (owners) in the collusion. He was the $2-million poster child of this whole thing."

In an interview he did with Matt Kelly of mlb.com for a story about Dawson winning the award, former PA executive director Donald Fehr said, "You had a graphic demonstration that one of the very best players of the game was of no interest to any team except his existing team (the Expos)."

Fellow Hall of Fame member and MLBPA special advisor Dave Winfield said this to Kelly about Dawson's stand: "That changed the circumstances of the way people looked at the entire thing that was going on with collusion. He could have had a bad season, but he didn't. He played under immense pressure. It was by hard work, dedication, going against the odds and playing in pain."

Dawson told me he "was honoured to say the least to be the first recipient to win the award." He commended Flood for what he did.

"He sacrificed a lot during his career. It takes a special individual to do that. It probably cost him his career for what he believed in," Dawson said. "It (Flood's stand) was frowned upon by the owners. He challenged (the baseball establishment) for what he believed in. He made an authentic mark on the game itself. It changed the game. It changed sports.

"For me as a recipient, it was history. With collusion, I took a stance (with the Expos) for what I believed in. I was subjected to the mercy of the ballclub. It was unfair treatment. I had a sense of leverage. With those collusion years, it (financial settlement) changed the whole concept of properly negotiating with players. The award speaks volumes. It's something I hold in high esteem."

How Jesus Frias became Pepe Frias

A Facebook friend of mine, Joel Passino of upstate New York not far from Montreal, had been telling me he really wanted to get an autographed ball from Pepe Frias. It was one of Passino's special quests to go along with the huge collection of bats and balls he has in his house.

Passino told me why he wanted to get a signed Frias' ball.

"I remember going to Jarry Park as a youngster, going to my first game in 1973," Passino said. "I was a shortstop in my town Amvets league so I was naturally attracted to the shortstop position and right away, I loved how he played the position on the team I loved and still love to this day. When I played shortstop, I was Pepe Frias."

So I took it upon myself to help Passino out and try and track Frias down. At the same time, I said to myself, 'Why not try to get an interview with him for this book?' Scouring the internet and typing in Pepe Frias for addresses down in the United States didn't seem to help.

But I studied his bio on the Baseball Reference website and I saw that his real first name was Jesus so I started typing in Jesus Frias. Up pops him as living in Tampa, Florida. I couldn't find a phone number attached to the Florida address so what did I do? I decided to write him a postal letter.

So the letter arrived in early February, 2021 and Frias' nephew Vic received it. He immediately let Frias know about my letter and that I wanted to do an interview with him and find out his address so Passino could send him a ball to get signed.

So on Feb. 12, I see a call coming in on my cell phone from the area code 809 which I know is the Dominican Republic but I didn't know who it was. I picked up the phone and the caller said, "Hey, Danny, it's Pepe Frias."

I couldn't believe my ears. I found out that Frias lives in his native Dominican Republic full time so I began talking with him about his career and how he ended up with the Expos. It's quite the story. Frias' life is one of resilience and patience and perseverance.

Jesus Frias was one of 15 brothers born to his parents in the famous baseball town of San Pedro de Macoris, which sent the likes of Tony Fernandez, Sammy Sosa, Robinson Cano and George Bell to the major leagues. Only four of his brothers are alive.

Frias started his pro baseball career in the San Francisco Giants organization in 1966 and he suited up to play in 1967 in Decatur, Illinois in the Midwest league. That same year, the Giants sent him to play with their team in Salt Lake City. After playing in four games, going 1-for-8, the Giants let him go.

"I had sprained my right ankle and they released me," Frias said in an interview.

So here was Frias in the middle of nowhere in the United States on his own and out of a job. He got into contact with his brother Pablo in New York City and Pablo told him not to go back home to the Dominican. Pablo told Jesus to come to New York and get work with him as an electrician. So Jesus gets on a bus that takes him to NYC.

When Frias wasn't helping out his brother, he would go to Central Park in downtown New York and play pick-up ball. In the meantime, the Dodgers signed him to a minor-league deal on Nov. 13, 1967 but he was released on April 1, 1968 without having played a game either in the minors for the majors – or at least that we know.

In this dizzying array of signings and releases, I tried to piece together his story, going back and forth to statistics at Baseball Reference. Frias ran into a scout, who knew Joe Silva, who recruited players and sent them to play in semi-pro leagues in Canada, including Québec.

So that is how Frias ended up in 1968 in Thetford Mines, Québec which is located in south-central Québec more than two hours east of Montreal and 90 miles south of Québec City. I was there in the spring of 1979, covering Ontario's Hawkesbury Hawks in the Centennial Cup Tier Two junior hockey playdowns for the Ottawa Journal.

Thetford Mines, with a population of roughly 16,000, is situated on the Becancour River in the Appalachian Mountains and is best known for its reputation as one of the world's largest asbestos-producing regions. The town was founded in 1876 after the discovery of large asbestos deposits. But nowadays, asbestos is not chic because of the medical dangerous it poses.

A scout in the Dominican Republic had somehow got a hold of Thetford Mines Mineurs general manager Joe Setlakwe, whose family ran a large department-store chain, to see if he would be interested in taking Frias.

"I'll pay for his way back home if he doesn't make the team," the scout told.

"You gotta be kidding me. How old is he?" Setlakwe replied.

"He's 16," the scout said.

In the end, Setlakwe agreed to take Frias, who said he can't remember how he got to Thetford Mines, probably by bus.

When Frias showed up, Setlakwe was asked by another team's GM, "Where did you get this kid? I was supposed to get him."

In 244 at-bats, according to Maurice Dumas, a retired writer who was working at the time in Thetford Mines for La Tribune, a paper based in nearby Sherbrooke, Frias batted .262 with 11 doubles, four triples, a homer and 38 RBI. Pretty decent statistics. You will see in looking at Frias' Baseball Reference statistics, that the year 1968 is blank. That's because he was playing for a team not affiliated with a team in MLB.

Despite Thetford Mines' inability to keep a minor-league team in town for very long, players who were honed there included future major-leaguers such as future Expos player Ken Macha, who won the 1984 Eastern League batting championship and was voted MVP and all-star with the Pittsburgh Pirates affiliated team.

Setlakwe and his family operated a chain of clothing stores in Québec called G. Setlakwe Ltd. and often he would be in Montreal as a salesman. So one day, he's at the Windsor Hotel in downtown Montreal where the Expos had temporary offices.

"I'd be in Montreal every Tuesday and Wednesday so I met Expos GM Jim Fanning. I told him what Frias did," Setlakwe was telling me.

"There comes a point where Pepe after a season is wasting his time in the minors," Setlakwe told Fanning. "You better send a scout up there. He's got what it takes. He's got all the capacity. He's got tremendous range, good hands, good arms. He makes an easy play look hard and a hard play look easy. He was trying to hit home runs when he's not supposed to hit a home run."

But Setlakwe never told Fanning that Frias was "really a hot dog", who liked to "impress all the time" and show off. In any event, Fanning wasn't interested.

"Nothing happens until a year later," Setlakwe said.

In the meantime, though, the Giants found out what Frias did in Thetford Mines and signed him again on Oct. 22 of that year to play the following year. So what do the Giants do? They send him back to Decatur, where he had played in 1967.

Like he did in 1967, Frias didn't hit so good in 1969: he batted .188 with no homers and 12 RBI. He was let go again on July 1, 1969. The first time Frias was released, it also so happened to be on July 1, according to his Baseball Reference transactions.

"I got released twice by the Giants," Frias said.

Frias returned to Thetford Mines in 1969 as an independent player but his stats in the league aren't recorded by Baseball Reference because it's not considered organized ball. So Dumas kindly told me Frias' batting average jumped to .293 and he collected seven doubles, five triples, six homers and 33 RBI. Another solid season.

"He was hitting first or seventh and eighth," Dumas told me.

During that season in Thetford Mines, Silva, at the urging of Setlakwe, called up Fanning and told him about Frias so Fanning got into his car, hopped on Route 112 and drove to Thetford Mines to see him.

Fanning came up to Frias and said, "Pepe, tomorrow, you will belong to the Expos."

So the next day, Aug. 27, as his career Transactions say, he was signed by the Expos.

"It was a rainy day and Pepe came into my office and told me he just signed with the Expos," Dumas recalled. "I replied, 'Pepe, I have no time to waste with you.'"

Dumas thought Frias was being mischievous and trying to pull his leg.

"But I phoned the team's president Gilles Turcotte and he confirmed the signature. I had the scoop that he signed with the Expos, "Dumas said.

Frias recalled his signing this way: "Fanning was very nice. I signed on the condition I go to the Florida Instructional league that fall."

And what did he sign for as we continued our conversation by text messages? "Notein," he said, as in nothing. Meaning no signing bonus was given him. Oh shit, the Expos gave him no money. Unreal.

So all this time, Frias is still known by Jesus, but that would change once he got to West Palm Beach for Instructional league play. The team manager was J.W. Porter, who didn't want to call him Jesus. Porter saw a glove on the ground that Frias had brought along and it was signed, 'Pepe.' It was a glove that had belonged to Frias' brother Pepe. So Porter said, 'Hey, Pepe, go to shortstop."

So the name Pepe Frias was born and he was known by that name in baseball after that.

In the following years, Frias found continuity in the Expos organization. After being released twice by the Giants and once by the Dodgers, he could finally call one organization home. He spent the 1970 season in Jacksonville, Fla, the 1971 season in Winnipeg and Québec City and the 1972 season in Evansville, Indiana.

In Québec City, Frias began to earn a reputation as somewhat of a party animal so Setlakwe got wind of his behaviour and told Fanning about him.

"What's the problem?" Fanning asked Setlakwe.

"It's your friend Pepe Frias," Setlakwe replied.

"Why?" Fanning asked.

"He's acting and doing things he shouldn't be doing. He's doing too much partying. He's a manipulator. We're going to fire (release) him,"

Frias family photo   *Canadian Baseball Hall of Fame*

Pepe Frias, right, poses with his son Victor, daughter Brenda and wife Felipa

Setlakwe told Fanning.

So Fanning agreed to come to Québec City and talk with Frias.

"Shit, get off the pot or you're fired," Fanning told Frias. "Get a hold of yourself. Quit the fooling around."

Said Setlakwe, "He was a good kid. You gotta understand, he's 16-years-old coming from a poor family and doesn't have any money."

Frias went to spring training in 1973 and cracked the Expos opening-day roster and spent the entire season with Montreal, making his debut on April 6 as a late-game replacement.

Frias, for the most part during his career, couldn't hit worth a lick but he was a crackerjack infielder. He took a great liking to manager Gene Mauch, who took a great liking to Frias and accepted Frias for his frailties at the plate because he was nifty at short. Frias played a pivotal role as the team almost made it to the playoffs in their fifth season of operation.

As they would say in French, Frias was "un peu faible au baton, excellent défensivement arret-court."

"I didn't make much money, about $4,000 that first year," Frias said. "In the old days, that was a lot of money. I was a nice person. I would take whatever they gave me. I never argued. I couldn't hit but I could play good defensively. I didn't miss a lot of balls. I established a role. Gene Mauch was the greatest manager I ever played for.

"They called me Cat. Gary Carter and Ken Singleton would take me out to get something to eat and buy me clothes. They made a lot of money."

Frias would hang around with the Expos as a part-time player for six seasons before getting released. Boy, he sure had a good run with the Expos. One story he likes to tell is the day in 1975 when Larry Bowa of the Phillies gave him a new Rawlings glove. Frias headed home to San Pedro de Macoris and ran into fellow major-leaguer Tony Fernandez.

"Here, Tony, you take this glove. You're going to be better than me," Frias said. "I was his first teacher back home."

Frias would go on to play for the Braves and Dodgers before packing it in 1981, some 40 years ago.

As for Passino, who lives near the Québec/New York border, he got an address from me for Frias in San Pedro de Macoris and he was looking forward to receiving an autographed ball. How about that? Same with Burton Peck, who resides not far from Passino.

As we kept talking, Frias told me he had heard that he qualified for the Québec Pension Plan, a topic I had written about back in the summer of 2020 so I made arrangements for him to get signed up to receive a pension.

"I need to have that pension," said Frias, who told me his pension from his playing days is $800 U.S. per month.

Frias and several hundred former Expos born outside Canada qualify for a little-known stipulation in the QPP fund. Some of these players are aware of their eligibility, but Jim Gosger and Mike Vail, who played for Nos Amours, weren't familiar with it until just recently.

The bonus pension is one reward for the Expos players because they were taxed so heavily when they played in Montreal. In essence, they are getting back some of the money they paid out. Québec is the only province in Canada that boasts its own pension plan, which is administered by the Caisse de dépôt et placement du Québec. Taxpayers in other provinces have their pensions rolled into the Canada Pension Plan.

"Professional athletes who meet the criteria may be eligible," QPP spokesman Frederic Lizotte said, in confirming the benefits for former Expos not born in Canada. "Workers can receive a retirement pension as of age 60, provided they contributed for at least one year. They do not need to have stopped working. The age at which the contributor begins receiving a retirement pension will determine the amount of the pension for as long as it is paid."

Months after he gave me information for my story for the Montreal Gazette, I asked Lizotte if he would help me in getting help from one of his colleagues to get Frias set up with forms he could sign in order for him to start receiving the pension. So on Feb. 15, that happened. Frias was thankful.

Macha's dream season in Thetford Mines, Québec

Like Pepe Frias, Ken Macha used Thetford Mines, Québec as a springboard to the major leagues and he sure had a dizzying season. A Season of All Seasons, the best campaign he enjoyed in all his time playing in the pro ranks in Canada, the U.S. and Japan.

On the last day of the 1974 Eastern League Double-A regular season, Macha went head-to-head against future Expos teammate Warren Cromartie of the Québec Carnavals for the batting championship. That's how good Macha was. That's how good Cro was.

So prior to the final game, Tim Murtaugh, the manager of the Thetford Mines Pirates and son of Pittsburgh Pirates manager Danny Murtaugh, asked Macha if he wanted to sit out the game because he was likely going to win the batting title anyway. Macha said no.

"I have 99 RBI. I want the 100 RBI," Macha told Murtaugh. "I went 0-for-2 to start the game and then I got a hit that locked in the batting championship. It's a fairy-book story. I hit a solo homer in the eighth inning. That's how I got my 100th RBI."

Said Murtaugh of Macha, "When he hit that home run to reach 100 RBI, I thought that was so impressive. He was a most impressive clutch hitter. He wasn't a great defensive catcher but his offence would let him play. He became a valuable player. He was one of the most intelligent players I was around. If I was going to be late or something, he'd take over until I got there. He had intelligence, high baseball intelligence."

Beautiful. When I emailed Cromartie, who bypassed Class A ball, to get this thoughts, he replied, "That was my first year of professional baseball. The last 10 days of the season, I started to notice the opportunity (batting title). I really wasn't chasing it. I just wanted to have a good year."

Macha was indeed a Pirates prospect. He also contributed 21 homers in only 386 at-bats and as he proudly told me, "I had 22 stolen bases. " That Thetford Mines team was a powerhouse that won the league title despite allowing a league-high 682 runs during the season. Macha, the team's catcher, admitted the team's pitching "wasn't that good."

Thetford Mines won the league championship with sweeps in the playoffs of Bristol, Conn. and Pittsfield, Mass. Among the other members of that potent squad were Willie Randolph, Omar Moreno and Tony Armas Sr., the father of former Expos pitcher Tony Armas Jr. That season, Moreno pilfered 67 bases. Six years later, he stole 96 in the majors for Pittsburgh.

Macha, who had signed with the Pirates for a mere $2,500 in 1972, had also played in Québec the season before at Sherbrooke where he hit .267 with 12 homers and 52 RBI. So he was merely just heading up the road about 110 miles to Thetford Mines.

"When we got there to Thetford Mines, we didn't have much of a field," Macha said. "Four of us got together, Frank Frontino, Dennis Malseed, Jim Minshall and I, and we got the top part of a house," Macha recalled. "Each guy had his own bedroom so that was nice. It was actually half a mile from the stadium (Bellevue). Frank was an avid golfer. He bought a bicycle and many times he would ride to a nine-hole course called the Thetford Golf and Curling Club. He'd play nine holes and then come back in time for our game.

"I can remember when we were in that house, we'd wake up to the smell of the Kentucky Fried Chicken place. Just to give you a thought right now, three years ago, my wife Carolyn and I took a vacation to Québec," said Macha, who lives near Pittsburgh. "We went to Québec City, Sherbrooke and Thetford Mines. And that Kentucky Fried Chicken place is really right where it was. How about that? And that nine-hole course became an 18-hole course."

That's right, the KFC joint is still located at 31 Frontenac Blvd. West, right smack in the middle of downtown Thetford Mines. It's been there 50 years.

That season, Macha also got playing time in Triple-A with Virginia's Charleston Charlies and got his first taste of MLB action following the championship season in Thetford Mines. He made his MLB debut Sept. 14 at Jarry Park against the Expos. But he didn't travel to Montreal from Thetford Mines. He met his Pittsburgh teammates in Chicago, meaning he took his own car, one given to him by his father Edward, for a long drive.

"I got into my car and drove to Pittsburgh. It was about 13 hours. When you get called, you drive anywhere," Macha said. "Then I flew to Chicago."

Macha guessed that he was told about Sept. 8 of his call-up but didn't play in any of the games at Wrigley Field. On Sept. 14 in Mon-

Thetford Mines Pirates photo

Québec's Thetford Mines Pirates won the 1974 Eastern League Double-A championship. Left to right are Tony Armas, guy behind Armas is unknown, Frank Frontino, George Whileyman, Ken Melvin, Dennis Malseed, Jim Sexton, Ken Macha, John Hall, Cal Meier, Rich Anderson, Ron Mitchell, Odell Jones, Mike Kavanagh, Willie Randolph, manager Tim Murtaugh, Omar Moreno. Some players are missing from the photo because they were called up to Triple-A or were transferred elsewhere.

239

treal, he pinch hit in the eighth inning for catcher Manny Sanguillen and singled. Pretty good debut. He stayed in the game as a catcher.

"We got beat 17-2. We got the daylights beat out of us," Macha said of his debut game.

Macha, a right-handed hitter, went 3-for-5 with a few pinch hits that month and with Pittsburgh's stacked deck, he got very little playing time. He was proud that he got a pinch-hit single to left off tough lefty Al Hrabosky of the Cardinals. From 1975-78, Macha spent most of the time in Triple-A for Pittsburgh.

He got a break on Dec. 7, 1978 when he was claimed in the Rule V draft by the Expos. He was getting lost in the shuffle with Pittsburgh so going to Québec to play with his third team in that province was fine with him.

"I was elated to be drafted by the Expos," Macha said. "There was a comfort level there. I had played against Gary Carter, Larry Parrish, Jerry White and the list goes on, all those years. They knew me because I was on the other side of the ball. I think they had a certain amount of respect because they knew I could play. If I had gone to San Francisco or any other teams, they would say, 'Who is this guy?'

"I was happy to be out of the Pirates organization. Even if I had stayed with the Pirates, I wouldn't give up those years in the Expos organization. They had all-stars (almost) at every position. Pittsburgh had Willie Stargell, Dave Parker, Al Oliver, Rennie Stennett, Richie Hebner, Manny Sanguillen was the catcher. They were all products of their farm system.

"Then you looked at Montreal, they had guys like Parrish, Valentine, Dawson, Carter, Rogers, they played through the organization and into the big leagues. What Pittsburgh did was trade guys like Armas and Randolph and in the long run, that led them to getting to winning the World Series in 1979."

So yes, Macha was glad to be gone from Pittsburgh, even if it meant not getting much playing time, even if it meant spending time on the Expos fabled BUS Squad, otherwise known as Broke Underrated Superstars, during spring training and getting on buses that would travel a few hours to a destination while the regulars stayed back at home base in Daytona Beach.

While it was perceived that the BUS Squad concept was a fun thing put together by Tommy Hutton, Macha looked at it another way, something that directed a critique if you will of the established players. Macha tended to wanted to kid and needle the regulars.

"It was more or less a sarcastic kind of a deal," Macha said of the BUS Squad. "It was a little rallying cry for the guys, the bench players. It became a big deal."

In 1979, Macha spent some time at Triple-A for in Denver and a bit of time in the majors. In 1980, he spent the entire season with Montreal but got little playing time, appearing in 49 games with a homer, eight RBI and a .290 BA. Like the Pirates, the Expos were loaded with talent at many positions as they almost gained a playoff berth in both 1979-80.

"I enjoyed playing for Dick Williams. I told him that. He was very demanding," Macha said. "He tried to teach us the game. He was tough on the guys but you knew where you stood with him. Actually, he drew up all the charts, where to position players. He was before his time.

"I can't say enough of my time in Montreal, the excitement. It's the reason my wife and I would go on vacation there. We were pretty tight knit. Gary Carter is in the hall of fame. Larry Parrish was hitting 30 home runs. Tony Perez is in the hall of fame. I was a stop-gap catcher, infielder, wherever. I hung out with Woodie (Fryman). When we went to Cincinnati, I'd go to his house in Kentucky. Him and I got along pretty good. I lived in the same building down by the Forum in Montreal as Scott Sanderson.

Courtesy Donruss/Panini
Ken Macha

"I remember we were in Cincinnati and I hadn't played in three weeks. So I was put up to pinch hit with the game on the line and the Reds gave me an intentional walk," Macha recalled, chuckling at the memory. "I said to Johnny Bench, 'I haven't had an at-bat in 21 days and you're walking me?' It was a good story."

Following the 1980 season, Macha had a chat with Expos president and GM John McHale, who was positive with what he had to say. McHale ventured to tell Macha that the Expos wanted to keep him in the organization, take him off the roster and the kicker was that Macha would earn the same money in the minors as in the majors "or we can try to trade you."

Furthermore, McHale told Macha "we would like to have you become a manager" in the organization at some point. Macha didn't think about this situation very long. He told McHale, "I think I can still play. I hit .290 that year." I had a pretty good year manage int eh minor leagues.

So this is what McHale did. He swung a deal to sell Macha's contract to the Blue Jays on Jan. 15, 1981.

"When you're done playing, let us know," McHale told Macha.

Like he did in Montreal and Pittsburgh, Macha got little playing time with Toronto. He got into 37 games, batting .200 with a homer and six RBI.

"In Toronto, I was the extra guy. Danny Ainge was at third, Ernie Whitt was the catcher. They were pretty well set," Macha recalled.

In the off-season, Macha learned of an opportunity to play in Japan so he went for it, playing full time in the course of four seasons with Chunichi Dragons. For the first time since Thetford Mines and Charleston, Macha was back to playing full time, instead of being on the bench most of the time.

"I wound up hitting a lifetime .300 with 82 home runs over those four seasons in Japan," Macha said, proudly. "At the end of my fourth season, I'll say with about three weeks remaining, they had told me I was not going to be invited back. On the last day I was there, I pinch hit and when the game was over, I was coming off the field and a few of the players threw me up in the air. I think you can find it on YouTube. There's a Japanese term for that."

It was Macha's teammates telling him how much they appreciated his time with the team. Was that an emotional experience for him?

"I think it was more emotional that it (Japanese career) was over," he said. "The next day, I came to the ballpark, got my stuff and packed up to go to the airport to go home. A bunch of the guys came to the airport to send me off. It was pretty cool."

In any event, what Macha did in Japan was what he couldn't do with the Pirates or Expos because he was a part-time player on teams that were stacked with players at most positions. In a full-time role in Japan like he was in the minors, especially Thetford Mines, he excelled.

Not long after he got back home from Japan, Macha called up McHale and true to McHale's word after the 1980 season, he arranged to get Macha a job coaching with the Expos under manager Buck Rodgers. Macha admitted that being away for five years, "to be truthful is a long time", meaning he couldn't really expect that McHale would still have a job for him after such a long absence.

McHale told Macha "we have a radar gun." So prior to games, Macha would help out with pre-game workouts and during games, he would be behind home plate running the gun on pitchers. By 1987, he was the bullpen coach and would spend six years with the Expos, then three years as a coach with the Angels and another four with Oakland sandwiched around time spent in Boston's farm system as a manager.

Then came a big break when he was named A's manager for four years and then another two with the Brewers.

"I had 23 years in the majors as a player, coach and manager," Macha said. "Tremendous years. I saw a lot. I saw Kenny Rogers' perfect game, Lenny Barker's perfect game and Dennis Martinez's perfect game."

Best player he ever saw?

"Tough question," Macha said. "There was Ozzie Smith at shortstop. In 1979-80 with Montreal, anytime you'd try to steal a base against us, Gary Carter was throwing out runners. Dave Parker, Ellis Valentine, they could pretty much do anything. And Bo Jackson – I swear he could pretty much dictate what he wanted to do. He was pretty awesome. I remember his last at-bat (Aug. 10, 1994). He got a base hit and he was at first. He was pissed because he wanted it to be a home run."

Thank you, Ken, for the memories.

Stoney belongs in Canadian hall

How is Bill Stoneman not a member of the Canadian Baseball Hall of Fame?

In a way, it's like asking why Paul Henderson is not in the Hockey Hall of Fame for scoring three consecutive, game-winning goals in the final three games of the 1972 Team Canada-Russia Summit Series won by Canada?

Stoneman not only pitched two no-hitters for the Expos but he was an Expos administrator from 1983 to 1999. He's an easy choice for the hall of fame selection committee.

Stoneman pitched for the Expos from 1969-73 and was noted for a nasty curve and still holds the Expos club record for strikeouts with 251 in 1971.

Stoneman's curriculum vitae, as I wrote it up in the Montreal Daily News on Feb. 15, 1989., is mighty impressive. Not long after 'retiring' as a player in 1974, he joined a Montreal-based group headed by Norm Caplan that represented athletes. He serviced clients and advised them on their tax situation. He remembered driving to Toronto to meet New York Islanders GM Bill Torrey and pick up forward Clark Gillies' first contract.

In early 1975, Stoneman joined the Canadian financial services company Royal Trust in a head office marketing position. Less than a year later, he was appointed the company's national advertising manager. In 1981, he became manager of a Royal Trust branch in Mississauga, Ont., west of Toronto while living nearby in Georgetown.

Two years later, he was back in Royal Trust's marketing department at head office. That same year, word got out that he was on the short list for the general manager's job with the North American Soccer League's

Toronto Blizzard.

Then his career took a turn back toward the Expos. He was passing through Montreal from a vacation in Prince Edward Island when his wife Diane Falardeau suggested they stop in Montreal for a few days.

One thing led to another and Stoneman attended an Expos game at Olympic Stadium and was in the press box chatting with a couple of people when Expos president and GM John McHale tapped him on the shoulder. McHale told Stoneman he wanted to see him later. They got talking about Stoneman returning to the club in some fashion.

But it wasn't until two years later that he did come back – as McHale's assistant. The official date was Nov. 14, 1983. Less than a year later, he was appointed vice-president of baseball administration on Sept. 18.

Then a few years later when GM Murray Cook was let go, Stoneman was appointed vice-president, baseball operations and GM on Aug. 11, 1987. Less than a year later, he relinquished those duties to assistant GM Dave Dombrowski and stayed on, tackling a lot of contract negotiations.

Stoneman was more comfortable behind the scenes, engaging in such functions as financing, budgeting and salary negotiations. He wasn't that comfortable dealing with the media whereas Dombrowski loved kibitzing with reporters. But what also entered into the scheme of things was the fact that him and his wife were raising kids still growing up: Jill and Jeff, who at the time of my story were 16 and 12, respectively. He really didn't want to be on call for possible trade talks when he would have preferred to be taking his kids to sports or school functions. Dombrowski, on the other hand, was single.

"I wasn't going to change a personality to suit a job," Stoneman told me back in early 1989. "Maybe I was too stubborn to recognize what a burden it was being GM. I didn't mind at all when the change (to Dombrowski) was made. Being a GM was not a very fun side of the job. I always was a low-profile person, even when I played, and I always will be. I'm not all that comfortable dealing with the media. Dave was a natural to take over. He's more at ease with the media. He's more outgoing.

"The financial end is my strength, my enjoyment," Stoneman continued. "My overall function is interesting. I have more control over what happens in the final end. I enjoy the salary negotiations. It can be stressful but it's really not all filled with pressure."

GM duties for Stoneman took a dramatic turn in the late 1990s when the Angels came calling, asking Expos president Claude Brochu for permission to chat with Stoneman. This time, Stoney was up to the task because Jill and Jeff had grown up and he had the time to devote himself to the position. He took the Angels up on their offer and stayed with them as GM through the 2007 season, although he was appointed interim GM years later.

Stoneman dipped into the rival Dodgers' pool of personnel to hire

Bill Stoneman
V.P. Baseball Operations

David Dombrowski
V.P. Player Personnel
and General Manager

Dan Duquette
Assistant G.M.

Gary Hughes
Director, Scouting

Frank Wren
Assistant Director,
Scouting

Kent Qualls
Administrative Assistant,
Player Development

Erik Ostling
Director, Team Travel

Rob Rabenecker
G.M. West Palm Beach
Operations

René Marchand
Administrative
Assistant & Scout

Expos brochure photo from late 1980s

their long time catcher Mike Scioscia as manager and presided over the Angels American League championship and subsequent World Series title in 2002. Stoneman was also the GM, who handled the team's ownership transition from the Walt Disney Company to Arturo Moreno.

Perhaps Stoneman's biggest player transaction was to convince Expos superstar Vladimir Guerrero to sign a free-agent contract following the 2003 season. Guerrero had spent $7\frac{1}{4}$ seasons with Montreal before leaving.

Until recently, I thought that Stoneman was Jewish because of the 'man' at the end of his name but I have been told otherwise. As it turns out, 1980-81 bit-player Steve Ratzer is the only Jewish player in Expos history.

I emailed Stoneman in February, 2021 to get the record set straight.

"Danny, my Dad's family (the Stoneman side) originated in Cornwall in England," Stoney said in an email. "My Mom's maiden name was Hennessey, and her side of the family originated in Ireland. I'm thinking that there must have been more than one former Expos player who was Jewish, but none come to mind right now."

Expos fan's collection astounding

Talk about Expos fanatics.

Take Don Rice, a reporter and copy editor with the Star-Phoenix, a daily newspaper in the Canadian city of Saskatoon, Saskatchewan.

"I could be wrong, but I believe I have the largest, or certainly amongst the largest Expos video and radio collections of their games in the world," Rice said. "If I am wrong, I would be overjoyed to meet the person who has a larger collection.

"I have been collecting Expos videos as long as my family had a VHS in our house. Unfortunately in the early days (mid-1980s) I wasn't as enthusiastic about collecting games, and didn't realize how rare or significant some of these games would become later."

Rice has been trying to find old Expos games for over 30 years, from others who have recorded Expos games. He somehow managed to track down people and make trades with those who had Expos videos online. He owes a lot of his early collection to another huge Expos fan with a large video and radio collection – Alex Weeks from Ancaster, Ontario.

Rice, 50, figures Weeks originally must have had the largest Expos collection in the world and would trade Rice dozens of games to help him increase his collection. In recent years, Rice has continued to add to his collection though, and Weeks hasn't been as active in collecting. But Weeks still also has one of the biggest Expos collections out there, other than Rice's.

Rice boasts about 500 full-game videos, 350 partial-game videos, 950 full radio games and 50 partial radio games. He has at least one full Expos video for every year since 1979, has at least one video clip from every year the Expos ever played (1969-2004) and has at least one radio broadcast for every year.

Hugh Buckley photo
Don Rice of Saskatoon, left, poses with former Expos executive Jim Fanning

The year he has the most videos and radio calls for is 2003 – 60 full videos and all 162 radio broadcasts. Rice remembers one of the early games he was very excited to get in a trade on VHS was Game 2 of the 1981 NLDS won 3-1 by the Expos in Montreal against the Phillies.

"I wore out that tape playing it," Rice said. "One of my proudest moments was recording El Presidente's perfect game. After making trades with various people, I believe my recording of that game was the one that ended up getting widely circulated.

"Then eventually games started to become available on DVD. That made it easier to trade. Since MLB has been allowing videos on YouTube, that has also increased the amount of games available. Games in MP4 or other digital formats are a lot easier to trade now because games can be transferred online with no need to mail them."

The best game broadcasts, Rice said, are the ones done by Expos broadcaster Dave Van Horne – especially those with some of his long-term partners like Duke Snider and Ken Singleton. Rice grew up listening to Dave and Duke on the radio and has many fond memories of their broadcasts.

"Unfortunately, we moved from Ottawa to Saskatoon in 1983. And although I had heard that Expos radio broadcasts were available in Saskatoon, I never found them. That was a huge disappointment," Rice said. "Thankfully, we would always watch all the Expos games we could on TV – both English and French broadcasts. But they never showed enough games."

Rice said the most coveted years for Expos videos are anything from 1981 or earlier – especially 1979-1981, and 1992-94 when they had such good teams. But the early years especially are very hard to find, he added.

"If anyone has or wants Expos games – video or radio – I would appreciate hearing from you and I'm sure we can work out trades," Rice told me. "I know there are Expos games out there that I don't have yet, which annoys me. But I'm doing whatever I can to get every possible Expos recording that exists, win or loss.

"I would also like to make sure that my Expos collection eventually gets preserved so this record of the Expos history will last. I'd love to eventually donate my collection to the Canadian Baseball Hall of Fame and Museum or some other baseball museum that recognizes the importance of maintaining the legacy of the Expos in video and audio format."

If you want to communicate with Rice, you can find him at: donwrice@shaw.ca

Ferreira synonymous with scouting

Fred Ferreira is known in baseball's scouting fraternity for being a valued assessor of prospects from high schools, colleges, universities and even kids, who weren't going to schools.

Overlooked, underrated, undervalued and underestimated. Such is the life of a scout like Ferreira, whose behind-the scenes work is cloaked in relative anonymity because scouts just don't get a lot of recognition.

What many people don't know is that Ferreira, in another life, was a tank commander for the U.S. army based in Fort Knox, Kentucky. He and some comrades were told to report to Korea to intervene in the brutal Korean War, a three-year-old stalemate between the North and South. North Korea was backed by China and the Soviet Union while South Korea had the support of U.S. and United Nations troops.

Luckily for Ferreira, only 18, when he got there, the war was ending. Unfortunately while he was there, he became very sick with Hepatitis C. He qualified for an honourable discharge and was sent home to New Jersey to rehabilitate. This convalescence meant he had to abandon his pursuit of a playing career, forcing him to miss his chance with the Red Sox.

Not long after he returned from Korea and following his recovery from his illness, Ferreira told me that he worked for a year or so as a ticket agent for Mohawk Airlines, a regional airliner operating in the Mid-Atlantic region of the U.S., mainly in New York and Pennsylvania.

Then he got lucky in baseball. It was a sport that he loved from early on in life. He used to play baseball from morning to night with his neighbourhood friends on makeshift fields and even in the streets. They sometimes used sticks for bats, improvised balls and old equipment when they could get it.

Eventually, Ferreira played organized baseball with the Little League, the Pony League, the Pal league and then in high school.

After getting healthy, Ferreira returned to his true love: baseball. He became affiliated with the Cuban All-Stars, who were playing in Miami. What did Ferreira do to get involved with that special team from Cuba? He played for them and helped coach them. He managed to catch the attention of the Dodgers and he began another pursuit of being affiliated with MLB.

Within a short time, Ferreira started working part-time as a scout with the Padres, Cardinals and Royals before he attained his full-time job with the Angels in 1972-73. In 1974-75, he was the head baseball coach at Fort Lauderdale College where he compiled a 92-40 record. He killed it as a coach.

"The impact of Fred Ferreira in baseball isn't limited to his work as a scout or with his time in Major League Baseball," his friend Ken Barnett said. "While the country was going through the Woodstock Generation in the 1960s, Ferreira was turning youngsters into players at his Fort Lauderdale Baseball School." Ferreira eventually sold the school to Bucky Dent.

Ferreira returned to scouting with the Phillies in 1975 full time and then from 1976-78, he was the owner and operator of the Pompano Beach Cubs in the Florida State League. His Play Ball Academy in Pompano Beach used the same blueprint as the Fort Lauderdale school and was responsible for turning Broward County, Florida into a nationally recognized hotbed of baseball talent.

Yet, for most of Ferreira's baseball career, the emphasis was on scouting.

In 1978-79, he was a full-time scout and director of international scouting for the Reds and then in a 10-year stint with the Yankees, he was a minor-league manager, scout, executive director of international scouting and Dominican Republic academy organizer and director. Busy man he was.

Working with volatile Yankees majority owner George Steinbrenner had its advantages and disadvantages as many people know. Ferreira recalls that while he was managing the Sarasota Yankees minor-league team, he received a call from Steinbrenner, telling him to sign a catcher for $5,000 to play for the team.

Steinbrenner had relayed this message because he had met an airline hostess, who told him that her nephew was a good catcher. So Ferreira, loyal employee that he was, signed the catcher and dispatched him to the bullpen to see what he could do. Hilariously, the bullpen coach phoned Ferreira in the dugout to tell him that the catcher didn't know how to put the catching gear on.

"I thought you said you were a catcher," Ferreira told the catcher upon visiting the kid in the bullpen.

Fred Ferreira photo
**Fred Ferreira, right, poses with Hensley Meulens of Curacao, who was
signed by Ferreira for the Yankees and who played for the Expos in 1997**

Vidro of Puerto Rico, Orlando Cabrera of Colombia, Javier Vazquez of
Puerto Rico and Guerrero.

"I liked Vidro's make-up and hard work from the beginning," Ferreira
said. "He wasn't a player with exceptional talent but he built himself up
with his hard work. Vazquez was a guy I drafted when he was 18. He
was throwing only 89-90 m.p.h. but he had a great body and make-up.
By the time he got to the majors, he was 95-98."

Without a doubt, Ferreira is the undisputed champion of all scouts
in baseball. That's why the Hurler Movie Production team just recently
tabbed him and Ed Bailey, another former Expos scout, as production
advisors for a feature-film project called Hurler. Ferreira and Bailey will
also participate in the movie.

Coming to a Theater Near You
Soon to be Major Motion Picture

Those are some of the headlines on a poster building up the movie
and Tony Wylder, the one-time Toronto resident and the film's writer and
director, said, "Fred Ferreira is the number one Cooperstown Champion
Baseball Scout. With 77 signings, he is the undisputed champ. That is
enough players to build out three Major League Baseball clubs or field
eight baseball teams."

Ferreira said he was contacted about getting involved and he said, "definitely, I'm interested. We'll see what happens."

Good job, Fred. You certainly deserve a plaque on the walls of Cooperstown. It could be argued also that Ferreira could be nominated for induction into the Canadian Baseball Hall of Fame in St. Marys, Ontario.

Poster submitted by Tony Wylder

Remembering Charlie Fox

Charlie Fox is a somewhat forgotten man in the annals of the Expos.

He was instrumental in helping to put together the team that almost made it to the World Series in 1981, going back and forth to Montreal from the family home in Phoenix.

Fox had been appointed Expos GM following the 1976 season by president John McHale. Fox had been hired initially by McHale as a special assistant and major-league scout heading into the 1976 season and was named emergency manager when Karl Kuehl was fired late in the '76 season.

Fox had a hand along with McHale in hiring new manager Dick Williams and they negotiated with free-agent Reggie Jackson before he decided on the Yankees.

"Dad had the opportunity to run his own team. He had free rein. Absolutely, Dad and Dick knew Reggie from his time with the A's," Fox's son Mike told me. "Reggie used the Expos as stopping leverage with the Yankees."

One of Fox's biggest moves as GM came April 27, 1977 when he acquired one of his long-time protégés, Chris Speier, a shortstop, from the San Francisco Giants. Speier had reached an impasse in contract talks with the Giants and proceeded to be a pivotal player in the Expos drive to attain elite status from 1979-83.

Fox was the Giants manager in 1971 when hotshot Speier came on the scene as a rookie. Speier helped Fox and the Giants to the NL West championship. Fox was voted NL manager of the year.

"They became close," Mike said about his dad and Speier. "Dad had two players he considered really key: Bobby Bonds and Chris. His relationship with Chris was almost like father and son. They had a long standing relationship. Dad really like Chris's confidence."

Ironically, Fox and Speier had a spat on July 20, 1978 in the Expos clubhouse prior to a game. Speier was scuffling badly in 4-for-31 slump and Fox came down from the executive suite and let Speier have it.

Speier's teammate and Expos player rep Steve Rogers didn't take too kindly to the confrontation. Fox hauled off and hit Rogers and threw him to the floor.

Speier took Fox's criticism to heart. What happened is the stuff of legends. Speier went out and hit for the cycle and collected six RBI that night as the Expos beat the Braves 7-3. Imagine that. You can't make this stuff up.

Mike Fox was chuckling about the threesome involving his father, Speier and Rogers.

"I won't call it a fight," Mike said of the confrontation between Charlie and Speier. "Chris was struggling a bit. Dad came down to motivate him. He got on him a bit. He told Chris to shake it off. Steve Rogers interfered."

Players association head Marvin Miller complained to commissioner Bowie Kuhn about Fox's role in the incident but Kuhn didn't hand down any disciplinary action. McHale stuck with Fox as GM until the end of the season at which time Fox thought it best that he step down. The general consensus was that a man in civilian clothes like the fiery Irish Catholic Fox shouldn't have done what he did to Rogers. It was conduct unbecoming an executive.

"It sure didn't look good," Mike Fox said of his father's behaviour. "Dad knocked Steve down. Dad stepped out of the GM role. Dad realized the role of the GM was a business role more than it was a baseball role. Dad loved the baseball role."

But that loss of the GM position didn't mean the end of Fox's tenure with the Expos. People forget that he remained with the Expos through the 1982 season when he departed for the Cubs as a special assistant to GM Dallas Green.

Like he did when he was initially hired, Fox worked behind the scenes for McHale as a special consultant on trades, player development and scouting major-league clubs. He was a de facto assistant GM. Nowadays, they call this kind of executive a special assistant to the general manager.

"John and Dad were having fun building the team. It was special," Mike Fox said. "They loved the fan base and loved working for Mr. Bronfman. They were really trying to build a championship for Montreal. It was a very enjoyable period of time."

Charlie knew McHale from his GM days in San Fran and that is how Charlie ended up with the Expos. Fox had joined the Expos after Giants owner Horace Stoneham sold the franchise to a group headed by Bob Lurie just when it was almost relocated to Toronto. Fox figured with new

Photos submitted by Fox family

Charlie Fox is seen here with Expos president John McHale and his wife Lola. Fox died in 2004 and Lola died in 2021.

ownership coming in that it was time to leave.

"Dad left the Giants under his own volition," his son said.

Fox was manager of the Giants Triple-A club in Phoenix to start the 1970 season but he was promoted to the major-league team as manager after a particularly difficult 17-16 loss in 15 innings by San Francisco at home to San Diego on May 23.

Fox was talking with Giants GM Rosy Ryan in Phoenix at a bar about the 17-16 game and Fox said, "(Manager) Clyde King burned through the pitching staff." Ryan replied by saying, "That is going to be your problem." In the next second, Ryan told Fox he was replacing King. True story.

After Charlie's first wife Eleanor died in 1984, he married restauranteur Lola Bertolucci in 1985 not long before he joined the Expos.

Charlie Fox died in 2004 at 82 following a four-year battle with Alzheimer's. Lola died Jan. 20, 2021 at the age of 95.

"It's a horrible disease," Mike Fox said of Alzheimer's. "It's hardest on the family than it is on the individual. The sad part is the original memories are not there (for his father). There are no conversations."

Appreciation to individuals, publications and organizations

Sherry Gallagher
Dawna Dearing
Herb Morell
Don Rice
Retrosheet
Canadian Baseball Network
Ottawa Citizen
Ottawa Journal
Ottawa Sun
Montreal Daily News
Montreal Gazette
Baseball Reference
Baseball Almanac

Wikipedia
Canadian Baseball Hall of Fame
MLB Productions
Associated Press
Canadian Press
Postmedia
Toronto Globe and Mail
Toronto Star
Stratford (Ontario) Beacon-Herald
Stratford-Perth (Ontario) Archives
Facebook
Twitter

Interviews

Mike Ahearne
Don Archer
Jim Baba
Earl Berard
John Boccabella
John Boquist
Barry Boughner
Steve Boutang
Ray Burris
Orlando Cabrera
Jolbert Cabrera
Sandy Campbell
Craig Caskey
Mike Cohen
Murray Cook
Victor Cupidio
Don DeMola
Larry D'Amato
Andre Dawson
Harriet Dues
Maurice Dumas
Ron Earl
Arden Eddie

Fred Ferreira
Ken Fishkin
Denis Flanagan Jr.
Jerry Flanagan
Pepe Frias
Jim Gosger
Russ Hansen
Perry Hill
John Hughes
Jackie Hunt
Ron Hunt
Bob James
Joel Kirstein
Darold Knowles
Doug Landreth
Larry Landreth
Ron LeFlore
Ken Macha
Bill MacKenzie
Dennis Martinez
Rudy May
Jim McCoubrey
Balor Moore

Wayne Morgan
Tim Murtaugh
Rich Nye
Dave Parker
Larry Parrish
Burton Peck
Barry Petrachenko
Cas Pielak
Don Rice
Martin Robitaille
Steve Rogers
Dan Schatzeder
Dennis Schulz
Larry Seminoff
Joe Setlakwe
Chris Speier
Brent Underdahl
Danny Upsdell
Larry Walker Sr.
Jerry White
Tony Wylder
Floyd Youmans

Photos supplied by Danny Upsdell

Larry Walker paid tribute years ago to his former B.C. coach
Lorne Upsdell by presenting him with a bat and plaque.
Upsdell died in 2018. The photo of a young Walker is from 1976 when he was 9.

Autographs

Autographs